Bandits, Peasants, and Politics:
The Case of "La Violencia" in Colombia

iLAS ILAS Translations from Latin America Series

Bandits, Peasants, and Politics

The Case of "La Violencia" in Colombia

BY GONZALO SÁNCHEZ
AND DONNY MEERTENS

TRANSLATED BY ALAN HYNDS

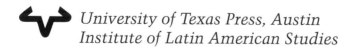 *University of Texas Press, Austin*
Institute of Latin American Studies

This translation was made possible in part by a subsidy from the Instituto de Estudios Políticos y Relaciones Internacionales (IEPRI) of the Universidad Nacional de Colombia.

Photos courtesy of *El Tiempo*, *El Espectador*, Archivos Judiciales, and Luis Gaitán (LUNGA).

Originally published in 1983 as *Bandoleros, gamonales y campesinos: El caso de la violencia en Colombia*. Copyright © 1983, El Ancora Editores, Bogotá.

First University of Texas Press Edition, 2001

Library of Congress Cataloging-in-Publication Data

Sánchez G., Gonzalo.
  [Bandoleros, gamonales y campesinos. English]
  Bandits, peasants, and politics : the case of "La Violencia" in Colombia / by Gonzalo Sánchez and Donny Meertens ; translated by Alan Hynds.
    p. cm. — (Translations from Latin America series)
  Includes bibliographical references and index.
  ISBN 0-292-77758-2 (hardcover : alk. paper) — ISBN 0-292-77757-4 (pbk. ; alk. paper)
    1. Outlaws—Colombia—History. 2. Brigands and robbers—Colombia—History. 3. Political violence—Colombia—History. 4. Colombia—Politics and government—1946–1974. I. Meertens, Donny. II. Series.
HV6453.C75 S2813 2001
364.9861—dc21   00–053517

Banditry, regardless of the perspective from which we view it, is a form of protest, a rebellion, a deviation, or a mere recourse for survival. It is a protest against the injustice of the powerful or the extortion of the strong; a rebellion against harsh social determinations hostile to the weak and appeasing to the strong; a deviation from individual ethics based on biological or hereditary factors; a recourse for satisfying needs, whether real or fictitious, good or bad, whether created by passion or vice, poverty or hunger. But, in the end, it is the handiwork of an imperious and decisive force.

And it is even more: the expansion of a sentiment, of a wild and exuberant freedom; an impulse of poorly restrained combativeness; an aftertaste of the anxious and wandering life of primitive man; a feudal replication and a manifestation of that latent communism that exists in the soul of all those who have been disinherited.

—*Enrique López Albújar,* Los caballeros del delito

Contents

Foreword

So crucial are the years of "La Violencia" in Colombia's history that for Colombian readers, the transcendence of any serious research on the topic will be immediately clear. This book is undoubtedly a very important contribution to the history of La Violencia, especially its dark, final phase, which began after the formation of the National Front. The authors have not only demonstrated their ability in this field, but they systematically use sources hitherto unexplored by historians, such as the notable legal investigations brought against the leading *cuadrillas* from 1957 to 1964. Nevertheless, and although the interest of this book is obvious for the Colombian public, it is still useful to emphasize the work's particular merits.

For anyone who belongs to what the authors call the "generation of La Violencia"—that is, for those who lived between 1945 and 1965—to see this social and political commotion in perspective is exceptionally difficult. Although it is true that there were several valuable early attempts to record, document, and analyze the phenomenon—think of the two volumes by Guzmán Campos, Fals Borda, and Umaña Luna published in 1962—it is also undeniable that they were written when the heat of battle had just begun to subside. To expect Colombians to have remained neutral vis-à-vis the events that took place in those years or to have no longer been involved in either the problems that led to La Violencia or its consequences would be absurd. It is, therefore, nothing short of admirable that a research project is now able to place the events that occurred between 1945 and 1965 in historical perspective—not common in countries where historians attempt to approach national episodes that took place in their own lifetimes.

Non-Colombian readers—and it is to be expected that this book will be read in various latitudes—should, of course, find interest in the events that took place during La Violencia. This phase of profound transformations in Colombia—little known outside its borders—constitutes an extraordinary chapter of the history of the twentieth century, a century that thus far has witnessed more and larger social revolutions—whether concluded, aborted, or barely under way—than any other. The focus of this work, nevertheless, covers a broader field of study, situating the research on the final years of La Violencia in the framework of a more general phenomenon witnessed in many parts of the world: banditry, studied not simply on account of its "criminal" nature but because of its relation with the politics and the society of a given era. Although the openly political guerrillas, such as the Liberal and Communist groups of the period, cannot be "included in the analytical category of *bandolerismo*," as the authors unequivocally point out, following the formal end of the civil war and the establishment of the National Front, the members of the *cuadrillas* that remained active in many regions of the country clearly can and should be described as bandits. Indeed, it is difficult to disagree with the authors when they state that Colombian banditry, from 1958 to 1965, constitutes the most widespread and formidable event of its kind in twentieth-century Western history.

To be sure, the armed *cuadrillas* of the final phase of La Violencia were overwhelmingly made up of bandits. Likewise, *bandolerismo* was unquestionably a social and political expression, for which reason it provides a unique body of materials that help understand and unravel the relations between *bandolerismo* as a mass phenomenon and economics, politics, and social protest, that is, the relations between *bandoleros*, campesinos, and *gamonales*, on the one hand, and between all of them and the state, on the other.

The most significant characteristic of "social banditry" per se is that it is locally acknowledged, tolerated, and even supported, and that it could not survive for long—at least in rural areas—*without* the acknowledgment, the tolerance, and the support of the populace. In the extensive historical literature on banditry, there is considerable debate, partially summarized by Sánchez and Meertens in Chapter 1, as to why social banditry is tolerated. Aside from reasons of terror, which, after all, prevailed for only relatively short periods, the controversy centers around why and when bandits cease to be considered simple criminals, just as has occurred with nearly all highwaymen in history, at least as long as they are alive and in the neighborhood. Whatever the answer, the authors show that between 1957 and 1964 most Colombian *bandoleros* continued to enjoy the support afforded to them in their areas of operation by the local peasantry, who labeled them *"guerrilleros"* or "boys from the mountains," that is, "rebels with a cause." Why? Sánchez and Meertens suggest—convincingly, in my opinion—that this popular banditry emerged in certain regions "as an anarchical and desperate peasant response" to a series of defeats, disappointments, and frustrations that had been in the making ever since the days of López Pumarejo's "New Deal." This type of banditry came to life amid the ruins of strong and well-structured leftist peasant movements, as indicated by its comparative paucity in areas where such movements were maintained despite all the attacks wrought upon them.

An even wider debate exists on the relative importance of peasant and *gamonal* support for this banditry or, in a more general sense, on the exact form of the *"bandolero-gamonal-campesino"* triangle. To my mind, Sánchez and Meertens conclusively point out that the banditry of the Colombian Violencia can only be explained by taking into account deeply rooted partisan loyalties that crossed class divisions and provided Liberal *bandoleros* in Liberal areas (and Conservative *bandoleros* in Conservative areas) with legitimacy, with the support of local political caciques—even against the manifest hostility of their national bosses—as well as with more than a few enemies, including the other party's peasants, for whom the peasants of the other side did not feel the least bit of sympathy. But the authors also show that the crucial factor that determined the *bandoleros'* fate was the support or hostility of the local power structures, which initially were in favor of "their" *cuadrillas*, not only for partisan reasons or for economic advantages—particularly in the coffee-growing areas—but also because of the repudiation by those local power holders of the growing centralization of the state machinery. And, conversely, the local power structures abandoned the *bandoleros* not only because of those structures' progressive integration into the new national political project but also because of the vague but discernible political radicalization of many *bandas*, which revived, on a smaller scale, the fears of the first period of La Violencia (1948–1953): that the autonomous action of armed peasants might escape the control of the two-party system and follow a revolutionary social path. In turn, when the local elites withdrew their support, *bandoleros* were not only deprived of the resources and the privileges that had kept them immune, but they also lost the—previously existing—possibility of reintegrating into the nation's political life. Terrified, powerless, ideologically confused, and increasingly forced to live at the expense of "their" campesinos, they ended up waiting to be eliminated amid growing isolation.

Consequently, Sánchez and Meertens's *bandolerismo* is more political than social, or to use an ambiguous term, it is "prepolitical." This is equivalent to saying that it cannot be understood except as a part of Colombia's history (regarding, for example, the role played in that history by the Liberal-Conservative dichotomy) and more precisely as part of the history of Colombia between 1930 and the Revolution whose "March" was, for so many poor Colombians, something more than a politician's phrase—but which was bloodily aborted after Jorge Eliécer Gaitán's 1948 assassination. In a certain sense, more than the primitive prelude to peasant organizing, it was a "postpolitical" phenomenon, so to speak, and the striking specificity of the Colombian context may make it difficult, based on "Chispas," Efraín González, "Capitán Desquite," "Pedro Brincos," "Sangrenegra," and the rest, to generalize on banditry in other parts of the world or from other historical periods.

Nevertheless, the authors' analytical ability, the wealth of their information, and the insight with which they place the Colombian phenomenon in historical perspective are such that all scholars of banditry and of the politics of preindustrial society will be deeply grateful. The authors provide invaluable material for comparative studies and, frequently, exemplary analyses of specific problems—for example, of the conditions that favored the exceptional concentration of banditry in the coffee-growing areas and of the social makeup of *bandas* and how *banda* members and their leaders were recruited.

The historical study of *bandolerismo* has developed rapidly over the last twenty-five years. The literature on the topic, already plentiful and often of high quality, is constantly growing. Sánchez and Meertens have made a remarkable contribution to it.

—Eric J. Hobsbawm
1983

Acknowledgments

The English publication of this book owes much to various persons and institutions, whose efforts we would like to acknowledge explicitly:

Aline Helg, Professor of History at the University of Texas at Austin, who was the true promoter of this project;

Ancora Editores, who published the successive editions of the book in Colombia and facilitated its translation;

The Institute of Latin American Studies at the University of Texas at Austin and the Universidad Nacional de Colombia, for their important contributions to the translation costs and other forms of support they lent to the project;

Alan Hynds, who translated the book, for his professionalism and creativity in seeking out equivalents for the most obscure regional expressions;

Nancy Warrington, the copyeditor, whose careful and demanding reading of the manuscript could have been provided only by a person who lived part of her early years in Colombia;

Virginia Hagerty, Managing Editor at the Institute of Latin American Studies, for her enthusiasm, patience, and dedication to this project.

Introduction

This book is intended, first, for an entire generation, the "Generation of La Violencia"—those Colombians who lived during the twenty-some years from 1945 through at least 1965 and who experienced this complex process in which government terror, anarchy, and peasant insurgency mixed with a rearrangement of social and political relations. However, this book is also written for subsequent generations, who have learned about the period solely from hearsay and are increasingly interested in studying the meaning of its decisive episodes, the impact of which continues to be felt in the nation's historical evolution.

The approach of this book responds to a long-standing need that has only been partially met. For many years, researchers of the period known as La Violencia, despite their distinct interpretations, gave too much weight to a single dimension of the process: its barbarity, bloodthirstiness, or repression, in a nihilistic or self-destructive re-creation of the colossal orgy of power the country experienced from at least as far back as the 1948 Bogotazo until the mid-1960s. The reduction of La Violencia to a simple bipartisan struggle for hegemony, or to a confrontation within the dominant classes that enmeshed the masses in a struggle that was not theirs, limited the inquiries into the multiple facets of the process. Had the masses, the oppressed, not put up their own struggle? Had they not, on many occasions, made a mockery of attempts to quell protest and rebellion?

The contradictory relationship between repression and resistance had to be re-created and, with it, the dynamics between "the bandits in power" and "the bandits of the people." The merely passive vision of that past—which, despite all its ambivalence, was also within the sphere of popular struggle—had to be forsaken in order to ask new questions that the prevailing ideology might not want asked. In this sense, this text is a challenge to what we have learned and been taught and to what has been carefully concealed.

Defining the subject matter—in this case, *bandolerismo*—was less a departure than an arrival. None of the available sources provided opportunities for reflection that broadened the debate on La Violencia beyond local and national episodes. Hence, we sought a connecting element that, without ignoring the concrete historical phenomenon, would allow us to make inroads into an issue that had points in common with other historically defined experiences. In this sense, the book contributes to comparative studies on banditry by examining the particular elements of the Colombian case—perhaps the Western world's most recent example of widespread banditry—and comparing them to those it has in common with its classical manifestations in Europe (Italy, Spain) or Latin America (Brazil, Peru). The book situates La Violencia in a specific, though not an exclusionary, theoretical field, since the analysis of this very complex and multifaceted topic required a definition of other specific theoretical fields.

Bandolerismo proved to be an exceptional strategic field from which to cast a retrospective and prospective examination of La Violencia— an examination that resisted facile, all-encompassing accounts. This was more than a mere method for approaching the topic. In concrete social practice, *bandolerismo* was also a result, the redefinition of the forces that competed in the first phase of La Violencia. For this reason, and to delimit the subject matter and avoid misunderstandings, we want to make clear from the outset that the issue of Liberal and Communist guerrillas during La Violencia, although it constantly intersects the topic of our study, is in no way included in the analytical category of "*bandolerismo,*" whose contents and makeup are examined in this book. *Bandolerismo*, an ambivalent and tortuous topic, is, then, at the crossroads of resistance. At the same time, its internal dynamics augured or engendered—however embryonically—new forms of violence: the revolutionary violence of contemporary Colombia.

Chapter 1 of the book reconstructs the general context in which *bandolerismo* arose as a specific topic for thought in the social sciences and outlines the current debate on its characterization, its meaning, and its insertion in Colombian society. It also refers to the possibilities for research afforded by an analysis of a case as unique as the Colombian one.

Chapter 2 sets forth the historical-political context of La Violencia and the overall interpretative framework used to analyze it. Chapters 3 and 4 use this framework to study the regional expressions and histories of the phenomenon in Colombia and to inquire into its origin within the evolution and complexity that characterize La Violencia. This multiplicity recovers its unity in Chapter 5, which examines the national impact of the interplay of the different regional processes and the various political and military strategies to eliminate *bandolerismo*. Last, the conclusion evaluates how evolving relations between *bandoleros* and the central government and other actors on the national stage—*gamonales* (local or regional bosses), hacendados, and peasants—led to the growing isolation of the numerous *bandas* and *cuadrillas*[1] and to their inevitable defeat.[2]

In our research we used extensive sources, including some that might be called traditional, such as national, regional, and local newspapers. However, oral testimony was also crucial, given the relative recentness of the processes and the prejudice with which city dwellers normally view people from the countryside, particularly dissident voices such as those heard here. Witness and participant interviews were, then, a part of this study also. Moreover, the prism through which the dominant classes viewed events as well as the concrete actions they took in response to them were at times an integral part of a social phenomenon or, in any event, allowed us to better understand it. In this regard, a careful analysis of the congressional debates was very revealing. Still, the most reliable and informative sources were the court records of the trials of the most important *bandas* and *cuadrillas* of the period. Judicial archives include transcriptions of oral testimonies, gathered during the period and where the events occurred. They contain, for example, accounts of the daily lives of prominent *bandas* and famous *bandoleros* and contemporary appraisals of how the *bandas* and *bandoleros* were viewed by the different sectors of society (some denouncing, some giving declarations, some informing, etc.). At times, they are the protagonists' accounts of the events. A file with fifty or one hundred oral testimonies can shed light on many hidden aspects of a given social or political phenomenon. The court files also proved to be an unexpected boon in that they contain documents difficult or impossible to obtain by other means, such as confidential reports from the state's and the army's security agencies; letters and *boletas* (extortion notes) to the relatives of kidnap victims or the targets of extortion attempts; statements by hacendados; accounts by deserters; and so on. Additionally, these files contain another important resource in a peasant society: the voices of the illiterate, of those who can barely sign their name—a category that then included most of Colombia's rural people. A final, very valuable resource was the research by those who had previously studied La Violencia.

The Fundación para la Promoción de la Investigación y la Tecnología, part of the Banco de la República, and subsequently the Consejo de Investigación y Desarrollo Científico, which belongs to la Universidad Nacional, provided financial assistance for the completion of this long-planned project. The Facultad de Ciencias Humanas and the Departamento de Historia, also of the Universidad Nacional, released us from some teaching duties, allowing us to finish the work. Our assistants Octavio Ramírez and Inés Sánchez worked efficaciously and deserve heartfelt thanks. Professor Angela de López helped generously with the final revision of the text. Nevertheless, none of these entities or persons are responsible for the views expressed herein regarding this controversial subject.

Bandits and Society

At least since the birth of the Robin Hood myth in medieval England, banditry has been a worldwide phenomenon. It has grown and thrived most during periods of crisis caused by the transition from precapitalist to modern capitalist societies. Since banditry is an imprecisely articulated expression of social protest, its decline has also been associated with the emergence of modern organizations demanding vindication for grievances. Examples include peasant associations, political parties, and revolutionary guerrilla movements—tactics and ideology to which banditry is generally considered unadaptable except by the anarchists who, led by Mikhail Bakunin in the second half of the nineteenth century, idealized bandits and presented them as among the many steadfast opponents of all oppression.

Despite the well-known universality of banditry and its endemic nature in some regions, until the late nineteenth century it was almost always a favored subject of writers and artists but not of historians or chroniclers. During this first period studied herein, ballads, novels, plays, and paintings best expressed views about bandits. Famous plays such as Friedrich Schiller's *Die Räuber* (The robbers) and many paintings by Spanish artists who had been influenced by Goya—the best-known being one by Rafael Tejeo, completed in 1839—are from this first phase.

The ten volumes of narratives on *bandolerismo* by Julian Zugasti (1876–1880) are no exception to the literary and artistic treatment of the subject. The collection of anecdotes by this one-time civil governor of Madrid, who became a knight-errant and a cruel butcher of highwaymen in Andalusia and Toledo by institutionalizing the *ley de fuga,* takes the perspective of the policeman more than that of the historian or social analyst.[1]

In the early twentieth century, bandits began to draw the interest of researchers with a legal background—especially those who had been influenced by the teachings of Raffaele Garófalo, Cesare Lombroso, and Enrico Ferri, the leading exponents of the Positive School of Criminal Law in Italy. These researchers set out to bring the advancements of the social sciences to the legal disciplines. In those early decades of the century, Constancio Bernaldo de Quirós and Luis Ardila, drawing from the positivists, wrote their classic monograph ([1933] 1973) on *bandolerismo* in Andalusia, where well into the century it was an institution as deeply rooted as bullfighting throughout all of Spain.[2]

In Latin America, the new school of criminal sociology produced studies whose quality is still unsurpassed, such as one by Enrique López Albújar ([1936] 1973), a former judge, on *bandolerismo* in Peru.[3] Although these studies insisted on a certain psychosomatic determinism and spoke of "born criminals," "mentally retarded individuals," and "inferior adults," they were the first to link criminality to structural factors imposed by geography, societal organization, or, in particular, agrarian structures.

In the 1950s and 1960s the topic attracted renewed interest, in part because of the big-screen success of two Brazilian producers who continued a filmic tradition dating to the 1920s: Lima Barreto received an award at the 1953 Cannes Film Festival for *O Cangaceiro* (The bandit), and Paulo Gil Soares won an award at the First International Film Festival of Rio de Janeiro in 1965 for *Memória do Cangaço* (Memories of the Cangaço). Another prestigious film was Italian director Francesco Rosi's *Salvatore Giuliano* (1962), on post–World War II banditry.

Most important, however, may have been the 1959 publication of historian Eric J. Hobsbawm's *Primitive Rebels.* This was the first attempt to systematize some previous regional studies and monographs on Western Europe, principally Italy, where brigandage has recurred throughout modern history, including during the 1960s and 1970s in areas such as Sardinia. Within the broader context of social movements that he collectively defined as "prepolitical" or "archaic," Hobsbawm dealt with banditry alongside topics such as millenarianist movements, the Sicilian Mafia, and the urban religious sects that preceded the rise of the European labor movement.

A decade later, Hobsbawm extended his study to other continents. In 1969 he published *Bandits*, an attempt to classify brigandage that took an in-depth look at one particular expression of it: social banditry. In the introduction to that book, he states, "What I have sought to explain is the uniformity of the phenomenon, and I hope that its explanation will, generally, predict what might be discovered about the behavior and the legends that [bandits] give rise to in hitherto unstudied areas" (Hobsbawm [1969] 1981, 9). Hobsbawm was announcing, then, something akin to a theory of banditry.

In his analysis of social banditry, Hobsbawm points to what he calls the "remarkable uniformity of the phenomenon" (ibid.). His general conclusions are, to a certain extent, applicable to other expressions of banditry and can be summarized as follows:

I. Social banditry is, first, a form of rural protest with "archaic," that is, traditional and conservative or, at best, reformist, characteristics. Its main objective (gleaned from its exploits and not from explicit programs, which can be said to be lacking) is, more than to abolish exploitation, to impose certain moral limits on injustice, on the despotism of the state and the landowners, and to reestablish the broken order. To parody the title of López Albújar's monograph cited above, *Los caballeros del delito*, social bandits might be called "righters of wrongs" or "knights-errant of crime."

II. Ambivalence is the distinctive trait of bandits' actions. The expropriations and even assassinations bandits carry out are actions that the state and its agents, in line with prevailing social values—that is, those of the dominant class—deem purely criminal and therefore deserving of punishment by bullets or the law. However, the peasant communities where bandits operate consider the same actions legitimate reactions to an offense, to an unjustified persecution, or to an untenable social or economic crisis. Even when terror is part of these activities and the rural community expresses no more than a guarded approval, the ideals of independence and justice that they nonetheless represent are sufficient for peasants to explicitly or implicitly provide the bandits protection from the authorities. According to Hobsbawm, this relation between the ordinary peasant and the rebel is what makes bandits "social."

Social bandits' actions express another ambivalence: social bandits undoubtedly arise as rebels against the social system, but, paradoxically, the more economic or political power they acquire, the greater the danger that they will become pillars of the established order and be co-opted by it or will at least join the rich and powerful who protect them out of self-interest.

III. Banditry is a marginal phenomenon, not only in the geographic confinement to isolated, sparsely populated regions without means of communication—but also in the limited number of members that normally make up bands. Although examples such as Andalusia or the Brazilian Sertão (the remote interior of the country) illustrate this thesis sufficiently, the *bandolerismo* that appeared in Colombia in the late stages of La Violencia, for reasons explored throughout this book, emerged as a clear exception to this usual trait of social banditry.

IV. Banditry emerges in backward or precapitalist societies, particularly as they enter a period of transition or disintegration. The phenomenon tends, therefore, to disappear with economic and political modernization, that is, with the penetration of capitalism, the expansion of communications infrastructure, and the increasing efficiency of public administration.

V. Although banditry can, in general and in comparison with contemporary revolutionary movements, be considered an obsolete or "prepolitical" phenomenon, it nevertheless has very complex ties with these movements: sometimes it acts as their precursor; at other times it coexists with but is differentiated from them. However, it can also be assimilated into and transformed by movements that struggle to transform society or some of its fundamental structures, as demonstrated by the Mexican Revolution; Mao's Red Army during the early stages and during the Japanese occupations of Manchuria in 1931–1932 and of Peking, Shanghai, and Nanking in 1937–1945; or even the Cossack peasant rebellion in Pugachev in late-eighteenth-century czarist Russia, which was preceded by several decades of endemic brigandage. Another noteworthy transformation took place in India. Famine, poverty, the indebtedness of the peasantry, and British military penetration combined to bring about recurrent banditry in certain provinces of India as far back as the late eighteenth century, and it lasted well into the nineteenth century. The incessant peasant disturbances reached a fever pitch in 1832, with a widespread rebellion—hardly describable as a simple bandit revolt—led by Ganga Narain, who, in addition to expressing popular aspirations, personified the god of death.[4]

VI. Finally, myth and reality are two inseparable aspects of an analysis of social banditry, although Hobsbawm admits—and underscores with particular vehemence in answer to one of his critics—that social bandits may differ greatly from their usual portrayal in popular legends. The importance of these legends lies in the light they may shed on the role that, regardless of the facts, peasants ascribe to them. This, in turn, explains many bandits' efforts to protect their reputation and to adjust their exploits to the legends surrounding them.

Hobsbawm's work has had considerable influence on other valuable research, such as the anthropologist María Isaura Pereira de Queiroz's studies on bandits in her native Brazil.[5] The results of her undeniably original inquiry into the economic and social conditions leading to the rise and fall of Brazilian bandits, their ideological ambiguity, the various evaluations made of them over time, the multiple interpretations by different social sectors, and the emergence of the national figure of Lampião—the most famous Brazilian bandit—are, all in all, a tacit confirmation of the theses put forth by the author of *Primitive Rebels*. And Hobsbawm, in turn, relies on Queiroz for the subsequent development of his ideas, at least regarding Latin America.

Nevertheless, a drawn-out controversy arose between these authors regarding the role of the well-known bandits Silvino and Lampião. Hobsbawm, along with Rui Facó (1965), sees these bandits as an expression of peasant discontent vis-à-vis a *latifundista* society whose own crisis was ripening, but Queiroz insists that they acted independently and that they were moved primarily by personal motives rather than by a desire to serve as the voice of a given social class.[6]

But the influence of authors is seen not only through their admirers but also through their critics. Hobsbawm's critics took two paths: some questioned certain aspects of banditry; others took aim at his general approach to the phenomenon. An example of the first category is Pat O'Malley (1979), who wrote an essay attempting to show that the exploits of the Australian bandit Ned Kelly, between 1870 and 1880, although in line with Hobsbawm's definition of social banditry, took place in a context that was neither precapitalist nor characterized by the presence of a traditional peasantry, unlike what Hobsbawm would have expected. Quite the contrary, the context for Kelly's actions was an advanced agrarian capitalism in which modern means of communication had established a foothold. O'Malley was questioning not so much the concept of social banditry as the economic and social prerequisites for its emergence.

Examples of the second type of critic can be found in the closely linked works by Anton Blok (1972) from Holland and Roderick Aya (1975) from the United States, who used research on Sicily and southern Spain to propose theses that shifted the crux of Hobsbawm's analysis.[7] While Hobsbawm emphasized the links between bandits and peasants and the image peasants have of bandits, Blok, Aya, and other researchers used various case studies to stress the other pole of the ambivalence: the protection bandits receive from the powerful as a crucial factor in their haphazard careers.

We can summarize these researchers' arguments as follows:

a) Hobsbawm focuses too narrowly on bandits and peasants and divorces them from society as a whole, where they inevitably interact with other classes and groups.

b) Because of this narrow focus, Hobsbawm overestimates bandits' role as spokespersons of social discontent. He minimizes—contrary to all evidence, notes Blok—their role as agents of terror in the service of politicians and landholders against the peasant bases from which they emerge, which, in the end, leads these bases to collaborate with the authorities in eliminating bandits.

c) To understand their invulnerability, we must, therefore, consider not so much the degree of protection they receive from the peasantry as their dependence on the politicians and dominant powers that back them and use them for their own purposes. This support from the dominant power structure constitutes, ultimately, the secret of their survival. "The mystique of invulnerability so often ascribed to hero bandits, moreover, has its objective correlative in this political shield," concludes Aya (1975, 44).

d) When movements with a broader scope emerge against the established order, bandits easily side with or remain faithful to the forces committed to restoring that order. Consequently, rather than encouraging peasant mobilization or social protest, they suppress it and turn on their own class.[8]

We have described the different emphases within the unanimously acknowledged ambivalence regarding banditry. Nevertheless, underlying this debate is not so much a difference in nuance or emphasis as the need to characterize a new kind of banditry, *analytically* distinct from that of the classic Robin Hood and identified neither by Hobsbawm nor by his critics: *political banditry.*

For now we might say that this is a category of bandits whose very emergence was determined by dependence on one or more elements of the dominant power structure, such as *gamonales*, political parties that help legitimize the established order, or a faction of the dominant class. Unlike most cases studied in the literature mentioned above, here political subordination is not a mere accident in bandits' careers but the element that primarily motivates them and determines their actions and targets. This is a distinctive trait of *bandolerismo*, the maximum expression of which is the Colombian case in the period covered in this study. Because it is political, this banditry does not exclude a profound social crisis; rather, such a crisis is a prerequisite for its emergence.

The distinction drawn by Juan Reglá and Salustiano Moreta regarding Castile and Catalonia in the late Middle Ages implicitly points to the issue of the different forms of banditry. These authors differentiate between feudal and nonfeudal malefactors, in other words, between the banditry of the aristocracy, of the landlords, of the dominant classes, and the banditry of the people, of the powerless, of the oppressed, even though, in practice, the two categories are often intertwined (Reglá 1968; Moreta 1978, 20). The French historian Fernand Braudel perceived this same duality in the sixteenth-century Mediterranean, although he did not explore all its implications. Indeed, after stating that "banditry is, above all, a retaliation against the organized states that defend the political as well as the social order," and that "the people are invariably on its side," Braudel is forced to point out that banditry often receives the support of the powerful, as demonstrated by the links between the Catalan nobility and banditry in the Pyrenees and between the Neapolitan or Sicilian nobility and bandits in southern Italy (Braudel 1976, 125–131).

Hence, the Colombian case study has a twofold significance: (1) It sheds light on a still poorly understood period of the country's contemporary history. (2) It also puts us face to face with an extreme manifestation of essentially political banditry in a society dominated by a century and a half of two-party rule and with concrete knowledge of the factors that led to its emergence, the mechanisms by which it operated and changed, and the conditions leading to its demise. It thereby provides essential empirical elements with which to broaden the general theory on banditry and its different expressions.

From this perspective, the controversy about whether bandits are intrinsically "social" takes a new turn. In fact, we now acknowledge that social bandits and political bandits are different actors. And this differentiation between actors who are included in a broader field—bandits—does not, obviously, negate the necessary relationships between them or the possibility that either kind of bandit may evolve into the other.

Hobsbawm's archetypal social bandit may turn into—as Hobsbawm admits—a pillar of the established order. This process occurred during the second half of the nineteenth century in Andalusia: The social bandit of the first phase, surrounded by an aura of popular hero, was violently suppressed when the exacerbation of contradictions in the agrarian structure made him even more dangerous than before, and the vacuum created by the elimination of social bandits led to peasant uprisings. Social bandits later reappeared, but with a new face, along-side and supported by caciques and landholders in defense of property and electoral fiefdoms, that is, as instruments for containing popular insurgency (Brenan 1967, 156).

But the opposite process is also possible. A politically subordinated bandit, such as the one described by Blok or Aya, can be transformed into a revolutionary when—for a variety of reasons we will specify—he chooses or is forced to break those ties of dependency. This study of the Colombian case will illustrate this possibility. One of the most remarkable examples is "Pedro Brincos" (Pedro Jumps). After beginning in the late 1950s as a Liberal guerrilla fighter and being stigmatized as a *bandolero*, in the 1960s Brincos became a champion of social revolution, an advocate of the worker-peasant-student alliance, and a soldier in the struggle against imperialism.[9]

The task of our research is, then, twofold: to account for the similarities of the phenomenon with movements that developed in other periods and regions, and to discover the type of society and the political contradictions in which it emerged—that is, its specific traits. This twofold approach leaves open the possibility of formulating new hypotheses and asking new questions that future researchers may help answer. We hope only to clear the path.

CHAPTER TWO

La Violencia: Context for Political Banditry in Colombia

General Antecedents of La Violencia

Civil war and poverty appear to have been the two most important variables in the internal dynamics of nineteenth-century Colombian society. Nevertheless, each one of the innumerable civil wars left a paradoxical continuity in the structures of domination and a clear delimitation of certain basic identities of the two traditional political groups: the Liberal and Conservative Parties. Those nineteenth-century wars appear to have been caused by a disturbing irrationality that characterized these two large political forces as subcultures of daily life more than as parties (Pecaut 1979, 24).[1] For peasants, armed mobilization in support of one or the other side has commonly demonstrated incorporation into the nation's political life.

The armistice that ended the War of the Thousand Days (1899–1902) and the growing consolidation of the export-oriented coffee industry at the beginning of the twentieth century raised expectations that the nineteenth-century dream of stable linkage to the world market—considered a natural prerequisite for peace and prosperity—was beginning to be fulfilled.

By the end of the 1920s, incipient, yet firm, bases for industrial development had been laid; but new contradictions had also appeared, introducing greater complexity not only into society but also into politics. The economic expansion was accompanied by growing social disparities that led to the emergence of strong class movements outside the traditional boundaries of the two-party system. The workers' movement, which thrived in the 1920s, was linked to early attempts to bring together political groups that claimed, under various banners, to be socialist; in 1930 the Colombian Communist Party arose from one of these groups. The organized, and quickly politicized, peasant movement became more prominent between 1925 and 1935, and its growth, far from slowing down, intensified because of the 1929–1930 global economic crisis. Its dynamics not only changed the relationship between peasants and landowners, especially in the coffee-growing areas where the hacienda system still predominated, but also raised the "agrarian problem" to the category of national debate and became a key element in defining bourgeois strategies for economic growth.

In 1930, these processes, along with the Great Depression and the ruling Conservative Party's multiple internal schisms, ended fifty years of Conservative hegemony, and the Liberals, headed by Enrique Olaya Herrera, took power. During the preceding fifty-year period, the Liberals had shown contradictory tendencies whose extreme manifestations ranged from a permanent reconciliation with the adversary to the proclamation of armed insurrection as the only tactic for coming to power. This range of strategies allowed one Liberal faction to use the discontent of the masses to its advantage, thereby defusing the threat of a consolidation of nationwide class-based parties that might have competed with the long-standing two-party system. Meanwhile, the other wing advocated reaching an understanding with the Conservatives to ensure that any crises be overcome without major traumas.

However, not even when it came to power, at the beginning of the National Concentration (1930–1935) government under the presidency of Liberal Enrique Olaya Herrera, did the Liberal Party succeed in becoming a homogeneous force. With the same malleability as before, it again divided into a government faction and an opposition faction. The first was always ready to reach an understanding with the most recalcitrant Conservatives in the government, those responsible for managing the state's affairs and the economy. This Liberal government faction acted through co-optation or repression, for example, vis-à-vis the peasant movement. In the first years of Liberal rule, peasants suffered at least as much persecution as might have been possible under the Conservatives, in part because many landholders in areas of agrarian conflict who were targeted during the struggle were Liberals. The opposition faction, by contrast, made itself heard through one or more dissident groups, irrespective of party identification, and used class-oriented language in its fight against government policy and even the established order as represented by its Liberal rivals, thereby giving impetus to the struggles of the worker and peasant masses.

The Liberal factions briefly converged during President Alfonso López Pumarejo's administration (1934–1938), called the Revolution on the March, and the young and combative Communist Party was also caught up in the reformist groundswell of the initial years. This helped generate overblown expectations of political participation among the populace, given a regime that had limited the masses' role to that of pawns. In contrast, the far right, inspired by the Spanish Falange, viewed the Revolution on the March as a dangerous hotbed of social destabilization. The unrealistic popular expectations and the right wing's extreme apprehensions paradoxically converged to make the Revolution on the March something that it clearly was not, or that it never intended to be. The meaning and the scope of López Pumarejo's modernization program, especially of Law 200 of 1936 regulating land tenure, had been overestimated.

A closer examination of the events shows, however, that the historical role of the Revolution on the March can be summed up in the following basic goals: establishing a new legitimacy for large agrarian landholdings, insofar as the peasant movement had clearly demonstrated the frailty of the existing order; imposing a minimum level of agricultural productivity by encouraging the formation of an agrarian bourgeoisie capable of more adequately responding to the demands of the growing domestic market; introducing rational relationships between capital and labor; and promoting policies to strengthen the state's managerial role. This was, in essence, a landowner solution to the agrarian problem, based on gradually transforming *latifundistas* into capitalist entrepreneurs and consolidating the industrial bourgeoisie as partners of domination, without antagonizing the traditional oligarchy.

After Eduardo Santos's rule (1938–1942)—misnamed the Government of the Pause—López Pumarejo's second term (1942–1945) made even clearer that the gap between expectations and achievements was due not to the deferment of the program proposed by the Revolution on the March but to the inherent limits on the logic of capitalist development. For this reason, Jorge Eliécer Gaitán, a Liberal and radical politician with socialist ideas, took up the standard of popular discontent implicit in the recognition of that gap.

The failure of the Revolution on the March's political project, which became evident with López Pumarejo's early resignation in 1944, put the country at the brink of a catastrophic confrontation—as López Pumarejo himself sensed—and augured a revolutionary explosion of unforeseen consequences (Pecaut 1979, 467).

The critical question was what role the subordinate classes would play in the subsequent sociopolitical process. Following the one-year interim presidency of Alberto Lleras Camargo, Mariano Ospina Pérez's "National Union" government, under the slogan "Revolution of Order," thrust itself on the national stage, openly calling on dominant classes to regroup, regardless of party affiliation. Any attempt to independently organize a popular movement, especially among the working class, was proscribed through various repressive measures, such as banning urban protests, ordering massive layoffs, and dismantling the most combative labor unions. Gaitán, for his part, called for "the people" to unite against both the Liberal and the Conservative oligarchy, and with his defiant and characteristic cry of "Charge!" he triggered social and political unrest unparalleled in the nation's history.

In its most general expression, the *gaitanista* movement was an attempt to unite popular forces under a predominantly petit-bourgeois leadership and around a program that, although certainly not anticapitalist, was resolutely democratic. As such, it was the most advanced political option of the moment, since the Communists, who might have been tempted to go further than the *gaitanistas*, were duty-bound to López Pumarejo's bourgeois-landowner program.

Gaitán had been a symbol of workers' nationalist struggle ever since he convened the famous 1929 congressional debates on the United Fruit Company in the wake of the 1928 banana-zone massacre, and peasants had recognized him as a spokesman for and ally of their fight against landowner power since the days of the Unión de Izquierda Revolucionaria (Revolutionary Left National Union; UNIR), an attempt to form a third party in the early 1930s. Nevertheless, he had held high positions in the López Pumarejo and Santos governments. Within the bipolar division of the Liberal Party, Gaitán had alternately opposed and belonged to the government during the Liberal Republic, allowing his party's contradictions to shape the course of his own development.

In the 1946 presidential elections, Gaitán went up against the Liberals' official candidate, Gabriel Turbay, and this division within the Liberal ranks allowed the smaller but more united Conservatives, headed by Ospina Pérez, to regain the presidency. By the following year, Gaitán had become the undisputed Liberal leader and appeared to be a shoo-in for the presidential term that would begin in 1950. But the Liberal Party's internal contradictions produced unexpected consequences. Under Gaitán, the dissidents were in the majority, and the only question was which of the two Liberal Gaitáns would become the next president: the social agitator or the conciliator. The oligarchy, fearful of the revolutionary potential of the masses who followed Gaitán, found the uncertainty unbearable. Gaitán was assassinated on April 9, 1948, a landmark date in contemporary Colombian history, as it is generally associated with the outbreak of La Violencia. Gaitán's execution, however, culminated the first wave of repression unleashed in 1945 by Alberto Lleras Camargo, López Pumarejo's Liberal successor, and continued thereafter by Ospina Pérez.

The masses responded immediately to Gaitán's assassination with a widespread insurrection. Although known as the Bogotazo, it was more organized, had a stronger political content, and lasted longer outside the capital, where Juntas Revolucionarias (Revolutionary Boards), popular governments, and peasant militias were formed.[2] After the military, with the collaboration of the old anti-*gaitanista* leadership, crushed the insurrection, some opponents who had fled the government counteroffensive began to form the first nuclei of armed rural resistance: in Barrancabermeja, Santander, Rafael Rangel became the "revolutionary mayor" of the April Ninth movement; in the Llanos Orientales (Eastern Llanos), Eliseo Velásquez led an uprising in Puerto López; and in southern Tolima, Hermógenes Vargas, known henceforth as "General Vencedor" (General Victorious), and his father were among the leading protagonists of the April Ninth rebellion in the region of La Profunda, in the municipality of Chaparral. At the time, these men probably did not imagine that in a little more than a year they would be leading full-fledged peasant armies in the period's characteristic form of struggle: peasant guerrilla warfare.[3]

Forces and Contradictions at Play

We must, then, describe the general context in which the resistance arose. The most prominent characteristic of Ospina Pérez's National Union government (1946–1950), especially after April 9, 1948, was, as Pecaut notes, the economic unity of the dominant classes and the role of foreign capital in the nation's development. Politically, in contrast, the most relevant characteristic was antagonism and the irreconcilable positions regarding strategies to be followed against the oppressed classes, as political actors autonomous from government and traditional political parties.

The bourgeois and propertied sectors active in the Conservative Party were inclined to assume that the system could only be stabilized by "mercilessly" stepping up state repression; intensifying the offensive

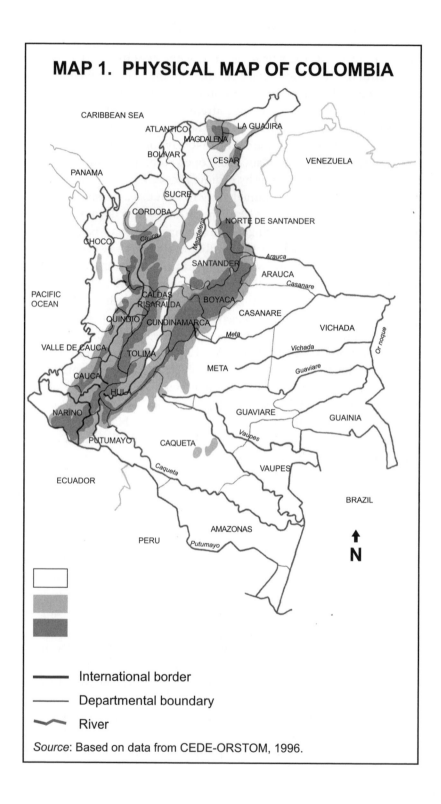

MAP 1. PHYSICAL MAP OF COLOMBIA

Source: Based on data from CEDE-ORSTOM, 1996.

that had been unleashed in 1945; promoting, at the same time, a Conservative union organization, the Unión de Trabajadores Colombianos (Union of Colombian Workers; UTC), to compete with the Liberal Confederación de Trabajadores Colombianos (Colombian Workers Confederation; CTC); and realigning the peasantry, with the support of the Catholic Church, around the anti-Communist Federación Agraria Nacional (National Agrarian Federation; FANAL). This repressive response, which excluded the participation of the masses from the political process, peaked during the dictatorship of Laureano Gómez. Starting in 1950, shortly after returning from Franco's Spain, Gómez set out not only to abolish all political freedoms but to promote a new constitutional order in which elections and other forms of political participation associated with a bourgeois parliamentary system would be replaced with a corporatist project, the cornerstones of which would be the Church, unions, and professional associations.

The Liberal Party's bourgeois and landholding sectors who, in the wake of the April Ninth uprising, had displaced or subordinated the former *gaitanistas* in their party's leadership, believed, despite recurrent hesitations, that the crisis could be solved or postponed only by incorporating—rather than excluding—the masses and subordinating them to the prevailing economic project or by neutralizing them, that is, by reviving the dream of the Revolution on the March. This was a desperate attempt to return to the days before Gaitán. The National Directorate of the Liberal Party, which advocated this position, was at first defeated. Later, however, it effectively imposed this strategy, but only after the popular-resistance movement had attained, on its own, a certain autonomy that threatened the dominant classes, making a pact among them inevitable.

Thus, in the vacuum created by these Conservative and Liberal options, the guerrilla movement spontaneously erupted, despite a lack of ties between the groups in the various regions of the country. Notwithstanding the calculated tutelage of the Liberal Party's oligarchic sectors, this movement quickly championed and symbolized a democratic alternative. Hence, the cycle of contradictions and confrontations between the basic forces that had defined the context in which *gaitanismo* emerged and expanded now appeared to reproduce itself, although this time the confrontation was more acute and the pro-democracy movement relied on the strength of its own arms.

The most salient characteristic of the first two governments during La Violencia (1946–1953) was, then, state terrorism. In the cities, this meant silencing the working class, which allowed industrialists and

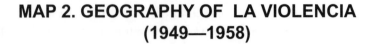

MAP 2. GEOGRAPHY OF LA VIOLENCIA (1949—1958)

- ●   Departmental capital

- —   Departmental boundary

- ▬   River   �█   Area affected by "La Violencia"

Source: Based on data from CEDE-ORSTOM, 1996.

landowning interests to freely appropriate the profits and accumulate the wealth of the postwar economic boom. Terrorism then spread to the countryside as an anti-Liberal and anti-Communist crusade to crush the peasantry's democratic aspirations and reverse the social gains peasants had won from the landowners. The working class had been practically silenced since 1948, and the anti-Liberal, anti-Communist crusade would become the Conservative standard after 1949. To this end, repression by the state's machinery—such as the sinister *chulavita* police from Boyacá—was not replaced but was complemented by paramilitary organizations such as the *pájaros* (birds) in Valle and Caldas, the *aplanchadores* (flatteners) in Antioquia, and the *penca ancha* (heavy whip) on the savannas of Sucre, whose victims would number in the hundreds of thousands.

But rural terror would have other visible consequences: the plunder of land and property whose owners had been killed or threatened into selling; the confiscation of harvests and livestock; the burning of houses, sugarcane crushers, and processing plants; the physical coercion of discontented rural workers, provoking massive migrations to the cities, or removing peasants to areas controlled by the party with which they were affiliated, until *veredas* (rural neighborhoods) and regions were politically homogeneous, or forcibly enlisting peasants into an armed group often made up of members of a single family. Ultimately, rural terror rearranged social classes in the countryside and relations of leadership and power in the different regions.

The persecuted had to choose between resisting or perishing. In many areas of the interior, rudimentary mechanisms of neighborhood defense and support emerged; nevertheless, structuring the resistance organically proved nearly impossible. Indeed, the resistance was concentrated in relatively well defined areas that became important poles of attraction and bonding for the recent migrants.

The first important guerrilla nuclei were formed in areas such as the Llanos Orientales that had the following in common: political homogeneity; frontiers of open colonization capable of productively absorbing a limited number of fugitives from the interior of the country; considerable distance from central power, affording protection from repression; and proximity to Venezuela, whose government was assumed to have befriended the resistance movement. In late 1952, the number of combatants in this area—the stronghold of the guerrilla struggle in the 1950s and the area with the most significant ideological transformations and the broadest perspectives for nationwide expansion—has been calculated at a minimum of 20,000. Other important Liberal guerrilla fronts included those in southeast Antioquia (the Pavón-Urrao Command); Carare-Opón in Santander; and Yacopí-La Palma in northeastern Cundinamarca. The Liberal guerrillas in southern Tolima—the guerrillas most directly manipulated by merchants and coffee hacendados—showed little interest in nationwide coordination and were conspicuously absent from the most important meeting held to achieve this. This gathering took place in 1952 in Sumapaz, a *gaitanista* bunker in the 1930s with a solid tradition of organized struggle against land tenure, and it was here that the former grievance-oriented associations were successfully transformed into a broad, disciplined guerrilla movement that was eventually victorious, because in the 1960s the government was forced to treat the region's problem not as a public-order issue but as a conflict mainly concerning land tenure.

The Communist Party initially announced it would resort to self-defense in the areas where it had the strongest presence: Tequendama and southern Tolima. In southern Tolima the Communists joined the struggle later than did the Liberals, whereas in Tequendama, particularly in Viotá, the Communists used fear of Liberal landowners to spread the war throughout the region and then joined these landowners in establishing a "diplomatic front" through which they negotiated a tenuous peace with the government. This, in turn, allowed the Communists to provide logistic support to the areas where war was inevitable.

In this context, guerrilla resistance emerged as a large-scale combination of various political expressions and of different levels of class consciousness, which historically have varied not only from one region to another but within each region. Its social makeup also varied greatly, both among low-level combatants and among leadership cadres. The leaders included, for example, migrants fleeing persecution (Eliseo Velásquez, in the Llanos Orientales); army deserters (Saúl Fajardo, in Yacopí, and Dumar Aljure, in the Llanos Orientales); former agrarian leaders (Isauro Yosa, in Chaparral, and Juan de la Cruz Varela, in Sumapaz); small landowners (Leopoldo García, "El Capitán Peligro" [Captain Danger], in southern Tolima); one-time policemen who had joined the April Ninth Movement; former prison inmates who had escaped during the Bogotazo; and impoverished peasants, such as Guadalupe Salcedo, who became a national symbol of resistance during this period.

Despite the splintering of these movements, the sometimes conflictive relationships among them (such as between Liberals and Communists in southern Tolima), and the difficulties they encountered in giving their programs a social, rather than a sectarian, direction, some manifestations of these movements caused significant anxiety among the dominant classes, including those members of the dominant classes aligned under the Liberal standard, who were much more familiar with the intimate details of these processes. Three main factors caused alarm. The first was the split between the guerrillas and the Liberal hacendados in the Llanos Orientales and the subsequent pact between the latter and the army against the insurgent peasants, in which the rebels for the first time were called *bandoleros* by members of their own party (1952 declaration by Sogamoso, cited in Franco Isaza 1959, 149–150). The second factor was the materialization of a project to coordinate the main fronts of the armed resistance throughout the nation, in what was called the First National Conference of the National Popular Liberation Movement ("Boyacá Conference"), held in August 1952. From this meeting emerged a National Coordinating Commission, composed mainly of members of the urban petite bourgeoisie. The third factor was a shifting correlation of forces in early 1953, when the guerrilla movement, at least in the Llanos Orientales, went on the offensive militarily. These processes were still in their early stages, raising a mere possibility of organized armed rebellion, although an ominous one.

It was then that the Liberal national leaders were finally heard, as members of the *ospinista* faction of the Conservative Party considered a new pact among the dominant classes to cover not only basic economic management but also the general management of the state and policymaking. This proposal was intended to isolate both those who viewed it as an unheard-of oligarchic ploy and those who considered it the expression of a reprehensible reconciliation. And since the antagonisms, hatreds, and inexorable confrontations at the grassroots level of both parties clearly prevented reaching a direct, immediate pact, a transition formula was opted for: arbitration by the armed forces, which, in the person of General Gustavo Rojas Pinilla, assumed power in June 1953. Rojas Pinilla had practically been forced to take power by the political bosses, who, except for those in the defeated faction, were unwilling to run any more risks regarding the potential for revolution or uncontrolled anarchy that was festering behind La Violencia.

Rojas represented a political solution to the crisis rather than a dictatorship in the usual meaning of this term, and his intervention was hailed as a "coup of opinion." With the simple, yet moving, slogan "peace, justice, and liberty," followed by an offer of unconditional amnesty, Rojas almost immediately scored a resounding victory and received widespread approval. This continues to be somewhat surprising, since "it was, curiously enough, a soldier without much merit who without using arms achieved the political objective where one of the country's most inured politicians had failed militarily. The general amnesty seemingly constituted a concession to the [guerrilla] movement, but was in fact its worst defeat" (Gabler n.d., 249). The military had calculated that once the combatants in the Llanos Orientales and Tolima had been demobilized, the rest of the problem would be quickly solved. Subsequent events show that the military was not altogether mistaken, although once the initial euphoria had passed, military repression would be felt selectively, and with particular severity, in areas where the guerrillas had been discerning enough to wait before surrendering.

An arbiter rather than a leading actor, Rojas attempted to resist the multiple and contradictory economic demands from the unions and achieved a temporary balance impossible to maintain in the long term, especially once the coffee boom that accompanied the first part of his government ended. The dominant classes sought to restrict and subordinate the military government's actions, rather than allowing it to present an autonomous political project. As a mediator who lacked his own political force and social base, Rojas attempted to fill this void with a "third force," an alliance between the populace and the armed forces that he hoped would receive their combined support. Confrontation was inevitable: the more Rojas attempted to become autonomous, the faster and more effectively the dominant classes united. After all, the two-party monopoly appears to be an integral part of social stability in Colombia. The direct pact, unattainable before the advent of the Rojas faction, would now be fully legitimized. In 1956, Alberto Lleras, representing the Liberals, and Laureano Gómez, the Conservatives, met in Sitges and Benidorm, Spain, and agreed on the basic principles: the two parties would alternate in power every four years for a minimum of sixteen years and would jointly control the entire state machinery. Lleras and Gómez united opposition to Rojas around a civil National Front; in May 1957 Rojas was forced to turn over power to a military junta, due in large part to the implacable pressure of a general strike called by industry, the banks, small businesses, and the Church, with broad popular backing.

The junta agreed to call a plebiscite to ratify the bipartisan agreement, and it turned over power in mid-1958 to the first National Front president: Alberto Lleras Camargo.

Officially, La Violencia had ended. This book will examine what actually occurred.

The National Front and Political Banditry

La Violencia had *not* ended. During the first two National Front governments, it would simply assume different characteristics. Hence, this was the beginning of a new phase, which would run from 1958 to 1965, the particular and dominant—though not only—expression of which was political *bandolerismo*.

The scope of Colombian political banditry is unparalleled in twentieth-century Western history. In 1964, once it had begun to decline, the movement included an estimated one hundred active *bandas* of armed peasants. In a more or less organized fashion, and ignoring the peace agreements between the official heads of the two traditional parties, the *bandas* prolonged the struggle between the Conservative and Liberal Parties. They received the militant or passive support of the rural communities that identified with their respective parties and on the protection and guidance of *gamonales*, who used the *bandoleros* for electoral purposes and pushed them into a war designed to weaken, contain, or exterminate their adversaries in the local or regional power structure.[4] In the initial phase of La Violencia, and particularly from 1949 to 1953, even a faction of the dominant class, through the Liberal Party, had reluctantly recognized that these peasant bosses or militants were guerrilla fighters.

The decisive factor in the insurgents' loss of precarious legitimacy was their reaction to the amnesty proposals, initially in 1953–1954 under the military government of Rojas Pinilla and then in 1958 under the first National Front government. Some rejected the proposals because they considered the guarantees insufficient, suspicious, or misleading; others tentatively accepted them but later found that the continual harassment to which they were subjected and the weight of so many years of life on the run made it difficult to readapt to normal life in the countryside. In addition, all the insurgents had understood the lesson of the murder of Guadalupe Salcedo, the most prestigious commander in the resistance against Laureano Gómez's dictatorial government, and they had fresh memories of many other former *guerrilleros* who had returned to civilian life and were later gunned down by the state's security apparatus. In these circumstances, a considerable number of former *guerrilleros* found no viable option other than to return to their precarious life in the mountains. For this decision, even their own party officially labeled them *bandoleros*, in retaliation for what the Liberals deemed an unacceptable insubordination.

Amnesty thus played an essential role in each stage of La Violencia: The purpose of the first amnesty, in 1953–1954, was to disarm the guerrilla movement. The second, that of 1958, had a twofold objective: to legitimize the bipartisan struggle against Rojas's "tyranny" and to rebuke, in the name of the National Front, the continued existence of that very struggle.

For all those who had taken up arms, two factors blurred the original motive of struggle against the government, that is, against the central power. One was the massive incorporation of adolescents into the armed struggle during this second stage—young people who had grown up in an environment of terror, who had seen their houses burned, their families massacred, their fields destroyed, their *fincas* (farms) abandoned. For them, the only meaning of their actions was retaliation and vengeance, which they felt was not only explicable but justifiable in light of the criminality officially protected or promoted in the first years of th La Violencia. The second factor was the fragmentation caused by the rebels' transition from dependence on national political leaders to a much more direct and compromising reliance on *gamonales*; the latter gave them a certain legitimacy, but only to the extent that the rebels yielded to the *gamonales'* provincial interests. Thus, no matter how much the *bandas'* influence spread through the interior of the country, they never had a nationwide profile. Provincialism emerged as one of the most prominent features of *bandolerismo*.

Bandolerismo cannot, therefore, be understood as a simple remnant of La Violencia, but as the armed expression characterizing one of its stages. As a particular historical construct, it stemmed from the changing relations between armed rebels and the state, the political parties, and the local and regional powerbrokers.

To be a *bandolero* meant, above all, to have lost political legitimacy. The same was true for the Brazilian *cangaceiros*, who, once their political protectors had been defeated, had to confront the entire state, police, and judicial powers.[5] However, the social contexts in these two countries were quite different. The bandits of the Sertão, the *cangaceiros*, moved about in a milieu characterized by dynamic alliances between competing families and factions; this gave them certain political options and a minimal possibility for independence, which often made their loss of legitimacy temporary and relative. In Colombia, by contrast, the two-party system introduced a much more static relationship between rebels and protectors: the political affiliation of both was practically determined at birth, by what has been called "inherited hatreds." Nevertheless, these relationships changed under the impact of the nationwide political reshuffling. The question of who would be defined as a *bandolero* was decided during a long process, the crucial moment of which was the establishment of the National Front.

In hindsight, insurgent peasants' political space was continuously being narrowed, even within their own party. In the early 1950s, only the opposing party—the Conservatives—and the government regime it had thrust forward called them *bandoleros*. Starting with Rojas Pinilla's military government, the army would also explicitly define them as such; and once the National Front had been established, the insurgents would also lose the support of their own party's national political leaders, although many local bosses continued to back them.

The continued tactical alliance between *gamonales* and *bandoleros*, and the hostility of both to a new project for political centralization, is reminiscent of the nineteenth-century Sicilian Mafia. Indeed, the Mafiosi, at the time barely distinguishable from bandits, tenaciously opposed the Bourbon occupation of Sicily at the beginning of the century and spearheaded the fight on behalf of the local bosses and landowners, who feared that the occupation would destabilize large estates as well as electoral fiefdoms. And, starting in 1860, during the Risorgimento and the Garibaldian Revolution that ousted the Bourbons, the Mafiosi supported the large Sicilian landowners who viewed the project for national political unification as a threat that could dislocate deep-rooted local power and land-tenure structures (Blok 1972, 97). Still, the spread of banditry in Sicily during this period was a response both to the economic crisis and to the Garibaldian Revolution's attempt to solve the southern problem, that is, the problem of the Sicilian peasantry, through sheer repression (Molfese 1979, 35)

Nevertheless, these similarities should not be overdrawn. In the Colombian case, alongside the disparities noted above and in addition to the always-underlying partisan ties, an essential continuity existed: peasant support for *bandoleros* in the areas where they were active. In these areas, people would invariably continue to refer to them as *guerrilleros*, that is, as rebels with a cause or, in a more familiar tone, as *muchachos del monte* (boys from the mountains).

This combined, contradictory support from peasants and *gamonales* caused the internal tension so characteristic of Colombian *bandolerismo*, which emerged both as the vague expression of defiance against the dominant classes' national political project and as these same classes' fulcrum for preventing discontent from following a revolutionary path. The acknowledgment of this contradiction, expressly intended to affect one of its two poles, allowed the tactical dissidents in the traditional parties, such as López Michelsen's Movimiento Revolucionario Liberal (Liberal Revolutionary Movement; MRL), to penetrate the rural areas and conduct campaigns to force the peasants to register for national identification cards. To this end, these dissidents offered to protect the dissident sectors of the National Front, including *bandoleros* and peasant grassroots' sectors influenced by *bandoleros*. During discussions on the MRL's return to the Liberal fold, López Michelsen expressed his awareness of his opposition movement's ability to channel resentment when he stated:

> [A] mechanical union under the present circumstances would bring no advantage to *liberalismo* and, in fact, would surely lead forces that today are bound together around the MRL to depart to other, non-Liberal camps. I have not expressed a personal dissent of the MRL with the Liberal Party so as to harm it but a dissent [based on political principles] to save it. If *liberalismo* continues to control a majority in this country it is because it has one flag on the side of discontent while others serve the cause of the government against the National Front. . . . If I were to do as I have been asked and bring about a union [between the government and the rebels], a large part of the rebel troops who now follow me would feel they had been discharged and would seek the protection of reds, of Communists, or of groups other than the Liberal Party. (*El Espectador,* May 11, 1965)[6]

The left, by contrast, with sectarian blindness, antagonized the *bandolero* leaders, since it overestimated the latter's role as agents of the regime and failed to understand until it was too late that influence could be exerted on the other pole of the contradiction to win the *bandoleros* over to the revolutionary cause or at least to neutralize them in areas where *bandoleros* and revolutionary movements had a conflictive coexistence.

In sum, *bandolerismo* cannot be understood in isolation or as part of a static relationship between peasants and the dominant classes or as a mere violent outburst in the nation's history. In its inherent fragmentation, and within the broader perspective of the country's social and political development, *bandolerismo* above all shows the dominant classes' success in sowing disarray among the ruled classes through a series of struggles as well as successive defeats. These include the political defeat and the failed expectations of the popular movement connected with López Pumarejo's Revolution on the March; the decapitation, with Gaitán's assassination, of a rising democratic-bourgeois project; the feeling of powerlessness after the heroic but thwarted nationwide insurrection of April 9, 1948; and, finally, the unexpected elimination of the guerrilla movement in the 1950s, which, despite its military effectiveness and the transformations that were under way within it, succumbed to the two-pronged strategy of amnesty and repression.

Given this backdrop of the popular movement's continual setbacks vis-à-vis the vigorous attempt of the dominant classes to reorganize through the National Front, *bandolerismo* understandably emerged in broad swaths of the countryside as an anarchical and desperate peasant response. And, since for desperate people the only program that makes sense is to destroy for the sake of destroying, terror became not only an integral part but also, in most cases, the overarching element of their actions.

This "negative program" of the frustrated and desperate—to use Hobsbawm's expression—joined another common element of the generation of the "sons of La Violencia": vengeance. Cruelty is inseparable from and is legitimized by vengeance. To the humiliated peasants who had been victimized by the official Violencia of the first phase and were unable to collectively organize and resist, disproportionate cruelty and massacres appeared as primitive but extreme expressions of power—as the only expressions available to them. Nevertheless, this thirst to kill and destroy had more rational roots, which to a certain extent were consciously controlled by the *bandoleros*: the need to instill both awe and fear, the two main sources of peasant complicity. Much of the *bandoleros'* success depended on correctly manipulating these two elements. As proof of this, when that fragile balance was broken, a social climate suitable for exterminating the once-invulnerable heroes was created.[7]

A product of this historical process, Colombian *bandolerismo* cannot be considered a prepolitical phenomenon nor can it even be understood as prepolitical in the chronological sense the term had, for instance, in Peru or even more clearly in Spain, where the Andalusian banditry studied by Bernaldo de Quirós disappeared along with peasant uprisings, as studied in Díaz del Moral's classic work ([1929] 1969).

Studies such as that of Camilo Torres (1963), which viewed rural Colombia prior to La Violencia as an archetypal society of submissive peasants—static, closed, and homogeneous—might encourage false interpretations of the Colombian case that would equate it with the historical sequence of countries such as those mentioned above. All recent research has demonstrated, however, the dynamism of union, agrarian, and political mobilization in the period before La Violencia, and, more specifically, starting in the 1920s, which to a certain extent marked the beginning of the movement's classic period.

Bandolerismo in Colombia, then, resulted not from a lack of previous class-based peasant organization, but rather from the disappearance or annihilation of this organization in the dominant classes' counteroffensive. A partial exception to this widespread tendency for previously existing, relatively autonomous, political and grievance-based organizations to be supplanted by *bandolerismo* was seen in the Tequendama-Sumapaz-southern-Tolima corridor, one of the main strongholds of peasant struggle in the 1920s and 1930s. In this region, although it sometimes made mistakes, vacillated, and backed down, the democratic peasant movement showed continuity until the early 1960s, and mass movements (agrarian unions, peasant leagues, democratic fronts) alternated with the guerrilla groups. Although *bandolerismo* was far from absent in these areas, its presence was comparatively weak. Still, these areas supplied a large number of leaders and *bandas* to other areas. When "Chispas" (Sparks), a *guerrillero* from southern Tolima in the early 1950s, became a *bandolero*, he could find fertile ground for his operations only in the neighboring department of Quindío. Moreover, to the extent that *bandoleros* existed in the areas mentioned above, they played a different role there than in other parts of the interior, where they were more akin to the *pájaros*, or paid assassins, in the service of politicians and landholders, who directed their actions precisely against organized peasants. The Communist Party's old antagonism to, and its lack of understanding of, *gaitanismo*, which reemerged in the well-known skirmishes between *comunes* (commies) and *limpios* (clean ones, that is, Liberals not infected by Communism) in the 1950s, naturally had something to do with the different role the bandoleros played in this region.

Political *bandolerismo* spread to nearly all the areas beset by official persecution or guerrilla struggles in the first period of La Violencia;

however, its intensity varied according to political and economic conditions. It failed to take root, for example, in the large strongholds of the guerrilla struggles of the early 1950s: Eliseo Velásquez's and Guadalupe Salcedo's Llanos Orientales; Juan de la Cruz Varela's Sumapaz and southern Tolima; Captain Juan de J. Franco's western and southeastern Antioquia; Rafael Rangel's Santander. By contrast, *bandolerismo* was pervasive in the areas where the peasant population had endured government terrorism and had failed to articulate its own resistance: the northern Valle, northern Tolima, and Viejo Caldas. The most renowned *banda* leaders of the period—"El Mosco" (The Fly), "Zarpazo" (Lash), "La Gata" (The Cat), "Chispas," "Capitán Venganza" (Captain Vengeance), "Desquite" (Revenge), and "Sangrenegra" (Black Blood)—were concentrated in the triangle formed by those three areas. In the same areas, *bandolerismo* most clearly reflected the dominant classes' disjointed attempt to mount a counteroffensive and most ostensibly showed its avenging nature. To paraphrase Pitt-Rivers (1961, 187), in idealizing *bandoleros*, the rural communities in these areas rejected the state and central power that they had associated with destruction, terror, and barbarity for the entire preceding decade.

Nor was *bandolerismo* most deeply rooted in areas exclusively dominated by latifundios. Rather, it reproduced like a Hydra head in areas where small, medium, and large landholdings existed side by side, and it was particularly visible in coffee-growing areas.

Dumar Aljure, a former comrade-in-arms of Guadalupe Salcedo's who found political protection in the faraway Llanos Orientales, might be viewed as an exception to the two aspects referred to above. However, since he operated in that large region of immense latifundios—the main center of resistance in the 1950s—Aljure's case appears rather marginal. In addition, as a one-time army deserter, Aljure was not eligible for amnesty, which played a decisive role in his choice to continue living on the run.[8]

Equally significant was the scarce *bandolero* presence in areas where, in terms of production relationships, either archaic forms or capitalist forms of social organization were relatively consolidated. Two examples of archaic social organization are the departments of Boyacá and Nariño. Examples of capitalist forms are the sugar-growing region of Valle and the mechanized-agriculture area of Espinal-Guamo (Tolima). In areas like Espinal-Guamo, where, before the outbreak of La Violencia, capitalist development had begun, the dominant classes avoided political interference at all costs; in others, such as Valle, they used particular forms of violence that reinforced the incipient capitalist development. For example, in Valle, violence was typically perpetrated not by *bandoleros* but by *pájaros*—true criminals for hire who clearly played a role in confiscating and plundering peasant land for ascendant sugar entrepreneurs.

Coffee-growing areas, the preferred stage of the *bandas*, merit a closer look. Above all, the municipalities that became centers of operations for one or another *cuadrilla* stand out because of their national importance for coffee output: Sevilla and Caicedonia in Valle; Armenia and Calarcá in Quindío; Chaparral and Líbano in Tolima, although in the latter, coffee output fell precisely because of La Violencia.[9]

Moreover, these areas—where, except for Chaparral, agriculture was generally carried out on small plots of land, although large coffee haciendas also exerted influence—were at an intermediate level of development. At least since the 1930s, they had undergone an unstable process of disintegration-restoration of different types of precapitalist agriculture. Thus, in some of these areas, coffee haciendas dominated local production, even though they were numerically insignificant compared to medium-sized and small landholdings. This was the case of Líbano and the region comprising Montenegro and Quimbaya (Quindío).

Various factors were at play in the crisis that had beset the hacienda system before the onset of La Violencia. The peasant struggles that began in the 1920s intensified with Law 200 of 1936, leading landholders to replace the precapitalist *aparcería* (sharecropping) and lease system with one of salaried contractors and laborers. However, rather than raising hacienda productivity, the new law accelerated their decline by causing an immediate shortage of labor and foodstuffs, which was not immediately offset by greater technological innovation.

La Violencia had a strong impact on the aging, weakened hacienda structure: in one manner or another, it ended the hacienda as an agricultural system, although only rarely did it do away with large landholdings. The decline of coffee plantations because of their owners' abandonment or absenteeism and, in some cases, because of a new correlation of power between hacendados and insurgent peasants put the old landholders at a disadvantage vis-à-vis the dynamic middle class, which, once La Violencia had ended, would make every effort to modernize coffee growing.

Nevertheless, the small- and medium-sized coffee-growing landholdings, which frequently changed hands or became part of the recently acquired assets of the new beneficiaries of the general disarray, were more vulnerable. In this regard, the role played by *aparceros* and *agregados* (sharecroppers) on medium-sized farms merits special attention. Their continued importance can be seen, for example, in the fact that in Quindío in 1954 they made up 52 percent of the economically active population.[10] This was true of the La Mina and Los Juanes *veredas* in the municipality of Pijao, which were the preferred territories of the *bandoleros* "Melco" (short for "Melquisedec") and Efraín González.[11]

The incursion of *bandolerismo* into the densely populated and highly integrated coffee-growing area would at first appear to run counter to *bandoleros'* proclivity, as noted in all the classic studies on the topic, to locate in areas cut off from most forms of communication. We know, for example, that Antonio Silvino, the forerunner of Lampião in northeastern Brazil, adamantly opposed the arrival of the railway to Pernambuco and even repeatedly expressed hostility to mail services in the area where he operated (Queiroz 1977, 76–77). Bandits frequently, and justifiably, see the introduction of communications as an enemy as dangerous as repression. Andalusian bandits are said to have been exterminated not only by the Guardia Civil but also by the wire, that is, the telephone and telegraph (Bernaldo de Quirós [1919] 1973, 210).

However, Andalusian *bandoleros* plied their trade in geographic and demographic conditions far different from those of Colombia. They operated not only in areas with large latifundios (considered by Bernaldo de Quirós [ibid., 228] to be the root cause of the phenomenon) but in regions where those who worked the land—day laborers, renters, sharecroppers, and even small and medium landowners—lived in relatively large villages rather than in the countryside. In sum, until the first half of the nineteenth century, Andalusian *bandoleros* and highwaymen typically moved about in a landscape of open fields with no population centers other than the solitary *cortijos* (farmhouses) where a few workers and hacienda foremen lived. Similar conditions, with large latifundios and vast deserts, existed in the Piura region of northern Peru, which was also a land of the "Knights of Crime" (López Albújar [1936] 1973, 329).

By contrast, and notwithstanding the spread of communications, some parts of Colombia's coffee-growing region were nearly impassable. For instance, *bandoleros* found refuge or moved about with ease on the inhospitable peaks of the Central Cordillera. These areas also afforded many conditions that partially or completely offset the dangers brought about by law enforcement's relatively greater efficiency in pursuing outlaws. The arrival of roads, for example, was offset by the greater ease with which *bandas* could obtain foodstuffs, clothes, and ammunition. And the dense, shady coffee *fincas* not only provided physical cover for *bandas* as they eluded the authorities but also made it possible, particularly during harvest periods, for them to take advantage of what Jaime Arocha has called "social camouflage," that is, to blend in among coffee workers and elude pursuit (Arocha 1979, 173–174, 177), similar to the eighteenth-century Dutch bandits who were highwaymen by night and held conventional occupations by day (Blok 1976, 22). But, in addition to purely logistical advantages, the area also afforded clear economic incentives. Hence, after 1954–1955, following the outbreak of *bandolerismo*, two practices emerged that would characterize the relationship between coffee and La Violencia: (1) the eviction of peasants from their land or the purchase of it at derisory prices just as a promising harvest appeared at hand; and (2) the theft or "confiscation" of coffee once peasants had harvested and processed it.

The first practice was carried out by non-*bandoleros*—hacendados, other peasants, but especially merchants—who took advantage of the prevailing apprehensions to frighten producers; the second became a typical means of support for *cuadrillas*. Sharecroppers would play a key role in both cases, since they were the only actors who continued to have an ongoing physical presence on *fincas* whose owners had been killed or forced to flee. For absentee landowners, the only guarantee of retaining a minimal portion of the harvest, or at least of forestalling the immediate loss of their property, was to contract a sharecropper who was accepted by "those who controlled the area." Sharecroppers had all the means of production at their disposal and would determine the fate of the harvests, though naturally under the pressure and manipulation both of merchants, with whom they were customarily in debt, and of *bandoleros*, who threatened them or simply convinced them of the advantages of complicity.

The sharecropping system, then, allowed *cuadrillas* to appropriate part of the harvests without affecting the interests of peasant collaborators. This eventually led sharecroppers to understand that cooperating with *bandoleros* meant less interference from landowners in their daily work and a greater share of the earnings from the harvests, or even the possibility, as many of them foresaw, of appropriating the *fincas*. From this understanding to an explicit pact was merely a matter of time. The *vereda* bosses, organically linked to *bandas* in Quindío, provide clear evidence of this phenomenon. Since booty in the form of coffee is easy to expropriate and market, *bandoleros* could not only survive but even become profitable. Thus, many occasional coffee hands were, not surprisingly, tempted to join a *banda*. Their status as semi-unemployed workers, and the growing disparity between coffee prices and day wages during the bonanza that lasted until 1954,[12] as well as the subsequent effects, toward the end of the decade, of the crisis on real wages, were powerful stimuli for peasants to enroll in different insurgent groups. Although *banda* leaders were predominantly the scions of small landowners, everything appears to indicate that their followers were mostly day laborers.

Behind the sharecroppers and *bandoleros* were the merchants who bought the stolen or "confiscated" coffee, who speculated with prices and fixed scales, and who, because of their familiarity with the community and the location of the plots of land, were in an excellent social position to seize *fincas* and harvests.

However, in addition to the economic interests of various strata of peasant society in tolerating or encouraging *bandolerismo*, there was another obvious factor that prevented Colombian *bandoleros* from being excessively hostile toward cities or other highly urbanized areas: given *bandoleros'* specific political nature, in urban areas they found their source of protection and legitimacy and consequently their guarantee of impunity. Here, once again, we need to stress the particular nature of political bandits vis-à-vis social bandits in classic studies. In Andalusia, and to a certain extent in Peru, social bandits were marginalized from the rest of society: they were "outlaws" who operated in uninhabited areas. The peasant communities they had left as fugitives or avengers of injustices considered them popular heroes deserving of protection. Their daily lives were not closely tied to their community; rather, social bandits were permanently absent, which facilitated the construction of a myth around them and their deeds. By contrast, Colombia's political *bandoleros*, whose actions were always related to their party affiliation; who had, during much of their careers, protectors of acknowledged social superiority; and who had woven within the rural population an extensive, specialized network of collaborators and abettors, were unquestionably an integral part not only of peasant society but of the larger society, as seen in their numerous linkages with the local power structure and their ongoing ties with the cities, about which they did not profess the usual fear felt by social bandits. Chispas's *banda* had so little hostility toward urban contacts that it put together and operated an urban network in Armenia and Calarcá.

It was, nevertheless, in the interstices of economic incentive that the peculiar class content of Colombian *bandolerismo* emerged. Liberal *bandoleros*, initially the enemies of poor and rich Conservatives alike, began to threaten or affect the economic interests of their own party's landowners. In so doing, they paradoxically did not broaden their social base, win the support of Conservative peasants, or extend their relationships and networks of support outside the Liberal Party. (Nor did Conservative *bandoleros* broaden their social base outside of their own party.) Instead, they acknowledged the division of classes within their own party, but not in society as a whole. We might say that there was a *fragmented class consciousness*, a social antagonism traversed by party dependence. Here the "political *bandolero*" encountered the "social *bandolero*" and the two were fused into a single protagonist. Both Chispas and Lampião personified this process, and Queiroz's observation on Lampião is also valid for Chispas:

> Antonio Silvino and Lampião had a certain awareness of social injustices, and they proclaimed that they were defending the poor, dividing the earnings from their robberies with them. . . . There was not, however, any element that denoted an ideal of equality of ownership, but a conception of helping the poor, which was the same as that of the *coronéis* [that is, Brazil's *gamonales*]: a paternalism that saw to it that the leftovers from the table of the rich were distributed to the poor. Many a *coronel* took pride also in being a protector of the poor. But both in this case and that of Lampião, it was *their* poor first, that is, those who helped them and supported them; the poor who supported their enemies ceased to merit that classification [and] were confronted in the same manner as were so many enemies, and persecuted as such. (1977, 207)

Given that evolution, which was tinged with partisan hatred, did the Colombian *bandolero* conjure up among the peasants the image of the social *bandolero*, the *myth* of the invulnerable fighter defending a cause that was with theirs, that of the peasants? The answer is as complex as the evolution of the protagonists themselves. In a first stage, Chispas, Efraín González, or Capitán Venganza, among others, represented—although less clearly so in the actual events than in legend—fundamental peasant aspirations, which brought them close to the image of the classic social *bandolero*: an ideal of "justice" and "liberty"; the possibility of experiencing a brief moment of wealth and power, putting them on the side of "those who earn respect for themselves," as the Sicilian expression goes; an example of social mobility that elicited the admiration of the peasants around them, etc. However, although the Colombian *bandolero* and the classic bandit partially share the descriptions given above, they are not equally concerned with cultivating a positive public image. Many of the bandits in classic studies even developed a certain skill at managing their image, although they possibly never surpassed the elegance of the Andalusian bandits of the romantic era or the Peruvian "Sambambé," who organized bandits in Piura and Lambayeque. Both the Andalusians and the Sambambé avoided direct participation in the killings, shared part of their booty with the poor, and even introduced the chivalric form of requesting tribute into their "profession," or robbed with hat in hand and expressed kind words and gallantries toward women. By contrast, the cruel milieu of La Violencia did not lend itself to such romantic frivolities. Even when political bandits evolved into a more social role, they made no attempt to imprint an aura of moderation on their violent acts, nor did they conceal their atrocities. Moreover, they did not need to as long as these atrocities were justified by being carried out against the enemy party, even if the victims were peasants from their own region. To the extent that it is a myth, then, the myth of the social bandit, the heroic defender of the poor, invincible and endowed with the gift of ubiquity, was not shared by an entire class, in this case, the peasantry as a whole.

Having arrived at a certain class consciousness, however fragmented, Colombian *bandoleros* began to suffer from an internal contradiction between their original status as political bandits and their actual evolution, which led them to propose new options that were opposed to the role they had played until then. How this evolution was structured in its actual process is the topic of the next chapter.

CHAPTER THREE

Regional and Sociopolitical Diversity of Banditry 1: Transitions

In this and the following chapters, we analyze the regional variations of *bandolerismo* during the period from 1955 to 1965. The purpose of this regional analysis is to account for the geographic differences in which *bandolerismo* emerged, the various socioeconomic and sociopolitical structures in which it took hold, and its particular dynamics and manifestations in the three regions studied. Hence, we construct a typology of the most significant processes found within the variations and dispersion that typified *bandolerismo*.

We have differentiated the following four processes, two of which are covered in this chapter and two in the next chapter:

1. *From Political to Social Banditry.* The process by which *bandoleros*, dominated initially by the oligarchy through bipartisan rule, gradually although incompletely came to a dynamic break with landowners and political bosses. This was the case in regions whose agrarian society had been decisively structured by precapitalist forms of production, particularly sharecropping. Thus, to the extent that they became the representatives of a multifaceted peasant discontent, they increasingly approximated the prototype of social bandits. The leading actors of this transformation were Chispas and Efraín González in Quindío.

2. *Banditry and Revolutionaries.* The process by which *bandoleros* dependent on local or regional power structures came into contact with or evolved into authentic revolutionaries and, given their ideology, organization, and objectives, adopted the characteristics of a revolutionary guerrilla movement struggling against the established order and the internal and external structures of domination.

This set of complex relationships and evolution in northern Tolima was exemplified by Pedro Brincos, an heir to the area's tradition of rebellion. The particular nature of this evolution will be better understood when compared to the other two most important examples in the region, Desquite and Sangrenegra.

The following variations will be analyzed in Chapter 4:

3. *Mercenary Banditry*. The process in the latter years of La Violencia by which a type of *bandolerismo*, because of its links to urban areas and its underlying economic motives and stimuli, became the rural equivalent of the dreaded *pájaros* of the first stage of La Violencia. This was the typical *bandolerismo* in the area of large coffee and cattle estates in Hoya del Quindío (the lowlands of Quindío, on the border with the department of Valle). We have also called this "late *bandolerismo*" because of its relative discontinuity with the first stage of La Violencia.

4. *Peasant Myths and the Crossroads of Banditry*. The process by which the most consummate expression of the *bandolero* myth, Capitán Venganza, emerged in the small- and medium-sized landholding area of Quinchía, Risaralda, as the invisible hero who protected peasants being persecuted.

One final category—landowner *bandolerismo*—outside the purview of this study, emerged in Sumapaz (between Cundinamarca and Tolima), which had a time-honored tradition of organized land-tenure struggles. In this latifundio region, La Violencia assumed the character of landholder retaliation, and resistance to it acquired the characteristics of revolutionary warfare. In this polarized context, *bandoleros*, prodded not only by landholders and *gamonales* but also by the army and secret service, acted as agents of terror against the peasantry's organized struggle. This was, unambiguously, the *bandolerismo* of the landowners, of the *señores*. The *bandoleros* of this region performed roles nearly identical to those of the official agents of repression, as had occurred in prerevolutionary Mexico with bandits and the rural police, known as the *rurales* (Vanderwood 1981).

From Political to Social Banditry:
Departments of Quindío, Tolima, and Santander

Efraín González Téllez

The transition from political to social banditry is epitomized by the life histories of two famous bandits: Efraín González Téllez, who acted,

MAP 3. STAGES OF "LA VIOLENCIA"

**First wave of violence
(1948–1953)**

**Second wave of violence
(1954–1958)**

N

—— Departmental boundary

Area affected by "La Violencia"

Source: Based on data from CEDE-ORSTOM, 1996.

first, on behalf of the Conservative Party and later on behalf of the ANAPO (National Popular Alliance, founded by General Gustavo Rojas Pinilla); and Teófilo Rojas (alias Chispas), who undertook his bandit life on behalf of the Liberal Party. The criminal career of Efraín González Téllez (alias Don Juan, El Viejo [the Old Man], El Tío [the Uncle], or Siete Colores [Seven Colors]) began in Pijao, a region of Quindío. This small coffee-growing town, where Liberals had been in the majority prior to Gaitán's assassination, became almost completely "Conservatized" during the first stage of La Violencia through various forms of coercion. It later became a magnet for Conservative families seeking refuge after being displaced through identical "Liberalizing" procedures in other regions of the country, such as Santander and Boyacá.

The González family also came from the department of Santander, but their migration from the municipality of Jesús María, where Efraín had been born in 1933, was presumably motivated by the wave of (Liberal) partisan violence that scourged the region during Enrique Olaya Herrera's government (1930–1934). Efraín's father had started out in Quindío as a farm administrator and later, through much effort, came to own a small amount of land.

Efraín attended three years of primary school; he entered the army around 1950 and later deserted, holding the rank of first corporal. He became an administrator for an hacendado in Armenia. Years later he witnessed his father's death during an army raid. The trauma of this unforgettable event propelled him, as similar events had done with so many of his contemporaries, into a legendary life of crime. As one of his biographers writes, "thereafter the orphan organized his *cuadrilla* and set off on the paths of robbery and plunder" (Alba 1971, 15).[1] He hooked up with the *cuadrilla* of the dread bandit Jair Giraldo, as did his three brothers, who ended up in the emerald-trafficking mafias of Muzo and Otanche, in Boyacá.

Still, González remained only a relatively short time in Quindío. The law and the army were following him too closely, especially after he was charged with murdering Celedonio Martínez, the editor of *Diario Quindío* and an enormously prestigious journalist in the region. He was captured (the only time he is known to have been) in Armenia, but he escaped under what court reporters normally called "undetermined circumstances"—generally a euphemism indicating complicity of prison authorities.

Two additional events buttressed his determination to return to Santander, the department of his birth, and particularly to the region of Jesús María-Puente Nacional, from where he would later broaden his radius of operations to Chiquinquirá and other areas of Boyacá. First, Liberal politicians in Quindío and coffee growers—especially those of Calarcá—had collected funds to finance the transfer of Chispas, along with numerous former combatants from the initial period of La Violencia, to southern Tolima. The presence in the region of the by-now-renowned Chispas, coupled with González's persecution by the authorities, threatened the image of invulnerability that González doggedly defended until his death. Second, around the same time, in the area of Vélez, Santander, the Liberal *bandolero* Carlos Bernal, allied with the MRL, was accused of massacring Conservative peasants. In exchange for armed protection, Bernal offered Efraín González much stronger solidarity than he might have found anywhere else in the country.

Despite—or perhaps because of—González's sinister past in Quindío, where he had been accused of fourteen murders by the time he left for Santander and had been given a sixty-three-year jail sentence in absentia, the Conservative peasants of his native region welcomed him with exultation and political fanaticism akin to religious fervor, rapidly constructing his myth. Some disseminated the legend that González could turn into a tree or stone; others proudly displayed his portrait and burned candles before it; and many carried out public collections in Garavito, Puente Nacional, and Chiquinquirá to finance a criminal crusade, although they did not consider it as such. All hid him and informed him of the movements of the authorities who pursued him. Around González, then, a network of links, legend, and economic and political complicity was woven, which constituted the natural milieu of *bandolerismo*.

In addition, the campesinos naturally interpreted the support given to González by regional priests as a moral sanction of his actions. A common trait of these Conservative *bandoleros* was their militant adherence to the church, expressed in practices that revealed a primitive, naïve religiosity best described as superstition. During battles, González would wear images of the two national religious symbols of Colombia for protection: the Virgin of Chiquinquirá and the Sacred Heart. When "El Mico" (the Monkey), another Conservative bandit, was gunned down, he reportedly was carrying a book with the following petition: "I am Manuel Cedeño. If an accident befalls me, take me to the priest." Likewise, Efraín González is not only said to have tried several times to become a monk, but he even disguised himself as a monk for a time near La Candelaria, in Ráquira, to elude the authorities. This can only indicate an open tolerance by the members of this religious community, who saw him as a faithful soldier of Christ.

Besides the support of the Conservative masses and the clergy, González found in Santander and Boyacá the protection of his party's regional political leaders, such as a lawmaker named Sorzano González, who in May 1964 praised Efraín in the Senate. As if this were not enough, the deliberate sluggishness of law enforcement in pursuing him was, at least initially, notorious.

When Efraín González left Quindío, fellow Conservatives Melco and "Polancho" replaced him. They and their most famous Liberal adversary, Chispas, reached a tacit understanding to divide the area that runs along the Central Cordillera, including part of Quindío and two large coffee-growing centers of northern Valle del Cauca: Sevilla and Caicedonia. Melco and Polancho set up their base of operations in *corregimientos* (an administrative designation for villages lying outside a *cabecera*, or municipal seat) in Pijao and in Caicedonia. This area formed a politically homogeneous Conservative zone, referred to sardonically as the "Independent Republic" or "Sovereign State" of Aures. Chispas established Quebradanegra, at that time within the jurisdiction of the wealthy coffee-growing municipality of Calarcá and today part of the municipality of Córdoba, as his center of operations.

These rival *bandas* generally used the same technique to defend their areas of control or to penetrate those of their adversaries: physical elimination, usually of innocent peasants, and with a deliberately competitive brutality so as to sow terror. Within their respective dominions, the social bases of their militants and the support networks were not very different either. One printed comment regarding Chispas's *cuadrilla* could be considered valid for all *cuadrillas*, at least in their initial stage: "[I]t exercised an illegitimate power discussed neither by the landowners nor by the illiterate laborers" (*La Nueva Prensa* 96, May 3, 1963, 25). And the *finca* administrators, who appear to have been the persons most able to obtain an economic advantage from the anxiety that had taken hold in the countryside, discussed this "illegitimate power" even less.

Bandoleros on both sides were equally inclined to resort to procedures that would become classic, such as the *boleteo* (extortion through the delivery of a letter) to pressure the owner of a *finca* to sell or abandon it or even to upgrade it—either by planting new crops or by building new structures. On other occasions, *boletas* were delivered to force the dismissal of a day laborer or the administrator of a *finca* whose

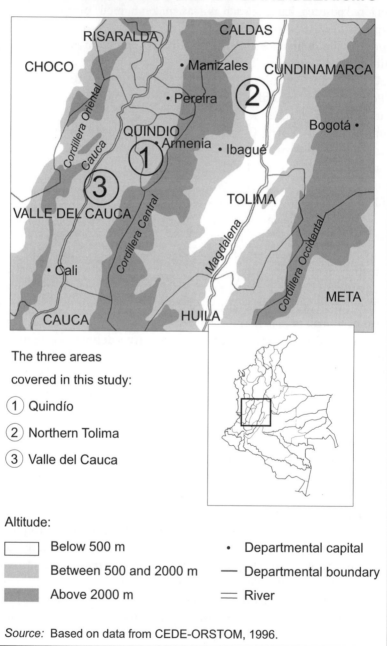

MAP 4. THIRD WAVE OF "LA VIOLENCIA" (1958–1965): MAIN AREAS AFFECTED BY *BANDOLERISMO*

RISARALDA

CALDAS

CHOCO

• Manizales

CUNDINAMARCA

• Pereira

②

Cordillera Oriental

Cauca

QUINDIO

Armenia

Bogotá •

• Ibagué

①

③

TOLIMA

VALLE DEL CAUCA

Cordillera Central

Magdalena

Cordillera Occidental

META

• Cali

CAUCA

HUILA

The three areas covered in this study:

① Quindío

② Northern Tolima

③ Valle del Cauca

Altitude:

☐ Below 500 m

▨ Between 500 and 2000 m

■ Above 2000 m

• Departmental capital

— Departmental boundary

= River

Source: Based on data from CEDE-ORSTOM, 1996.

owner the *bandoleros* wanted to harass. After the *bandoleros* would come the *usufructuarios* (literally, "beneficiaries"): local merchants, neighboring landowners who wanted to extend their boundaries, bosses who wanted to get rid of a sharecropper or avoid paying wages. The most conflictive relationship linked to La Violencia appears to have arisen between landowners and sharecroppers, whose presence was common on small- and medium-sized holdings. The owner of a farm in Génova—an area where these three different *cuadrillas* would test their capacity to retaliate and where in mid-1962 Melco carried out one of his most notorious massacres—complained that in the preceding year he had gone through four sharecroppers: the first had been killed, the second had worked "about fifteen days picking coffee . . . [then] he picked up the coffee and ran off and didn't give me any accounting, all he gave me was one *arroba* [about 25 pounds] of coffee. And the next one did give me a little coffee and told me he wasn't staying any longer, and gave me the *boleta*." The landowner had not been able to appear on his *finca* for a year (Sumario 9, 109). Taking advantage of this climate of terror, many administrators came to own not only the harvests but also, although temporarily, the land they administrated or adjoining parcels.

By contrast, in predominantly *minifundio* (smallholding) areas, such as those controlled by Efraín González in Santander and Boyacá, the most obvious economic effect of the *bandas'* actions was to transfer property from the peasants of one party to those of the rival party, until the regions were politically homogeneous. (With regard to González, in one noteworthy case of redistribution, the Liberal owner of some 200 hectares in Puente Nacional was forced by the *banda* to break up his property and sell it to Conservative peasants [Aguilera and Ramos 1980, 9].)

But the motives for peasants' support of *cuadrillas* were not solely economic. They also felt safer protected by the informal and illegitimate power of the *cuadrillas* than by the state, simply because they saw the state personified daily in the police and the army that persecuted and tortured them or, if they were lucky, that merely harassed them in the zeal to discover the authors of crimes or their accomplices. Hence, a vicious cycle was being created: the greater the harassment, the greater the peasants' complicity with *bandoleros*, which in turn led to a new, increasingly desperate reaction from the army, until repressive measures were unleashed that were as disproportionate as those used in investigating the aforementioned massacre by Melco. The following order is an example of this type of army reprisal.

Génova, July 7, 1962

CAPTAIN IN COMMAND OF THE MILITARY GROUP
[...]
   I most attentively request that you see fit to capture the following individuals who reside on the Bogotacito, California, and
Trinidad *fincas*, in the *vereda* of El Cairo:
[Names omitted by the authors]
   Likewise, it is indispensable to lead all residents from said fincas,
including the women and children, and gather them in the town's
public plaza so that they may be submitted to an interrogation and
review. Naturally, when this raid is carried out, it is necessary to
have vigilance on the affected haciendas, to avoid plunder and robbery.
   This massive [effort] must be carried out next Wednesday, the
eleventh day of the month.
   Having nothing else to add, I send you my best regards, attentively,

Investigating Judge
(Sumario 9, 19)

Such reprisals against entire peasant communities were inevitably repeated often during the army's fight against the most prominent
bandolero leaders, since the real target was an "invisible" enemy.
   Nevertheless, *bandoleros* also copied the army's disproportion between objectives and the means to attain them. One explicit intention
of the massacre alluded to above was that of "clearing Liberals" from a
certain *vereda* to shorten the distance between two deployment bases
of Melco's *cuadrilla*. To wreak the greatest havoc possible among the
peasant population, Melco deliberately carried out the operation at
the height of the harvest season—a common practice in incursions
into territory deemed to belong to the enemy, but not in the *cuadrillas'*
own areas of support, where they were careful not to "cause damage"
during the coffee harvest. This is a clear example of the *cuadrillas'*
distinctive behavior in areas they considered to be under their jurisdiction and those they defined as targets to be attacked.
   Although Conservative *bandoleros* were relatively isolated, their
internal dynamics and their evolution were similar to those of *bandoleros* defending the Liberal standard. As happened with their Liberal counterparts, the Conservative *bandoleros'* elimination roughly

coincided with the transformation of their original political linkages. This can be seen in the demise of Efraín's two successors in Quindío, which occurred before that of their leader. Polancho was killed in mid-1962, and a few months later (March 1963) Melco, the protégé of the Conservative *gamonales* in Caicedonia and of the parish priest in Génova, was gunned down. As was *de rigueur* for Conservative *bandoleros*, Melco was wearing medals of the Virgen del Carmen (Our Lady of Mount Carmel) and the Virgen del Perpetuo Socorro (Our Lady of Perpetual Help) around his neck.

In any event, Melco's and Polancho's Conservative peasant supporters, believing that this denouement resulted from their heroes' personal shortcomings, failed to notice the irreversible loss of legitimacy by their most eminent protectors. They once again turned to Efraín González, as if this were the most natural thing in the world. They are known to have taken up a collection, "demanding from each and every *finca* owner in the El Dorado *vereda* one *carga* of coffee" to finance his return and "consequently to fix this town up for those who have contributed" to the cause (Sumario 9, 152).

Unlike his successors in Quindío, Efraín González still enjoyed a controversial popularity in Santander and Boyacá because, after two members of the legislature broke a campaign promise to give him amnesty, he had had the foresight to slip into a fundamentally city-based opposition movement—the Alianza Nacional Popular (National Popular Alliance; ANAPO)—giving his struggle a new source of legitimacy. Unlike that of most *bandolero* leaders, González's network of urban contacts was not limited to well-heeled politicians; it was so widespread that one step taken by military intelligence in February 1965, when the army tried to encircle him with motorized troop movements, was to wiretap telephone lines in his area of influence, western Boyacá (Comando del Ejército n.d., case 59, 229).

González's new links to ANAPO were first made public well into 1965, when, following his *banda*'s kidnapping of the heirs of a prominent landowner, Martín Vargas, González named two ANAPO legislators, Benjamín Burgos and Alfredo Cuadros, as his intermediaries. Curiously and significantly, upon the death of González's political rival Carlos Bernal, and after González's one-time protectors had joined the pro-government ranks of the Liberal Party, Bernal's followers joined ANAPO. Hence, an old, implacable, partisan rivalry was resolved at the grassroots level, in a new political project (Aguilera and Ramos 1980, 12).

Chispas (Teófilo Rojas)

The career of Chispas, Efraín González's political adversary and the most renowned Liberal *bandolero* leader, ended in the same region of Quindío where Efraín González had made his début. The most reliable account of Chispas's childhood and adolescence is the autobiographical report he gave in 1958 to José María Oviedo, "General Mariachi," under whom he had operated in southern Tolima. This document may be the most complete account given by a *bandolero* of himself, and it exemplifies the personal and political career of most "sons of La Violencia": a childhood lived amid terror, which generally meant the loss of family members and property; the premature entry—in early adolescence—into a fundamentally defensive armed struggle; an insurgency continually betrayed by its intellectual backers, the *gamonales* and the "notarial *guerrilleros*" (those who encouraged and benefited from La Violencia from the safety of their urban offices); the patent difficulty of transcending the narrow limits imposed by the latter on the uprising; and the absence of effective guarantees to encourage a return to a normal life of work. The document begins as follows:

My given name is Teófilo Rojas, and I am going to tell you how I had to live, even when I was a very young boy, as far back as around the year 1949 and 50, when I lived next to my parents, on a *finca* we called La Esperanza, owned by my father.

Question: And where is that *finca*?

Answer: It is in the region or jurisdiction of Rovira [Tolima], where we worked and lived very peacefully until when, I recall it as if it were now, people in uniform started to come with some private individuals [and they] mistreated those of us who had the misfortune of being with them; the least they would call us was "son-of-a-bitch *collarejos*"[2] and other swear words that were, moreover, offensive—when they didn't hit us or threaten us. This kept us terrified, and our terror spontaneously increased when they killed some men, and they murdered many others so unjustly. And, not only that, but they trampled on the children and raped the women, doing whatever they liked to them. They [the victims] didn't dare utter a word, to avoid greater torment; and I especially remember everything they did to a cousin, grabbing her in front of her parents and doing things I would rather not remember, ignoring the pleas made to them. I remember that nearly all the people who committed those atrocities lived [near] the checkpoint at La Selva; and I remember well a certain Ricardo Prieto, who, taking advantage of my stupidity and fear, since I was young, suggested that I switch from being a *cachiporro* [Liberal] to a *godo* [Conservative]. He said that way I would live in peace and would lack nothing and that, on the other hand, if I did not accept, he hinted that he would kill me. And they did that with all of us, men and women, old and young, and [he explained] how they killed, burned, insulted, robbed, raped, and did so many things because we were Liberals; and at that time I was no more than thirteen (13) years old. I was very afraid and was hurt by everything they did. I resolved to get away from those very despicable people, to see if in that way I could finally avoid dying at their hands.[3]

Chispas, like so many *banda* leaders, was the son of a small land-holder from a Liberal area where a couple of sinister outsiders arrived "in uniform" and in the company of "some private individuals"—that is, *chulavitas*[4] and *pájaros* who, with official impunity, unleashed wide-spread terror on a peasant town that initially did nothing but express its impotence in the face of events whose nearly unimaginable cruelty paralyzed witnesses to this daily tragedy.

This cruelty, typical of the entire period of La Violencia and not yet sufficiently understood, was expressed in such ways as the infamous *corte de franela* or the *picada de tamal* and horrendous crimes with sexual overtones, such as mutilating victims' genital organs and disemboweling pregnant women.[5] Psychiatrist José Francisco Socarrás (1958, 7) says these acts, along with symbolic castration—decapitating and gouging out eyes—express a desire for destruction and self-destruction linked to the Freudian wish to die. The root, in this case, is individual and collective frustration: frustration regarding basic needs; frustration of one's personality in a repressive family setting; cultural frustration; and, last, frustration caused by a religion that demands constant privations.

Nevertheless, passivity in the face of cruelty and violence, Chispas tells us, has a limit:

[A]nd since I could do nothing against so much, I fled from one place to another until I finally came to a place near the Andes, where Leonidas Borja was as well. He also had to flee from that violence and persecution [although our] only sin was being Liberals. And because at that time no one even talked about a guerrilla movement, we didn't know how to defend ourselves or where to hide to get away from so much ferocity, and since poor families whose loved ones had been killed, or who had been mistreated, or whose belongings had been stolen, or whose small landholdings had been burned continued to arrive[;] then with our friend Borja, they began to organize to defend those poor families and those of us who had no other protection than what they offered and to find a way to be protected and far from so much evil. In this way and out of sheer need and with great sacrifice, they managed to gather some small shotguns, all of which had been haphazardly repaired and were unreliable, since they even had to use a piece of rubber to make them work. In addition, with some machetes we were able to get meat in the wilderness, and since there was also firewood, we could take care of urgent needs. . . .

It was then that those villains followed us all the way to where we thought we would be in less danger, although we were hungry and cold after everything we had to endure on the flight, [instead of being able to be] happy. [W]ith so much evil, they cornered us and forced us to answer the shots they were firing at us.

The formation of guerrilla groups, as the typical expression of resistance in the second phase of the first period of La Violencia, was, then, highly spontaneous, inseparable from the widespread sequence of families fleeing, of the need to survive in the wilderness and to defend oneself from continual persecution. Moreover, as a result of this process, the initial nuclei of the *cuadrillas* frequently consisted of the members of a single family: the Borja brothers in the case reported by Chispas; the Fonseca brothers or the Bautista brothers in the guerrilla groups in the Llanos Orientales; the González Prieto brothers in northern Tolima; or the five Loaiza brothers, headed by their father, in the southern part of the same department. One of the Loaiza brothers summarized this experience as follows: "Guerrilla groups were not formed out of choice; they were created by La Violencia" (*Tribuna*, August 28, 1953). The prevalence of kinship ties in the *cuadrillas* also explains the widespread use of nicknames to avoid the persecution of other family members ("El Lobo" [the Wolf], for Leonidas Borja; "Córdoba," for his brother, among many others). The number of families was so large, said Chispas, that they decided to divide into two groups "to see if this would make it easier and more efficient to save so many innocent ones."

The guerrilla groups justifiably felt that their own party's hierarchy had given them only passive or token support. Nevertheless, they maintained an irrational or principally sentimental loyalty, based on "inherited hatreds," to their party's standard. And, encouraged by their success in obtaining weapons and foodstuffs by robbing and pillaging their enemies, they surpassed the initial, defensive phase and gradually became a clearly offensive force.

The dominant classes' fear of this new development led to a reshuffling in the nation's power structure. Chispas described this in the following terms:

That, I remember quite well, was when the planes that had once fired their guns at us now [dropped] flyers and newspapers telling about the fall of then President Laureano Gómez, who, because he was evil and corrupt, had been overthrown, but [they claimed that] a very good man would now rise to the presidency, one who preached peace, justice, and liberty for all, who would see that our persons and properties were respected, who would end all this killing, and since he was the one in charge of the Armed Forces and his name was Gustavo Rojas Pinilla, he would put things in order and we would be able to return to our land and work and live peacefully with our families, and he would be the sole savior of the fatherland. Those *guerrilleros* who defended us were then informed that they would have to surrender their weapons if they wanted us to be left alone and to be able to go back to work in peace, because, [if they] turned over their weapons, the government would help us and would give us many guarantees so we could work, would see to it that we recovered what we had lost. So, with all those promises, which we never saw fulfilled, our good defenders surrendered the few shotguns that they carried as defense weapons, as I explained before. We proceeded in good faith; our good leaders thought we would be left alone and could return to work and to peace, since the persecution against us was so unjust, what else could they continue to do to us . . . [?]

I didn't know which direction to go in, until I decided to head out to Guadualito to work on the farm of don Servando Gutiérrez, with a son of his, in agricultural work, where I remained for about a year.

During that year, Chispas says, Córdoba, one of the Borja brothers, two Cantillo brothers, and even Chispas's boss, the son of Servando Gutiérrez, were all killed.

Then the horrible wave of persecution returned against all of us who did not give in to the proposals that we switch sides, since they kept inquiring about the *guerrilleros* and those of us who were with them seeking protection, as I have explained. So, then, with the surviving Cantillos and Borjas, once again we had to organize to see how we could defend ourselves. We were not trained to take arms against the police and the army—who were called the *pájaros*—who received weapons, ammunition, and money to persecute all of us Liberals who wandered from place to place in search of guarantees, peace, and work. But [their] idea was always to completely finish us off, while preaching Peace, Justice, and Liberty. In this way, they forced us to seek refuge in the mountains. . . . And, since my life was once again threatened and in danger, far from my protectors, I had to look for them again and put myself in their care in around 1955, more or less in the month of November, and accompany Lobo once again, given the danger that threatened me.

As Chispas recalls, after the June 13, 1953, coup d'état, the senior military commanders set out to weaken the guerrillas in the two main areas where they had concentrated, the Llanos Orientales and southern Tolima. Given the course of events and the number of troops committed to the resistance in both of these areas, the degree to which the military regime would either be legitimated or called into question depended largely on what occurred on those two fronts. Although the consensus Rojas had obtained from the outset among the political leadership facilitated his task, it was not enough. The existence of forty distinct fronts of resistance against the ousted government of Gómez (and his replacement, Roberto Urdaneta) was also relevant, despite their dispersion throughout the country. In addition, many insurgents did not learn of Gómez's overthrow until the moment they surrendered, because freedom of the press was nearly nonexistent and there was excessive zeal to conceal or downplay the real dimensions of the dispute.

The guerrilla commands were flooded with flyers dropped from helicopters promising PEACE, JUSTICE, AND LIBERTY, and numerous government emissaries went to the different regions to explain the specific promises directly to the guerrilla leaders. Brigadier General Alfredo Duarte Blum and the governor of Tolima, Colonel César Augusto Cuéllar Velandia, directed the operation. On June 19, 1953, Duarte Blum sent a circular to the different army commands authorizing them "to give complete freedom to all those individuals who in one way or another have been implicated in subversive acts against the public order and who voluntarily appear before the military authorities surrendering their weapons, to protect their lives, to help them return to their work activities, and to assist them with their most urgent needs when circumstances so require and you deem it necessary" (Guzmán 1968, 141).

The first mass surrenders took place in the small town of Rovira by the armed groups mentioned by Chispas: one, under the command of Tiberio Borja (Commander Córdoba), operated in the Riomanso region, and another, from the area of La Estrella, was led by David Cantillo Elías ("El Triunfante"). Although the true number of ex-combatants probably did not reach 200, the army commanders, hoping to have a strong psychological impact on other regions and on the cities, organized transportation to Rovira for the elderly, women, and children— that is, noncombatants who were in poor physical condition. For a guerrilla surrender, this was a politically profitable spectacle, and it needed to be accompanied by multiple promises of rewards and benefits, to set an example. The preparations had begun as early as mid-July, just one month after Rojas came to power. On August 2, 615 persons ("guerrilla elements," according to the jubilant press) were gathered in the schools of Rovira.

However, the Liberal guerrilla groups of southern Tolima had attained neither the independence nor the political vision to convincingly demand guarantees or conditions for surrendering to the military authorities. By contrast, the guerrillas in the Llanos Orientales and southwestern Antioquia and the Communist guerrillas, whose headquarters were also located in southern Tolima, at times made varying demands simply to give themselves time to dissolve or demobilize. Hence, the case of Tiberio Borja is among the most disappointing. The account he gave to the *Tribuna* newspaper about his first contacts with the army does not indicate that he made any demands prior to formally agreeing to surrender his men and weapons; on the contrary, the tone indicates an unwonted submission by the former combatants, who asked for nothing more than compassion regarding their misfortunes:

> We would like to tell you in this letter many things regarding the interview [we had] over there with the colonel, but we will talk of that later on, when we are in the capital with our men and with the

sick, the invalids and the wounded and the elderly whom we will take on the day of the surrender. When we told our comrades about the things we saw there, the guarantees offered us by the colonel, and we showed them the medicine the army gave us, many did not believe [us] and thought we were deceiving them, and some even imagined that we were betraying them. None of this is strange, because after so much suffering and so many deceits and persecutions throughout these times, people have become very distrustful and incredulous regarding the word of the authorities. . . . The children are happy with the syrups the military sent them and since they like them so much we have to hide them so they don't drink them like soft drinks. The tonics have already changed the appearance of many of the convalescents and the elderly who were listless. All this has been received as a blessing from God, and the women keep saying that it is an absolute miracle of the Virgin and Santa Rita, whom they call the advocate of the impossible, and they do nothing but burn candles to them. . . . We beg you to tell all this to the governor, to tell him that we distributed all the peace information that he gave us and that we also hung the general's portrait in many places. (*Tribuna*, July 29, 1953)

Two weeks after the surrender they returned to their places of origin, with their tonics and their poverty.

Since there were no mechanisms to guarantee that the promises of credit, medical assistance, and other aid would be kept and that the requests later made by the *guerrilleros* through the press would be attended to, these promises and requests naturally came to naught. Gerardo Loaiza, another of the principal Liberal leaders of southern Tolima, acknowledged as much in a request he sent Rojas Pinilla from Rioblanco in March 1954.

When, at the beginning of the second half of the year before last . . . I said in a solemn ceremony for the surrender of the revolutionary forces under my command, "I exchange my rifle for a hoe," I believed that the reciprocal promises made by the representative of the National Army, Colonel Convers Pardo, would be happily and quickly fulfilled. Today, after months that have brought a situation of greater urgency for the inhabitants of the region, the promises are nothing more than a memory and a hope that we will see them kept. . . .

We were told that the Office of Rehabilitation and Relief would provide each head of household residing in the region a minimum sum of one thousand pesos ($1,000) with the backing of the state, plus two breeding cows and agricultural tools, with a reasonable period for repaying that amount. . . .

[W]e ask no other [help] than what was offered at the moment of reconciliation of the armistice. If we surrendered our guns that had allowed us to defend our lives, we expected to receive the tools that would make it easier for us to obtain our daily sustenance. (*Tribuna*, March 31, 1954)

The broken promises soon gave way to a new wave of government-sponsored violence, which was particularly acute in 1955 and 1956 and was felt most dramatically in the region of Sumapaz and especially in Villarrica. The destructive, lethal action of military planes, the incessant bombing and machine-gunning, the burning and ravaging of sown fields forced the peasants, after resisting heroically, to embark on a massive, organized exodus that touched the nation's public opinion and erased the dubious prestige Rojas Pinilla had initially enjoyed (Fajardo 1979, 120).

The government's failure to keep its word, the relentless harassment, and the frequent murder of former, amnestied *guerrilleros* made the latter increasingly wary of promises of peace and contributed to the lumpenization of many of them, who continued to live as *muchachos del monte*. They did so not out of a conscious commitment to a particular form of struggle but simply as a modus vivendi. This allowed those who continued under arms for more complex reasons to also be included under the blanket term *bandoleros*.

In any event, the undeniable fact is that the dynamic of the initial process was repeated: government-sponsored persecution was followed by the insurgents' reorganization for defense. Hence, the end of Chispas's account is quite similar to its beginning:

Once Lobo was dead, all eyes turned to me. As an account that I must give to God, until then I had not had to act, but they began to persecute me horribly; I now imagine that this was probably because they knew I had been with all [the insurgents] for some time. They could have assumed that I had learned defensive ways from them, and they might have considered that I would follow the tactics of those good men who gave their lives defending so many families and innocent ones. We saw death so close, just for the sin of being Liberals. And, in fact, it was in this manner that all those people placed their trust in me, probably because I knew how to get along with everyone and I obeyed orders. It made me sad to see those unfortunate people, companions in disgrace, suffer. By common accord, they decided to put me in charge of things so that we wouldn't be caught off guard and all of us finished off, as [our enemies] had long ago set out to do.

Chispas felt, nevertheless, that he lacked experience and knowledge, and he sought the support of the guerrilla groups in southern Tolima under the command of General Mariachi. In the conclusion to his July 1958 statement to Mariachi, he said:

I was not able to leave sooner because the army and the *pájaros* stepped up their persecution; I then had to confront them and defend myself when they cornered me . . . they have done nothing but hold me accountable for all the deaths that occurred, [even] natural deaths. They say I'm the one and they have to kill me. No longer could I, nor can I, allow myself to be killed like a tethered sheep. Since [self-]defense is permitted, I have done nothing but defend myself and defend the defenseless. . . . And in so many comings and goings after the March 16 elections, I received some commissions and communications from General Mariachi, giving me more information about the political situation and the guerrilla groups. This seemed to me to be a definite invitation to come where he was, to hold talks, as in fact I have done. Because of [these *guerrilleros*] I came to Planadas, where I now am quite content.

Nevertheless, the national press and the army had not portrayed Chispas as a protector of the defenseless, as he considered himself, but, quite the opposite, as a socially incorrigible criminal. He was accused, whether with justification or with fabricated evidence, of having led or taken part in more than 50 robberies between 1954 and July 1957, with a toll of nearly 500 dead and 50 wounded, several kidnappings of minors, and the theft of livestock in the municipalities of Ibagué, Rovira, Cajamarca, and Ortega, all in central Tolima. A closer look at the number of yearly robberies and fatalities shows, moreover, that these occurrences were on the rise, except for a significant decrease in 1955. The statistics went as follows: 1954, 8 robberies and

101 fatalities; 1955, 6 robberies and 69 deaths; 1956, 16 robberies and 148 fatalities; 1957, 20 robberies (in just the first half of the year) and 162 deaths. If these statistics were reliable, Chispas was nothing less than a symbol of terror and death.[6] And this was how he and most of his peers were perceived in the cities. If Efraín González later succeeded in changing this perception, it was because his grassroots support in the final phase came from a political movement that drew on the marginalized masses of the large departmental capitals and because he died in combat against the army in the nation's capital. He was one of the few who, once dead, captured the attention of popular troubadours (in fact, a widely distributed record was dedicated to him).

Chispas's public image was used to undermine the support General Mariachi was still capable of marshaling. And the worsening relations between Chispas and Mariachi had enormous implications for the links between the former *guerrilleros* and the official wing of the Liberal Party, and, consequently, undermined the credibility of national Liberal Party leaders who defended the *guerrilleros'* cause. Mariachi, a former *guerrillero* who had been in command of the Liberal resistance in all of southern Tolima during the first stage of La Violencia, enjoyed the complete confidence not only of the party's directorate but also, following the creation of the National Front, of the army, with which he cooperated in the fight against some of his incorruptible comrades-in-arms.[7]

Mariachi, whose headquarters were in the *corregimiento* of Planadas, in the municipality of Ataco, had negotiated with none other than General Navas Pardo a sort of monitored freedom for Chispas in 1958. Under this agreement, Mariachi assumed responsibility for protecting (and controlling) his subordinate. In September of that year, Mariachi wrote the governor of Tolima, Darío Echandía, saying, "If this poor wretch were not persecuted, he would not persecute anyone else," adding that Chispas had returned to his old ways because La Violencia continued to take innocent victims, forcing him to defend himself and others (*Tribuna*, September 20, 1958).

During the first National Front government—that of Alberto Lleras— a new amnesty was declared, with the stated purpose of "facilitating the consolidation of peace in the departments where the State of Siege remains" (Cauca, Caldas, Huila, Tolima, and Valle del Cauca). Decrees 0328, of November 28, 1958; 2582, of December 11 of the same year; and 006, of March 2, 1959, called for suspending prosecutions and sentences for political crimes. Chispas availed himself of the decree in

March 1959 and made his decision formal through a ceremony held in the municipality of San Antonio. Before a public gathering, he submitted a document read by the president of the Liberal Party's directorate for Tolima, Rafael Parga Cortés:

> From Guadualito, March 8, 1959, for the tranquillity of the region and of all my fellow citizens, I declare publicly that:
>
> 1. It has never been my desire to have a territory under my exclusive command, since I understand the government has the right to control and to oversee all locations in the Republic. The authorities may go through Guadualito canyon as often as they like, provided they do not go [there] to commit outrages against the honor, lives, and property of the peasants. Today Guadualito is not a war zone but a field of work and peace.
>
> 2. I expressly repudiate those who have ordered honest Conservatives to evacuate the *fincas* and estates that legally belong to them. The persons who have proceeded in this manner have abused my name. I myself was in the jungle looking for harmony and peace, and I talked with individuals opposed to my policy. Several men are witnesses. Our common agreement was to live in peace in order to work in tranquillity reconstructing what was destroyed yesterday by barbarity.
>
> 3. It is absolutely false that I have been sowing anxiety and fear, violence and death, since my arrival in Guadualito. It is, likewise, contrary to all truth [to claim] that I have demanded money or portions of harvests as a tax [to be paid] to a leadership inspired by the terror, poverty, and death of many innocent persons. Those who think and say these things are the ones who go around looking for the right occasion to once again unleash destruction on the peasants. It is possible that many persons want to commit outrages under the protection of my name; for that, I am not responsible.
>
> 4. I repudiate all those who, in my name, have engaged in the theft of livestock, so as to create conflicts for me with the authorities. I am the first to understand that, through my upstanding conduct as a citizen, I render a loyal service to the government of Dr. Alberto Lleras Camargo.
>
> 5. I warn that I will turn over to the authorities anyone I catch attacking the property or the lives of peaceful and honest persons.
>
> 6. I emphatically state that I have no checkpoints, or command centers, or advance parties, as my detractors unfairly want [people] to believe.

7. I state once again before the governor of the department, Dr. Darío Echandía, and before the people from one and the other party gathered here in the town of Playarica, that I am availing myself of the amnesty decree and that my only aspiration, and I wish it intensely, is to live in peace, engaged in honest work. Therefore, I make a call on all Liberals and Conservatives to put an end to the hatreds and set up a barrier against violence, so that on a basis of peace we may work and protect our mothers, wives, and children.

8. I sincerely invite the parish priest in Playarica to visit the region so that he may give testimony that in Guadualito we honor God and that its residents yearn only to fulfill this ideal: peace and work for all.

Teófilo Rojas (Captain Chispas)
(*Tribuna*, March 10, 1959)

The statistics from the July 1963 military report of his death and criminal record show that Chispas was signaling his genuine desire for the peace and tranquillity afforded by work: in 1958 he was blamed for 75 deaths and 20 injuries; in 1959—the year he accepted the amnesty offer—only one death was attributed to him (*El Tiempo*, January 3, 1963). The authorities, however, did not respond sympathetically to his evident conversion. A short time later, the army fired at the house where his pregnant companion lived. In July 1959, in a message sent to correct information published by an Ibagué newspaper, *Tribuna*, Chispas complained, "[Y]our newspaper also prints offers of large rewards for my head, which I could not care less about" (July 17, 1959). An army officer responded with the following threat: "I warn you once and for all that within [my] battalion's jurisdiction, no authority other than that elected by the people, that is, the legitimate authority, will be accepted, and that you and only you will be responsible for any bloodshed that may occur because of your unconsulted, disloyal, and uncontrolled actions" (Guzmán 1968, 302). But who was the true assassin? Guzmán reports that the officer who wrote this was himself responsible for several murders, including the massacre of peasants in front of their wives and children in Topaipí and La Palma (Cundinamarca), and that he had falsely accused Chispas of cattle rustling. In any event, Chispas's response was emphatic: "What has happened is that the Conservatives are uncomfortable with my presence in the region and they are spreading gossip, wanting me to be persecuted and a merciless war declared against me. If this should come to pass, I cannot sit back and do nothing, allowing them to assassinate me; the instinct for self-preservation forces me to defend myself" (Guzmán 1968, 302).

Chispas, of all people, could not have believed that such relentless persecution stemmed from the government's sincere desire to make good on the promised amnesty. Given these circumstances, his return to life on the run was understandable and, for him, fully justified. It naturally entailed a break with Mariachi, who had remained loyal to the orders of pro-government Liberals. In November 1959, Mariachi stated publicly that Chispas, "Triunfo," and "Sevillano" had rebelled against his authority. Sevillano had previously broken with another leader and former *guerrillero*, Leopoldo García ("General Peligro" [Captain Danger]), for which he had been expelled from the municipality of Rioblanco. Mariachi, who had assimilated the language used by the military, denounced an alleged "subversive plan" being hatched by Chispas and his comrades against "peaceful former combatants" in southern Tolima. To show that his accusations had the explicit support of his party's national leaders, he traveled to Bogotá, where the newspaper *El Tiempo*, to which he gave the following account, warmly welcomed his viewpoints:

> Let me tell you everything about the subversive plan. As you know, when the "war," or La Violencia, as you call it in Bogotá, ended, I and my comrades from the Liberal guerrilla groups put down our arms and devoted ourselves to work. By agreement, southern Tolima was divided up, to maintain the peace, into zones in each of which a former guerrilla leader would act as commander. Hence, "General Peligro" was put in charge of the Herrera zone; "Vencedor," the La Profunda zone; "Arboleda," Chaparral; and I, the Ataco region, which includes part of the territory of Huila. My base since then has been Planadas.
>
> We, the heads of the former guerrilla groups, imposed a new order. According to our code, robbery, murder, cattle rustling, and any other form of crime would be punished. We even decided to impose the dry law [banning liquor consumption]. Our law was strictly abided by and, consequently, southern Tolima was completely pacified, as the Conservatives themselves can attest.
>
> That was several years ago.
>
> In the meantime, I received news at my base in Planadas of Chispas's activities. Holdups, crimes, robberies, and all kinds of out-

rages were attributed to him. [But] I was not sure that the former comrade-in-arms was a wicked person, as he was being portrayed to me.

On one occasion I told Chispas that if what was being said of him was true, he could count on my rejection. I offered him refuge in Planadas, so that he could be rehabilitated, and I practically took on his defense. I took charge of his case before the authorities, and I took him to Planadas with all his men, hoping he would return to honest work and to peace.

But Chispas and his men betrayed my hopes. While I was in Ibagué, Chispas and his men devoted themselves to stealing, to drinking *aguardiente* [Colombia's national liquor], and to treating their neighbors disrespectfully. Chispas was to be expelled from Planadas. And, indeed, he was expelled, and the traitor then headed for Monteloro, where the plot was already being developed. . . .

Finally, Chispas' plans became known, and I immediately informed the authorities. And I thought it was necessary to repel those bandits. . . .

Now . . . Chispas and his friends want to sow terror. They intend to revive La Violencia by establishing a single leadership, which was agreed upon at a meeting in La Profunda called by Vencedor, who has become the *bandoleros'* Maecenas: There, after many former guerrilla commanders were disqualified, Vencedor appropriated for himself the "single leadership."

In La Profunda, the plan for violence was agreed upon. Hence, since December 18, Chispas, Vencedor, and Triunfo have been sending groups to kill and steal, the only thing they know how to do . . .

So . . . these *bandoleros* I have spoken about want once again to disturb the peace in southern Tolima.

I want to warn Liberals so they will not let themselves be fooled. I know that people from the capital of the Republic and Communist leaders and leaders of a dissident sector of the Liberal Party are behind this subversive plot. Liberals and Communists identify with each other's purposes and methods.

Regarding me . . . , I want to make it clear that I support the order and work and justice implicit in the National Front, because the most prominent leaders of the Liberal Party are the authors of said political system and I don't believe they can all—collectively—be mistaken. (*El Tiempo*, January 3, 1960)

In essence, the rupture merely reflected the Liberal Party's two currents and further divided the party. Mariachi had become a faithful and submissive spokesman of the policy of using the National Front to defuse La Violencia, whereas Chispas felt it could only be contained through "his" war. Henceforth, Chispas would be officially and publicly identified as a *bandolero*, which shows that *bandolero* status was not an intrinsic quality but depended on a relationship, and more specifically, a political relationship.

Chispas, knowing that his break with Mariachi would mean the loss of his last center of protection in Tolima, initially denied the disagreements with his former boss to give himself time to coordinate a new plan of action. Months later he definitively crossed the Central Cordillera and set up camp in the coffee-growing region of Quindío, where members of his *cuadrilla* had been operating for some time and where, in addition, Liberals who were being hounded by Efraín González, Melco, and Polancho urgently needed his presence, as noted at the beginning of this chapter.[8]

Nevertheless, the transfer of his base of operations to Quindío, along with 105 men—according to a member of his *cuadrilla*—did not imply a complete severing of his ties with the remaining *guerrilleros* in southern Tolima, such as Mariachi. His new protectors, wealthy landowners and leading politicians around Calarcá who had asked him to move to the region, were also militant members of the governing wing of the Liberal Party. This translated into a tenuous, and short-lived, truce in Chispas's dispute with his former commanders, who were now members of the National Front. Mariachi could no longer dismiss the armed protection offered by Chispas to his partisans as *"bandolero"* protection, since these partisans were in dire straits because of incursions into their territory by Conservative *bandas*.

Newspaper accounts and court records indicate that the remaining ties were reflected, at least formally, in the organizational structure extended to the *guerrilleros* in both departments. This structure had the same hierarchical ranks as the regular army: the Supreme Chief, with the rank of Brigadier General, was Leopoldo García (General Peligro), whose central command was in Herrera, Tolima. Six command positions—five in Tolima and one in Quindío—answered to the central command: Planadas, headed by General Mariachi; Rioblanco, headed by Silvestre Bermúdez, "Mayor Mediavida" (Major Half-Life); La Profunda, led by Hermógenes Vargas, "Segundo Vencedor" (Second

Victor); Loma de la Pava, led by Aristóbulo Gómez, "General Santander"; and Cañón de las Hermosas, under the command of Luis Efraín Valencia, "General Arboleda." The command center in Quindío was at Córdoba on the Guayaquil finca, under the leadership of Teófilo Rojas, "Chispas," who held the rank of major. Later on, after sending a letter to the owner of the Flor de Café finca, Chispas promoted himself to the rank of colonel, and his trusted brother Mario ("Incendio" [Fire]) was given the rank of major (Sumario 2, cuaderno 2, tomo 2, 135–140).

Nevertheless, despite the apparent unity in the command structure, the *cuadrillas* were not homogeneous in either their actions or their thinking. The ongoing rivalries between *quindianos* and *tolimenses* regarding greater autonomy were only part of the problem. Mid-level *cuadrilla* commanders would often carry out operations on their own, and for their own benefit, violating the norms established by their immediate commanders. In addition, *cuadrilla* members often had divergent political opinions or preferences. The politically talented Chispas was obliged, in order to preserve unity in his *cuadrilla*, to remain ambiguous regarding the latent internal struggle between pro-government Liberals and MRL dissidents. In the last elections held before his death, he reportedly allowed his subordinates to vote for the slates of their choice, as a clear show of his neutrality. Still, the results were also a clear indication of the path he should have taken, and which he presumably did take, near the end, when his views were changing rapidly: his peasant supporters voted overwhelmingly for the slates of MRL dissidents.[9]

This lack of internal cohesion frequently had high political costs for the commanders as well as for the *cuadrillas* overall. For example, two members of Chispas's *cuadrilla*, "Franqueza" and Triunfo, apparently acting on their own, committed the grave mistake of murdering Ramón Cardona García, a teacher and the director of the Universidad de Caldas's conservatory, whom, after a confusing verbal exchange, they mistook for their real target, Jorge Leyva, head of the Conservative directorate. The crime, which sparked the indignation of society in Quindío and throughout Viejo Caldas, was attributed to Chispas, with the intention of furthering his reputation in Tolima as a merciless *bandolero*.

From another angle, the public debate regarding the murder of Cardona and six other people traveling on the same bus—who were later identified as being affiliated with the Conservative Party—exposed, and clearly juxtaposed, the two most important ways of describing or formulating *bandolerismo*. The two positions were expressed, at different moments, in the same newspaper. Shortly after the tragic event, *La Patria* of Manizales blamed the Rehabilitation Office, which, through the Caja Agraria (Agrarian Bank), had given Chispas a loan for 100,000 pesos. Chispas had used the money to buy a farm in the Cañón de Chili, which straddles the municipalities of Rovira and Playarica. The newspaper suggested that the loan had helped finance the *bandolero*'s career of crime (June 30, 1959). A year later, a less indignant and more analytical editor of the same newspaper, who had interviewed one of the assailants in jail, wrote:

> A glimpse into the obscure souls of those *bandoleros* is a surprising adventure. To personally meet those human beings, when the notoriety of their infamous deeds has made them into legendary beings of an almost incredible existence, is an experience that leaves one with a bitter aftertaste of amazement and repugnance. The ages of most of these criminals range from 18 to 25. They are the product of a corrupt environment, of a childhood without affection, of an adolescence without teachers, of a youth of hunger, hounded by the enticements of a life of pleasure that they see within their reach, without the arduous fight for daily sustenance, [and they believe that] crime and rebellion against all laws, against all human and social repression is an easier way out. Are they the only guilty parties? Did they not, perchance, lack a friendly hand, fraternal love, an opportunity to receive an education and to become part, under normal circumstances, of a society they were later forced to leave aside? (September 22, 1960)

This shift from a purely individual and repressive view of the phenomenon to an attempt to explain the type of human being that La Violencia had created introduces structural variables that define these criminals in multiple ways as the products of a decade of *campesino* frustration, family breakdown, the closing of normal channels of social mobility, the state's failure to devise policies other than those carried out by "fire and sword"—in sum, a widespread social crisis that few dared acknowledge as such.

Still, our emphasis on the biographical profiles of central figures such as Chispas in no way negates the social dimension of the phenomenon; rather, it takes this aspect as a given, to the extent that, as noted by José Varallanos (1937, 41–47), it is the leader who imprints his personality and idiosyncrasy on a *banda* or *cuadrilla*. Nevertheless, the analysis would be incomplete if it left out characteristics related to the constitution, operation, and internal structure of the armed groups. Before proceeding, we need to note a fundamental distinction between *bandas* and *cuadrillas*. *Bandas* were made up of between three and nine individuals, and *cuadrillas*, of two or more *bandas*, as noted by Varallanos in his study on this phenomenon in his native Peru (in Colombia, the largest number of members in a *banda* was fifteen). Though this would appear, then, to be merely a quantitative distinction, a larger or smaller number of members would generally determine a greater or lesser possibility of dividing duties within the group, that is, its relative complexity.

Moreover, although numbers are not normally very precise, this imprecision is often the result not of a dearth of reliable sources but of variations in the manifestations of a phenomenon. In the case of the raids attributed to Chispas, the number of attackers varied greatly, from a low of 4 to a high of 60. However, the total number of *cuadrilla* members was somewhat higher, around 100, by the late 1950s, without including, naturally, the broad, amorphous logistic-support networks that, in any event, constituted an essential component of *bandas* and *cuadrillas*. In addition, since *bandolero* commanders could resort to using prospective militants in various areas, depending on their movements and needs, the advantages they hoped to gain, as well as tactical considerations, the real number of active members was often unclear. We cannot, then, use the number of participants in a given assault to extrapolate the number of members in a *cuadrilla*, which, as noted, is a set of *bandas*.

A notable uniformity did exist in *bandoleros'* ages: most were *pollos* (youngsters), between 18 and 30 years old. The presence of older men was quite rare, as was that of children such as the dread "Teniente Roosevelt," who was no more than 11 or 12 years old. In this environment of young men without long-term commitments—most were single—and with a low cultural level, women almost inevitably had purely sexual or domestic roles, such as cooking and making clothes for their companions of the moment. Their most direct role in the struggle of the men who accompanied them or visited them at irregular intervals may have been making uniforms for the *cuadrillas* when they found it difficult to use the services of local tailors.

Clothing presented a strange paradox in this deadly confrontation between *bandoleros/guerrilleros* and regular troops: each side tried to resemble its enemy as much as possible, with *bandoleros* wearing uniforms and military insignias and soldiers disguising themselves in campesino attire. In this trading of each others' identities, the only distinctive sign was the prints left by *bandoleros'* tennis shoes. But the victims tended to be campesinos who did not know who had come to their house. Each side assumed the other's identity to test the loyalties of the peasants. They, in turn, did not naïvely fall into the trap, since they understood the game and acted with a reticence that irritated insurgents and soldiers alike.

Peasants were caught in cross-fire from several sides. They were victims not only of the fighting between the army and the *bandoleros*, but also, if they were close to an area identified with a political party other than their own, they suffered from the concomitant effects of the retaliation of both sides. A mayor from the municipality of Pijao described their situation as follows:

> In these regions, there have been two rabbles with distinct political colors: one Liberal and the other Conservative. Both highly dangerous. . . .
>
> As I was told by the inspector from Córdoba, who is of Liberal persuasion, they were very fearful that the *godos* of Buenavista and La Mina would attack Córdoba and its surrounding regions. And, by contrast, the Conservatives of La Mina have lived in total dread, making the army run out of fear it would be attacked by Chispas's riffraff and by that of Córdoba. Just this week they have evacuated houses of both Liberals and Conservatives, fearing reprisals from both sides for the crimes that have been committed. (Sumario 2, cuaderno 4, 58)

Significantly, the duels for local or regional control between these *bandas* or *cuadrillas* were not waged in direct confrontations but were always settled through the brutal punishment of defenseless peasants of the opposing side (Octava Brigada 1965, 62). Their war-making had something else in common: both sides were careful to avoid carrying out punitive operations within their area of support—a golden rule for the survival of any armed rural group. Bandits—and this appears to be a universal experience—normally distinguish between the "interior" and the "frontiers," with the latter defining the boundaries for what is illicit.[10]

One member of Chispas's *cuadrilla,* "El Murio," demonstrated how this principle was unconsciously applied in the region of Córdoba

(Quindío), where the *cuadrilla* had its headquarters and even a military training center for *finca* workers: "In this region, I haven't had to deal with any attacks; we have gone out on armed expeditions, but nothing has happened. In Pijao alone we attacked four guys" (Sumario 2, cuaderno 2, 462).

When, later on, and because of a lack of political clarity on how to respond to the government's armed offensive, they abandoned this unconscious or poorly rationalized practice and began to carry out violent actions in their former strongholds, their days were numbered. In any event, the rival *bandas* also had a common target in the army, not only because they saw it as the armed wing of the state against which they were both fighting but also for military considerations, such as obtaining radio equipment, uniforms, etc. This, and the black market in weapons—in which soldiers also became involved—allowed many *bandas* to achieve a technical parity with the army, in addition to their advantage of being irregular armed groups.

However, to suppose that these men's lives were reduced to roaming as *bandoleros* or in *cuadrillas* would be a mistake. For some, these activities were relatively marginal: they worked on farms in the region during the week and plied their trade as *bandoleros* on Saturday and Sunday. Those more or less permanently enrolled in a *cuadrilla* would often spend their weekends in the villages and towns drinking or visiting bordellos—activities requiring reliable urban linkages. Moreover, they were integrated into the local market, since they had permanent dealings not only with the shopkeepers who supplied them with their necessary foodstuffs but also with the merchants who bought their ill-gotten merchandise or products, principally coffee. For these forays to the municipal seats, at least in Quindío, they would use motor vehicles, getting rides from friendly drivers who didn't charge them. In sum, they were very far from classic outlaws working on back roads. In many instances, they might instead be described as modern highwaymen and bus robbers, which is not surprising, given their establishment in a zone as highly urbanized as are the coffee-growing regions.

Their many urban and rural links gave these Colombian *bandas* a complexity not normally seen in other countries, if the available information is correct. This necessarily led to greater diversity and specialization of duties within the *cuadrilla*'s general structure. Their duties corresponding to their rank within the military hierarchy—which went from corporal to general—were complemented by other, clearly defined duties. The practice of extortion known as *boleteo*, for example, was conducted by a four-person specialized urban cell, the *tumbadores de la calle* (street goons): "Bombero" (Fireman), "Tuso" (Pockmarked), "Estudiante" (Student), and "Conejo" (Rabbit), under the command of Chispas's brother, Major Incendio.[11] Another specialized group, known as the "meat distributors," gave slaughtered cattle to peasants. A third important cell, the *tumbadores de pájaros* (*pájaro* shooters), was in charge of executing members of paramilitary groups. The network of couriers, generally adolescents, and the *aguantadores* (sharecroppers or landowners who housed the couriers on a more or less permanent basis), was also vital to the *cuadrilla's* operation.

To maintain such an organization obviously required large sums of money. Where did they get this money? We can distinguish three analytically distinct sources from different times in the *cuadrillas'* existence: Initially, funding was not a serious problem because, as mentioned, Chispas had been recruited and bankrolled by Liberal landowners who had, more or less formally, agreed to pay a periodic "protection quota." Later, funding became more complicated, since the landowners began to renege on their original commitments or fulfill them only grudgingly, leading the *cuadrillas* to demand obligatory contributions based on the size of the landholding and to resort to the *boleteo*, that is, to issue death threats for those who failed to make the required contribution by the peremptorily established deadline. Finally, when the landholders attempted to transfer the burden of the payments to sharecroppers, and thus keep part of the remuneration that contractually belonged to them, the affected parties openly sided with the *cuadrillas*. In this alliance, they inverted the traditional relationship of domination, placing landholders in a position of subordination. The army's Eighth Brigade described this process as follows:

> If the landowners refused to hand over the fruit of their honest labor, they were notified that the *finca* administrators would henceforth be none other than those whom the *cuadrillas* assigned to them. Once the *antisociales* [criminals] had attained this objective, the administrator had to proceed to inform his respective employer that the *bandolero* leader in the region prohibited him from visiting his *fincas* and that consequently he would have to wait for his harvests in the city or village.
>
> So the administrator had to distribute the yield from the respective *finca* in three parts: one for the *bandolero* leader, another for

himself, and a minimal part for the owner, generally determined by agreement between the first two. (Octava Brigada 1965, 21)

Nevertheless, the financial obligations demanded by the *cuadrilla* varied according to not only social status but also political affiliation, although, here, fellow party members who "turned" or were deemed traitors were treated more severely than were adversaries, according to the principle that old friends are worse enemies than long-standing enemies. One peasant confessed, "'Nobleza' trusted me because I didn't give them money, but they said that wasn't my fault. Still, they said that the *finca* owners were Liberals and they would have to kick their asses because they didn't want to help now, [claiming that these landowners] had helped them before; that's why they killed Mario Tobón" (Sumario 2, cuaderno 1, 98).

Conservative merchants and coffee growers were subject to two characteristic forms of harassment: the former, to demands for cash payments, exacted through diverse threats whereby the (generally) absentee landowners sometimes were explicitly obliged to designate Liberal administrators, who, with the *cuadrilla*'s political and armed protection, would often seize the harvests. One person who was both a wealthy coffee merchant and the owner of several farms—a coincidence generally found in the first stage of La Violencia—exemplified this. In a single file, this merchant had three similar *boletas*. As a merchant, he received *boletas* from Mayor Incendio, who threatened him with "great harm" if he failed to pay (Sumario 2, cuaderno 2, 140). In one declaration he tells of the *boleta* he received as a landowner:

Last year, I was in Córdoba, on one of my *fincas*, La Flor del Café, on the boundary between Pijao and Córdoba. . . . Some friends in Córdoba warned me that, for the coffee harvest on that *finca*, I should name a Liberal element, since otherwise, I could be adversely harmed with regard to my politics since I am a Conservative. Therefore, I got in touch with Mr. [name omitted by the authors], whom my friends had recommended to pick up the harvest for me in *cargas*: *said harvest was lost entirely that year.* (Ibid., cuaderno 2, 145; our emphasis)

Regarding the *cuadrilla*'s direct or indirect control over production, a Bogotá weekly observed, after Chispas's death, that "not even one case is known of him distributing land, although it is known that one of his most reliable sources of income was the share of coffee sales he received" (*La Nueva Prensa* 96, May 3, 1963, 25). A "de facto partnership" had, then, been formed among administrators, sharecroppers, and the members of Chispas's *cuadrilla*.

In addition to motives common to other regions, in Quindío a well-known incentive for campesinos to join or establish links with *cuadrillas* was the possibility of economic and social mobility. Affiliation with a *banda* could even constitute an alternative to seasonal unemployment, as explained by one protagonist:

> In Córdoba, I failed to find work, and no one gave me food [or] anything else either. So one day "Venado" [Deer] and I went to Rioverde to look for work. We ran into that guy Chispas in La Miranda, and Venado told him to take us over there even just to [have us] unsaddle animals. This was a Monday and Chispas told us to go on Wednesday, and we went on Wednesday and we stayed there and we went to unsaddle animals. This was just after the harvest. . . . More precisely, they are in the business [to demand] many rights because their *fincas* were taken from them or their parents killed, that's why they're united like that. (Sumario 3, 75)

Within a single *cuadrilla*, members had distinct motives for joining, depending on which of two different areas they came from. Statements by members from Quindío indicate that the most important factor in their decision to join the irregular armed life seems to have been economic advancement. By contrast, those from southern Tolima offered reasons mainly related to a political vendetta, the origins of which went back to April 9, 1948. Moreover, the latter, more experienced with both persecution and struggle, also had a clearer vision of the past, which guided their present actions. For this reason, Murio's experiences are very similar to those of Chispas and typical of *bandoleros* from Tolima:

> My father was in Ibagué selling some *cargas* of onions, and at about 10 P.M. the police came, asking for my father; then they tied me to a coffee tree and right there they killed my mother because she had cried the day [Jorge Eliécer] Gaitán was killed. When I was working in Quebradanegra, some boys came, friends of mine whose parents had also been killed, [and told us] to go to the mountains

because we couldn't work, since we weren't Conservative workers and we wouldn't be allowed to work and we lived under threat.

In March about five [years] ago, like I said before, I got tired of wandering and I came to Quebradanegra to work in the coffee harvest. Then one Sunday I met Chispas, who had come down from where it was cold, and since he had known me in Tolima, in Peligro's guerrilla group, he invited me to go with him.

By that time, Chispas had an organized commando of some 150 men. To pick up the shipments of munitions General Mariachi sent them on muleback; they would go down to the nearby towns, where they had collaborators:

> When we had a little money, we would come on Saturday and Sunday and sometimes on Monday to Córdoba, Calarcá, and Armenia, especially to the red-light district. . . . In Quebradanegra, some men would help us out with a small shipment and a little money, and in Córdoba, the man from the store would sell to us on credit, but we had to pay him almost all of it, since he was a good person. In Calarcá, one *finca* owner would send Chispas payments of fifteen hundred pesos cash. (Sumario 2, cuaderno 2, 471)

Some clarifications regarding the contrasts between La Violencia in Viejo Caldas and in Tolima should give a better understanding of the diverse elements that converged in Chispas's *cuadrilla*. Since this *cuadrilla* was not a mere transplant from Tolima to Quindío, it had to adapt to, and had been influenced by, its new terrain. As the National Police noted in 1962, the well-known economic motivations for La Violencia in Viejo Caldas and Valle were seen in such things as the preponderance of crimes against property, in both rural and urban areas. The most frequent crimes consisted of robbing agricultural produce and demanding money. In the latter case, when the target of the demand paid, his life was normally spared. The thirst for profits had, in addition, clear effects on the dynamics within the *cuadrillas*, since it inevitably generated individualism, which led to constant internal rifts, disloyalty, and the diminished effectiveness of the leaders. Therefore, despite the *bandas'* formal military structure, both the *bandas* themselves and their leaders had an unmistakable air of improvisation. The number of members of the different criminal associations

was normally quite small in these areas. Finally, the use of motor vehicles to transport victims in urban areas before killing them was a
distinctive trait of La Violencia in these departments.

By contrast, in Tolima, the same report indicates that La Violencia
was more political, although not in a predominantly partisan sense,
but rather insofar as it was "antidemocratic" and "anti-institutional"—
terms used in the report to describe the regime's opponents. By comparison, *cuadrillas* there were larger and better prepared, their internal structure was stronger, and their leaders' control both over their
followers and over the rural community in general was much greater
in Tolima than in Caldas or Valle. Likewise, although these *bandoleros*
in Tolima had the sympathy of some lower-ranking administrative
officials and were protected or tolerated when they came to a town to
rest, they had an obvious peasant appearance, reflected even in their
low cultural level. Last, compared with the dispersion and fragmentation of the Valle and Caldas *bandas*, in Tolima—noted the police report—"contacts exist between gang leaders, which includes the obser-
vance of a rudimentary protocol, with internal diplomatic pacts and
agreements" (Policía Nacional de Colombia 1962, 125).

The data in Table 1, recorded in 1962, provide an idea of the size of
the *bandas*.

Thus, multiple factors determined a *cuadrilla*'s capacity to go on
the offensive and move about. In addition to those already noted, the
most important was the leader's prestige among the peasants in the
region. Even the army that trailed and fought Chispas was forced to

TABLE 1. *Size of Armed Groups in Caldas, Valle, and Tolima in 1962*

Department	Number of Armed Groups*	Total Members	Average per Group	Number of Groups with 50 or More Members
Caldas**	33 (37%)	513 (29%)	15	1 (Chispas's)
Valle	30 (33%)	512 (29%)	17	1
Tolima	27 (30%)	756 (42%)	28	7
Totals	90 (100%)	1,781 (100%)	20	9

Source: Based on *Policía Nacional de Colombia* 1965 no. 8 (Charts No. 8, 13
and 14, pp. 35, 40–41).

* Rather than distinguishing between *bandoleros* and *guerrilleros* with
different ideological orientations, the study includes all groups under the term
"*bandoleros*."

** In 1962, the present-day departments of Quindío and Risaralda were still
part of Caldas.

acknowledge this prestige, much to its chagrin, as seen in the Rifles Battalion's indignant response to a local judge's insistent demands that Chispas be captured:

> Report from the Rifles Infantry Battalion
> From: Barcelona (Fourth Brigade)
> To: Judge No. 280, Calarcá
> August 25, 1961
>
> 1. One of the specific missions of the battalion under my command is precisely that of capturing Teófilo Rojas (alias Chispas).
>
> 2. This outlaw, regarding whom the Government of the Department of Caldas is offering a reward of 30,000 pesos to whoever gives information leading to his capture, has operated for some ten years, initially in regions of Tolima and later in Quindío, without the troops capturing him or taking him out of action. This is principally because *the inhabitants of the regions where he operates are resolutely protecting him,* by notifying him of the presence of troops with sufficient advance warning to allow him to escape from the countless expeditions that have pursued him within not only this battalion's jurisdiction but also that of the Cisneros Battalion and that of the Sixth Brigade (Tolima).
>
> 3. For the reasons set forth above, I think that his informers, either naïvely or maliciously, have portrayed this individual to [Your Honor] as a common criminal who can easily be captured and brought to you. The truth is that said individual, the head of a relatively numerous and well-armed *cuadrilla, has a highly efficient information service among the inhabitants of the region,* which has allowed him not only to evade the troops but on occasion to conduct relatively successful ambushes.
>
> 4. Given the above considerations, the troops under my command shall spare no effort to *capture Teófilo Rojas* and his comrades in order to bring them before you, although I advise you in advance that *this will not be an easy task.* (Sumario 1, 1; our emphasis)

The investigating judge's accusation of the battalion's inefficiency was well founded, since it stemmed from the public knowledge that Chispas—like his peers in other regions—received the direct collaboration and tacit support of soldiers and mid-ranking officers. In the case of Chispas, this began to change in late 1961, mostly because of pressure exerted by Liberal landowners and *gamonales* who were no longer sure they could effectively control their old protégé and who increasingly saw him as a potential or real threat to their interests. However, the overarching factor that prevented repressive action was the intricate support network woven around Chispas and his "boys." This produced an undeniable sense of powerlessness in the army, whose members frequently discussed this powerlessness—a factor that was crucial to the survival and expansion of *bandolerismo*.

When the most ruthless military campaign against Chispas's *cuadrilla* began in December 1961, the commander of the Fourth Brigade, Colonel Guillermo Pinzón Caicedo, was forced to declare, with a mixture of impatience and resentment, that "the military command in Quindío has ascertained that Chispas's *cuadrilla* is supported and helped by people who use him for economic benefit, in particular, forming an organization divided into highwaymen and their supporters and harborers" (*La Patria*, December 15, 1961).

As part of this new offensive, by early 1962 the highest reward ever was being offered for Chispas's head. The incentive for informers was combined with brutal operations to punish the civilian population that protected him. These operations, in turn, were presented to the public as large-scale fighting with Chispas's *cuadrilla*, such as the battle in April in a location known as La Bella, in Calarcá.

Regional newspapers announced that the *banda* had been completely exterminated. The following month, to counter the image of invincibility that had been created around him, Chispas was described as ragged, wounded, repentant, and headed for Manizales to find a priest so that he could confess and seek "reconciliation with society" (*La Patria*, June 5, May 26, April 12 and 13, 1962). At the same time, however, the Third Brigade complained that "because of the citizenry's absolute lack of collaboration with the authorities, his capture has become impossible" (*La Patria*, July 18, 1962).

We know, however, that Chispas was giving clear signs of redirecting his struggle. In September 1962, in response to a message from a national beauty queen, Olga Lucía Botero, asking him to end his activities, Chispas responded as follows:

> Our struggle will henceforth be the poor against the millionaires, the oppressed against the oppressors; a social struggle without all those infamous atrocities that the oligarchy has committed with the armed forces at its service and that the "major press" has encouraged through its publications. . . . May the money wasted pursuing [the poor] be used to alleviate the tremendous poverty that our unworthy leaders have brought us. Death to the oligarchy of all

parties. Long live the social revolution. Our struggle, beautiful sovereign, is at the service of the exploited. (Guzmán Campos et al. 1977, 336)[12]

Although Chispas's message to the beauty queen was his first public statement announcing a new ideological justification for his actions, his adversaries gave a different chronology of his transformation. Long before, in 1958, businessmen from Tolima and Caldas said they had "received threats [from Chispas] regarding the alleged persecution of Communizing workers" (*Semana*, September 16, 1958).

Still, Chispas clearly did not know how to put into practice his now publicly announced transformation. Hounded by the army, denounced by his own party, isolated from the landowners who had initially supported him, he unloaded the burden of sustaining the *cuadrilla* on the peasants—not through persuasion but through force. Neither the campesinos, formed in the sectarianism that he had reinforced in his initial stage, nor much less the members of his *cuadrilla* could assimilate their leader's new perspective. Instead, they became informers, believing the false promises of rewards and pardon.

One informer confessed to the investigating judge: "I left Chispas's *cuadrilla* because I learned that they had killed Mario Tobón and Henry Gutiérrez, who were members of the Liberal Party, [and] I was angry that they killed their fellow Liberals. . . . And if they do so, it is for money and not for political ends, because when I did this, it was to finish off the Conservatives" (Sumario 2, cuaderno 2, 96 and 139).

Signs that the *banda* was disintegrating and that its old protectors had grown weary, creating a climate especially propitious for the army's offensive, undermined the leader's move toward a clearer political definition. Infiltrators and informers were increasingly common and finally brought about the famous *bandolero's* demise.

And so it was that one day an informer told the army of Chispas's exact whereabouts and movements in the vicinity of Albania, a hamlet close to Calarcá. Army troops began to patrol the area heavily, assisted by people familiar with the *bandolero's* favorite haunts. Aggressive civic and psychological campaigns to discredit his image were simultaneously unleashed on the civilian population that protected Chispas, and several military intelligence actions were carried out, reiterating the offer of "unconditional [amnesty] . . . to any of Chispas's trusted collaborators" who turned informer (Comando del Ejército n.d., 67–72). Reconnaissance operations were conducted by officers, noncommissioned officers, and soldiers familiar with every inch of the terrain, and three platoons of sharpshooters were assembled for the decisive operation. The final phase of the siege began on January 19, 1963. The plan called for the Cisneros Battalion, divided into four units, to communicate by radio, whistles, flares, and gunshots when it spotted the target. The soldiers marched through the coffee fields during the night of January 21, carrying weapons that presaged a major battle: eight .30 automatic rifles, forty-one .30 Belga rifles, three M-1 carbines, two Madsen pistols, and fifty-four MK-II grenades.

On January 22, at 5:30 P.M., a patrol spied Chispas walking toward the El Porvenir farm with his bodyguard and a woman. The army immediately gunned him down, using only six rifle shells and nine carbine shells. The decisive factor was the informer: the angry father of the woman who accompanied the *banda* leader.

Chispas's pockets reportedly contained two significant photographs: one of Efraín González, who, according to the journalist who disseminated the information, symbolized Chispas's hate; the other, "Che" Guevara, who symbolized his affection (*El Espectador*, January 23, 1963). To paraphrase poet Gonzalo Arango (quoted below), we might say that the first photo expressed the Liberal *bandolero* that Chispas was, and the second, the revolutionary fighter he was becoming.

The notary public in Armenia recorded the following account:

TEOFILO ROJAS VARON
In the Municipality of Armenia, Department of Caldas, on the twenty-third day of the month of January, one thousand nine hundred and sixty-three, Francisco Arango Q. appeared and stated that at 5 P.M., January twenty-second, Mr. TEOFILO ROJAS VARON died, [that the deceased was] a 32-year-old male, a native of Rovira, Tolima, Colombia, whose marital status was single, whose last occupation was that of a farmer, and that this death occurred in the *vereda* of LA ALBANIA, municipality of CALARCA, and that he [was] the legitimate son of (unknown) and of (unknown) and that the main cause of death was "violent death with a firearm," which was certified by the medical examiner. (Sumario 2, cuaderno 4, 129)

The army jubilantly celebrated "the elimination of the leading *bandolero*, who for more than half a decade had been a nightmare for the authorities." Chispas's death allowed the army to recover at least some of the prestige "diminished by its purported inability to eliminate him." An overall assessment of the operation noted that "the Don Juanesque spirit of [Chispas], an undue self-confidence [and] an erroneous evaluation of the ascendancy he exercised over his immediate subordinates led him to commit a mistake, skillfully exploited by the troops, which took him to the grave." The psychological pressure now had to be taken to its logical conclusion, "to end a myth that was destructively nurtured in the clouded minds of his collaborators and protectors, and even at times of the troops" (Comando del Ejército n.d., 67–72).

Nevertheless, testimonies from the region indicate that for many years the place where Chispas died was the site of pilgrimages by the area's campesinos, who showed their admiration through prayers, even though his antiheroic end had erased much of the myth that surrounded him while he lived. In this respect, Chispas was no exception. Most of his contemporary *banda* leaders died in similar or even less heroic circumstances.

Efraín González, by contrast, was one of the few who died in an all-out battle against the army, and in Bogotá no less, which only added to his legend. González was often seen in the San José neighborhood, in the south of the capital, where he apparently had not only amorous liaisons but political ones as well. In June 1965 he made one such trip, although it is unclear if the purpose was, as some say, to plot the escape of his lover, Cleotilde Mateus, who was being held in the Buen Pastor jail for her involvement in a notorious kidnapping, or if, as others claim, he simply was seeking treatment for a lung ailment at the San Carlos hospital, which he entered under an assumed name. In any event, the army was informed of his presence and surrounded the corresponding city block. In an uncharacteristic show of force, broadcast on radio to the entire country, hundreds of soldiers, police, and secret-service operatives took up positions in the vicinity, equipped with sundry forms of matériel, including tanks and machine guns. After a five-hour battle during which, according to the army's chief of staff, 70,000 rounds were fired, Colonel José Joaquín Matallana, who was in charge of the operation, delivered a report—if it could be called a *report*—of a humiliating victory. More than 10,000 persons swept through the area cheering the *bandolero* and calling the agents "assassins," while protest rallies were held in the Quiroga neighborhood (*La Patria*, June 10, 1965).

One subsequent account stated that popular reaction was so strong that

> the place where his bullet-riddled [body] fell became a shrine, with an abundance of sacred images, lighted candles, and fresh flowers.

Visitors from every social class came, [including] several hundred luxury automobiles. They say that from different regions of the country, especially Santander and Boyacá, buses and trucks have come filled with people to [join] the pilgrimage, and that his friends and countrymen intend to erect a statue in his memory where he died, as a symbol to his heroism and courage for resisting the terrible armed assault for so long, facing alone hundreds of soldiers and police officers equipped with powerful, modern arms. His battle lasted longer than some of the battles of National Independence, and, to execute him, the authorities shot [and threw] thousands of projectiles and stones. The *bandolero*'s admirers now repeat the refrain: "Efraín's death was a victory, Matallana's action was cowardly," and they add sardonically that the government was considering requesting reinforcements from the United States. (*Sistema*, July 1, 1965)

Under the circumstances, his body could not be put on public display, as had been done with some of his peers. Rather, it was taken to Yopal, in the Llanos Orientales, and officials ordered that neither his mother nor any of his relatives be allowed to attend his burial.

In his last year, González signed the messages and *boletas* he sent to landowners—Liberals and Conservatives alike—with the words "National Liberation Front" (Gilhodés 1974, 75–76). In shaking off the guidance of the powerful in his region and party, he had sought, perhaps more clearly than had Chispas, the support of the poor, to whom he distributed the land he expropriated. For this reason, he was protected longer—two and one-half years longer. Given the average time *bandoleros* were able to be active (three and a half years), the difference is significant. It also explains why the army promoted and decorated numerous officers who took part in the final operation, and why the Sociedad de Agricultores de Colombia (Society of Growers of Colombia; SAC) gave the army the "sincere recognition of the agrarian organization" for having liquidated the *bandolero* (Alba 1971, 211).[13]

Bandoleros and Revolutionaries: Department of Tolima

"Tell me, Ramoncito, why all that vengeance stuff?"
He stared at her anxiously.

"It's death for life, Miss Hartmann. If you don't kill, you'll be dead . . . you'll be pursued . . . they used to order us, they used to incite us, they paid us to defend the things they discussed all the way up in the political directorates. . . . Later on, we were alone and they formed a single army, a single persecution, because they demanded the arms that they had sent us and that we give up their own struggle . . . but they also took the breath away from those who surrendered their weapons . . . it is life for death, Miss Hartmann." (Pardo 1979, 102–103)

Three nationally known figures, at one point united by La Violencia on a common geographic stage, came from three different municipalities in Tolima: Desquite, from Rovira; Pedro Brincos, from Líbano; and Sangrenegra, from Santa Isabel. The pace of their political evolution also differed; hence, an analysis of their mutual relationships will facilitate an understanding of the complex nature of *bandolerismo* during that period.

When La Violencia broke out, both Desquite and Sangrenegra were teenagers: the former was born on March 5, 1936, and the latter around 1932. In 1950, they were 14 and 18 years old—which in the countryside makes one an adult. At the time of Gaitán's death, Pedro Brincos, born in the *vereda* of Coralito (Líbano) on March 11, 1922, was a man of experience, including the handling of weapons, since he completed his military service in the Ayacucho Battalion of Manizales before being sent to the Presidential Guard Battalion.

Each of the three had different initial motives for taking up arms against the established authorities. Sangrenegra, of Conservative affiliation, left home at the age of 10 and settled in El Cairo, in the department of Valle, where he spent his adolescence. Returning to El Cairo in 1948, after his military service, he killed the son of a local Conservative boss and, as a fugitive, returned to his parents in his hometown of Santa Isabel, Tolima. There he changed sides, since he no longer felt protected by the party that was pursuing him and because he identified with many motives of the Liberal peasants who had organized in *cuadrillas* (Sarria Mondragón n.d.).

As his nickname ("Revenge") indicated, Desquite took up arms for the most common reason at that time: in late 1950, the mayor, in cahoots with the police, killed his father and brother in Rovira. Along with the other survivors in his family (his mother and sisters), he had to flee the region. In 1962, he recalled his experience as follows: "I took up arms because of the murder of my parents, the plundering of [our] property, and the persecution unleashed in the municipality of Rovira against the entire Aranguren family" (*Revista del Ejército* 4, no. 26 [September 1966]: 161).

The personal motives that led Pedro Brincos to enlist in a *cuadrilla* in late 1949 are not known, although in the prevailing political climate, personal motives were not altogether necessary: being a Liberal sufficed. Moreover, in hindsight, his family members had a history of rebelliousness, and several had become leaders in various factions of the opposition, both legal and clandestine.

In the first stage of La Violencia, Pedro Brincos was second-in-command of the northern Tolima *cuadrilla* led by Agustín Bonilla ("El Diablo"). This group had shown its capacity for combat in an important and macabre episode that no one in Líbano would forget. On July 16, 1951, the police abruptly opened fire on a crowd of mourners at a cemetery gathered around the casket of one Antonio Almanza. Local residents later remarked, "Not even the dead can live in peace." The following day, the *cuadrilla* retaliated by killing several Conservatives near Coralito, practicing "an eye for an eye, a tooth for a tooth." Constant rumors that the *cuadrilla* was preparing to take over the town served as an excuse for an atypical increase of manpower, with the conspicuous participation of the dread *chulavitas*, or Conservative police. Frequent punitive expeditions were sent to the rural areas of Santa Teresa, El Convenio, and Tierradentro, triggering a mass exodus of terrified residents starting in March 1952. A visit by the department's governor, Francisco González, accompanied by the son of interim President Urdaneta Arbeláez, exacerbated the situation in Líbano. To the *cuadrilla*, this was an open provocation, and it responded by sending a note challenging González. The group made good on its threat by attacking the governor's retinue on April 5 as it returned to Ibagué, killing numerous soldiers and civilians. Meanwhile, intense fighting had broken out April 1 near Río Recio between troops claiming to be "pacifying" the area and hundreds of campesinos who thought they were simply defending their right to live. This operation was the spectacle the governor had come to inspect.

Referring to these events, José del Carmen Parra, a Conservative political leader and local medical examiner with a keen eye, wrote in his diary for April 11, 1952: "Good Friday. The troops that have been operating in El Descanso and El Tesoro returned, after nine days of fighting and destruction."[14]

In turn, Luis Eduardo Gómez, a well-known Liberal, who probably based his information on the meticulous statistics compiled by his friend, Dr. Parra, gave the following account and assessment:

> In April [1952] a truly large punitive operation was carried out this time around. Entire regions were leveled. That expedition was decidedly monstrous. The number of dead has been calculated at between 6,000 and 8,000. If we accept the lack of some statistical data indicating the names of the fallen, given the regions the expedition went through and leveled, the number still cannot be lower than 4,000. The destroyed property points to impressive numbers. Close to 1,000 houses burned or evacuated; agricultural equipment destroyed; livestock taken away. Household utensils that served as spoils of war. (Gómez n.d.)

A delegation of engineers estimated the value of the damages at twelve million pesos, an alarmingly high figure for a single region within the municipality.

It was to avoid even greater disasters—if there could have been greater disasters—that men like Pedro Brincos and his four brothers took up arms and that many peasants followed them. Two of these peasants would later earn entirely unenviable reputations: Sangrenegra and "Tarzán," who was barely more than a child—13 years old—when he took up arms. But at this time only the ruling party considered them *bandoleros*, since they had succeeded in legitimizing their actions both to the peasantry that was being attacked and to the Liberal Party as a whole, except for its national directorate. They were still publicly acknowledged as guerrilla fighters, as was, for example, Guadalupe Salcedo, even if their actions in this initial period would later be added to their "criminal record." If they were now called *bandoleros*, it was mainly because they had refused to accept the National Front's armed truce.

Desquite entered the stage later, around 1956. After his discharge from the military police in Bogotá, he and seven accomplices held up the paymaster of the Compañía Colombiana de Tabaco in Guamo. Convicted by the War Council, he was sent to the Central Penitenciaría de la Picota (Picota Central Penitentiary), one of Bogotá's largest prisons. In May 1957, he escaped, thus eluding a twenty-three-year prison sentence. Shortly before his escape, the newspaper *La Calle* (April 1957) had taken a picture of him with a copy of Franco Isaza's *Las guerrillas del Llano* on his desk, and with a picture on the wall of popular Liberal leader Jorge Eliécer Gaitán. Desquite resurfaced in late 1960 near Líbano, heading his own *cuadrilla*.

As noted, all three *banda* leaders had completed their military service. Not only did this enhance their abilities and authority but it also lessened, to an extent and for a time, the army's hostility toward them. Many soldiers and noncommissioned officers saw them as former comrades whose rebellion was justified.

Decisive for the transformation of the three *bandas* and the relationships among them was Pedro Brincos's temporary move to Viejo Caldas. On returning to northern Tolima, he brought new tactics and a new ideology that, despite its many contradictions, he would try to sell to his old comrades.

Newspapers reported that when Pedro Brincos first arrived in the coffee-growing region of Quindío in early 1957 he contacted a group of professionals who were attempting to revive a political movement that, although claiming inspiration from Gaitán, was decidedly in favor of armed struggle. Passing himself off as a rich hacendado ("Julio Calle") from western Caldas, Pedro Brincos obtained an interview with a member of the Quindío Military Board, who promised not only help but also—and what interested him most—safe-conduct and permission to help the government capture thugs in the hire of the Conservative Party (*pájaros*). From Quindío he went to western Viejo Caldas (Quinchía, Supía, Riosucio, Irra, and Marmato), where the peasants welcomed him warmly. He organized a meeting in La Cumbre to explain the objectives of his movement to a group of peasants, and he established a quota system to fund his "just cause." In the *vereda* of Palogrande, he set up a military training center for his followers.

Pedro Brincos's much broader concept and understanding of politics than his peers in northern Tolima is evidenced, for example, in the meeting he promoted in a Riosucio social club requesting help from the area's well-off, or by the support he obtained from a Quinchía priest, whom the church later punished by relieving him of his duties.

On March 26, 1958, the Servicio de Inteligencia Colombiana (Colombian Intelligence Service; SIC) apprehended Pedro Brincos on multiple trumped-up charges. In March of the following year, a Manizales judge threw the case out and released him. In the following months, Pedro Brincos applied for a "rehabilitation" loan. The Conservative press set off a nationwide scandal when he received 10,000 pesos. The Medellín daily *El Colombiano* denounced the loan as "the macabre symbol of a tolerance mentality," while *La Patria* (June 23–24, 1959), of Manizales, argued that the monies of the Rehabilitation Office—

created to deal with emergencies affecting La Violencia's victims and to help former *guerrilleros* return to peaceful activities—were really a "crime fund."

Because of this pressure, Pedro Brincos was arrested again in June 1959. This time he was sent to the Penitenciaría de Ibagué, charged with a holdup in El Aguila, Valle. From the vantage point of his prison cell in the capital of Tolima, he was forced to appeal to the public to solve his problem:

> I spent the months from March 20 . . . to June 6 of this [year] in Bogotá taking the necessary steps to obtain a rehabilitation loan, to which I am entitled as a victim. When the newspaper *La República* learned of this, it set out to take away my right. But I want the public to understand that as a Colombian I am entitled to the rehabilitation [loan] from the state. The losses I have suffered in the last ten years of violence include fifty-seven thousand pesos ($57,000) in burned houses, in livestock, and in harvests; three brothers murdered, plus the children and wife of one of them, [and surviving] children between the ages of twelve months and ten years. I [must] traipse about with them without being able to settle down to work in peace because of the continuous and very unjust persecution. So I ask myself, "Will I be given a loan to let me reorganize and work? Or will those who have persecuted me be entitled [to receive one]?" Nevertheless, I wait for the public to hand down its decision, and I am resigned to whatever suits Colombia for the good of the entire community. (*Tribuna*, June 24, 1959)

A month and a half later Pedro Brincos was released, through the intervention of the nation's attorney general, leading to a public debate in Congress on the role of the Rehabilitation Office.

Pedro Brincos was finally forced to flee western Caldas, where he was succeeded by the also legendary Capitán Venganza, discussed below. Between late 1959 and late 1960, Brincos appears to have set out to organize, politicize, and train peasants from different areas where he planned to relocate. Following this, he returned to Líbano. When the state secret service learned that he had come back to his birthplace, it described him as "more educated, well-trained in the formation of *cuadrillas*, [and] a committed militant of the Movimiento Obrero Estudiantil Campesino [Worker-Student-Peasant Movement; MOEC]," which was the first political organization inspired by the Cuban Revolution, established when Cuba still symbolized independence vis-à-vis the pro-Soviet Communist Parties (*Tribuna*, June 24, 1959). But Pedro Brincos and his four brothers' dealings with the Communist Party had been extremely tense at least since 1952—so tense that they were forced to leave the region (Fajardo 1979, 136).

Probably to exaggerate the danger he represented, the secret police also portrayed Pedro Brincos as the "leader and coordinator of the nine *bandolero* groups operating in the region." However, the strong personal power acquired by this time by Sangrenegra and Desquite made it unlikely that they would have submitted to a single regional command. Moreover, the different repressive state security forces disagree on the number of members in each *banda*. For instance, although in mid-1962 the Sixth Brigade of Ibagué estimated Sangrenegra's *cuadrilla* at 72 members, it calculated the military firepower of the three *bandas* as roughly equal, since all had submachine guns, carbines, hand grenades, revolvers, and, naturally, shotguns and machetes (Sumario 5, cuaderno 3, 1; Policía Nacional de Colombia 1965, no. 8, 40).

Pedro Brincos plainly did not yet raise much suspicion among Líbano's Liberal leaders, as demonstrated by his reception at the local club in early 1961 by political bosses, merchants, rural landowners, and others. This implied a social and political recognition that the other *banda* leaders must have envied. This deference probably stemmed from local Liberals' desperate need to strengthen their defensive and offensive capacities, since the area was reeling from incursions by the brutal *pájaros*. One *banda* of *pájaros*, led by "Cabo Yate," had committed a massacre in Alto del Oso, in the Murillo) *corregimiento*, in October 1959, and another in El Placer, which claimed 28 lives.

These mass assassinations, marked by boundless cruelty, left indelible wounds in the collective memory. Four years later, Sangrenegra retaliated for the El Placer massacre with an even larger slaughter of his own, in Totarito, near the Santa Isabel–Líbano boundary. A court order described this as one of the most horrendous acts of violence in the criminal annals not only of Tolima but of the entire country.

In most instances, however, vengeance brooked no delay and was carried out in a matter of hours or, at most, days. Various accounts agree that a wealthy landowner from upper Santa Isabel and Anzoátegui paid Sangrenegra 40,000 pesos to do a "little job." Still, *bandoleros* were less inclined than were *pájaros* to receive monetary compensation for genocide, except during "late *bandolerismo*," which is examined below.

At this point we should also stress some differences. Although the three groups undoubtedly conducted joint operations, Pedro Brincos is not known to have taken part in a single peasant massacre such as those described above—even though he was the most visible *cuadrilla* member and despite the addition, in December 1960, of another name to the list of his murdered family members. The death of Joaquín González ("Capitán Centella" [Captain Lightning]) caused indignation in Santa Teresa "against the Liberal oligarchy and against the *godos*," as Dr. Parra noted in his diary. Pedro Brincos did, nonetheless, take part in joint attacks against the police and army, such as one in the municipality of Armero and another at El Taburete, on the Líbano–Santa Teresa Highway.

The events leading up to the El Taburete attack merit examination. Armero's parish priest had been attempting to negotiate a cease-fire between the *cuadrillas* in northern Tolima and the Sixth Brigade. The *cuadrillas* had two basic demands: that the army withdraw from the area and that it recognize a shared form of rule in the area they controlled, "within a peculiar concept of *bandolero* sovereignty" (Comando del Ejército n.d., case 38, 172). The Sixth Brigade obviously could not accept the *cuadrillas'* enormous show of confidence in their own power. In addition, as was later learned, "a political leader in Líbano became interested in stopping the contacts between the priest and Desquite, since they jeopardized [the leader's] political activity" (*El Cronista*, March 18, 1964). The civilian and military authorities' rejection of the overtures immediately caused the *cuadrillas* to join forces. More than 120 men and women under Desquite's command attacked a military convoy in El Taburete, killing twelve soldiers and two civilians. They also captured weapons and left defiant notes for the Patriotas del Líbano Battalion. A report by the DAS (Departamento Administrativo de Seguridad) office in Líbano said that the *bandoleros'* precision in the April 7, 1962, ambush was made possible by their "transistor radios fitted for picking up military radio broadcasts in a radius of one or two kilometers, depending on the topography" (Sumario 5, cuaderno 2, 93).

This unification, however, was short-lived, despite the unsuccessful attempts of Pedro Brincos—who, of the three leaders, was the one with the broadest political vision—to make it last and to force his old comrades to see beyond blindly sectarian objectives. On October 23, 1962, Desquite met with Pedro Brincos, whom the authorities suspected of "seeking a union of the *cuadrillas* under Communist ideals." Desquite replied, however, that he "was not interested and ordered Pedro Brincos to leave the region" (*Revista del Ejército* 6, no. 26 [September 1966]: 160). Similarly, one woman who accompanied Sangrenegra said, "At Tapias they met with Pedro Brincos, and he wanted them to join the other two *cuadrillas*, but neither he nor his *cuadrilla* liked Pedro Brincos's conditions" (Sumario 6, 30). These conditions called for the *cuadrillas* to improve their relations with the peasants through practices as apparently inconsequential as paying for their meals during deployments, so their hosts, whether voluntary or coerced, would not see them as a burden. Another condition had to do with transforming the operations and organizational structure in line with a new ideology regarding their struggle. Specifically, Pedro Brincos advocated paying the "boys" in the *cuadrillas* a salary, that is, professionalizing them to eliminate the despotic and *gamonal*-like use of funds by the leaders and to end simple *bandolero* pillaging to meet basic needs.

Furthermore, Pedro Brincos was not negotiating or establishing contacts on his own behalf. He was a political activist and was representing his organization, the MOEC, which for several months had been calling for a meeting with representatives of all the guerrilla *focos* (clusters) throughout the nation that lacked a strategic plan and centralized coordination. The relevant parts of one official dispatch he sent Desquite from Bogotá, dated January 28, 1962, read:

Dear Desquite:

I am answering your letter dated January 19 of this year and at the same time sending you encouragement and wishing you much success in your daily tasks.

I am very pleased by what you say, since you have some sixty men under arms with some degree of determination to fight and some measure of ability not to let themselves be easily cornered.

Regarding unity, from what you tell me, it seems I do not agree with you on this matter. What I tell you is based not only on sensible analyses but also on experience. For some time I have been fighting in isolation without any effective results. Many regions of the country where I was organizing can attest to this. Now, not only from my personal experience but also that of all fighters in Colombia as well as the entire world, I am convinced that the struggle will be fruitless as long as it is not a strictly national one in which all political movements of the left, armed groups and everyone fighting and who wants to fight for the liberation of our Colombian people are grouped under a collective leadership. . . .

You speak disparagingly of leaders, [yet] there are revolutionary movements that want to organize the revolution, especially the MOEC, which has made more headway and is directly organizing the armed struggle, with some results. . . . In this movement you can [verify] that there are no leaders: there is a collective leadership, and since we are fully convinced that the revolution can only be carried out by the people as a whole, we are contacting the men who thus far have stood out in their fight, so that with all of them [we may] form the collective leadership of revolutionary unity. This is a condition for, a need of, the revolution so that it may come to a propitious conclusion. . . . The desire of the movement is for you— or anyone from [your *cuadrilla*]—to participate in some talks that will soon be held in this city.

I can tell you that the movement appreciates you and holds you in high esteem; it has realized that your efforts are not in vain, the tireless struggle you have engaged in for so long, despite the isolation in which you have fought against international coordination. Among us here, I am the one who knows a little more about your activities, have pressured so that the region will not be left to its own devices, and so that you can be part of a national organization. I have insisted that in the national organizations or organization that assumes the military leadership there must be men who have some practical knowledge of this. Of course, as you say, the men who make up the leadership must be in the mountains, that is, next to the armed men, [and] this has already been resolved. For this reason I [would] like you to participate in the talks that will be held soon, since from [those talks] will come concrete plans on a nation-wide scale. (Moncada 1963, 215)

In his response, Desquite comes across as particularly suspicious of the urban leaders who advocate revolution—doubtless because of his negative experience with the traditional urban *gamonales* under whose guidance he began his career. Nevertheless, although he was distrustful, his general attitude until this time revealed a certain agreement with those who favored reassessing the struggle. Along with San-grenegra, he was now a member of the MRL, which had filled the vacuum left by traditional *gamonales* and which both locally and regionally was making room for the most diverse interpretations of its revolutionary discourse, despite the strategic integrating role its leaders had assigned it.

Desquite gave a comprehensive answer to Pedro Brincos's proposals, arguing that the isolation of his struggle was not precisely his fault and expressly alluding to his difficulties with Sangrenegra, who had put many of his people "at the service of the oligarchy." Although he recognized the need for a national directorate, he said military circumstances in his zone prevented him from leaving the region and attending the meeting. He added:

> I have struggled until today, when I have won over those people who had gone completely astray, and I have more than one thousand men integrated into our struggle, not [all], of course, under arms, but ready for any difficulty. They go out and then return to their work, and, so, by strictly following the "one hundred and fifty questions for a *guerrillero*," we have been making many gains. (Moncada 1963, 216–217)

However, Desquite was not the only leader with whom this approach was attempted nor was the MOEC the only group to attempt to do so. Emissaries from a dissident faction of the Communist Party were nearly killed by Sangrenegra when they made similar proposals.

Despite these *cuadrillas'*, or at least their leaders', common backgrounds, they had evolved politically in different and at times slipshod ways. This is seen not only in their reactions to movements that sought a complete social transformation but also in their daily actions. Sangrenegra was clearly a typical avenger. A statement attributed to the best-known of his mistresses convincingly illustrates this side of his personality: "[T]he people he is going to kill ask him to please not kill them and Sangre says that since no one felt sorry for his family. . . . " (Sumario 5, cuaderno 2, 188). Desquite was also largely an avenger, but his notable concern for projecting a certain image as a protector and benefactor was at times reflected in his reluctance to admit having participated in acts with which he did not totally agree or that had escaped his control. Although an exaggeration, the claim by Sangrenegra's mistress that Sangrenegra was a Liberal and Desquite a Communist is telling (ibid.). Desquite's apparent adherence to norms different from those of his followers is also seen in the trials against him and "Avenegra" (Black Bird): several kidnapping victims, both men and women, testified that they had repeatedly complained to Desquite of the abuse (especially sexual abuse against women) committed by Tarzán and other subordinates, and that Desquite had used his authority to intercede on their behalf (Sumario 4, 11 and 62).

Their different behavior, attitudes, and ideology could also be seen in some small details. Pedro Brincos's *cuadrilla*, for example, used pseudonyms, but not aliases. The nickname by which he, as a leader, was known was given to him outside the *cuadrilla*, and his systematic use of his given name (Roberto González Prieto) in communiqués, proclamations, and *boletas* shows that he did not want to go by his nickname. By contrast, in the other two *cuadrillas*, not only the leaders but all the members had aliases—generally names of birds or wild animals, revealing the degree to which these campesinos saw themselves as part of the "wilderness" rather than of a society from which they felt excluded. In Sangrenegra's *cuadrilla*, to take a paradigmatic case, eight aliases referred to birds, such as "Pájaro Verde" (Green Bird), "Gavilán" (Sparrowhawk), "Golondrina" (Swallow), "Aguila Negra" (Black Eagle); four were jungle animals, such as "Zorro" (Fox) or "Pantera" (Panther); six were war instruments, such as "Metralla" (Grapeshot), "Cartucho" (Cartridge), or "Gatillo" (Trigger); the rest ranged from those alluding to their dangerousness ("Cianuro" [Cyanide], "Almanegra" [Black Soul]), to their agility and dexterity, such as "Zarpazo" (Lash) and "Despiste" (Mislead), or to their personal traits ("Tranquilo," "Insoportable" [Unbearable], "Invencible").

This practice, largely to avoid reprisals from the army or other armed groups against their family members, was offset by another, equally common: having one's picture taken in military garb, expressly to gain publicity and prestige. To this end, *cuadrilleros* would send their photos to newspapers or leave them on the bodies of their victims, whether civilian or military.

Pedro Brincos, who did not follow these practices, was said to have made plans to "tax the farm owners" and was more interested in silently raising the consciousness of the peasantry than in gaining publicity. Even the other *cuadrillas* had this perception of him. One member of Desquite's *cuadrilla* said: "Pedro Brincos is a follower of Fidel Castro and goes around with a few books and propaganda, which he distributes to the people" (Sumario 5, cuaderno 3, 202). His followers dressed like "Cuban militia." In the wake of the November 1962 kidnapping of the owner of the Lutecia farm, near Líbano, Pedro Brincos made explicit his objectives, which the victim reported as follows:

"What they have told you, that is what we need, ten thousand pesos. In giving it, you will not go hungry, nor will your family." I asked him for what purpose it was that they needed that money and he answered that it was for the purpose of carrying out a revolution, since they had connections throughout the republic and even internationally. (Ibid.)

Internationally, Pedro Brincos's contacts stretched to Mexico and Cuba; within Colombia, they extended to the major cities: Bogotá, Cali, and Barranquilla. His links with the MOEC and the Frente Unido de Acción Revolucionaria (United Front for Revolutionary Action), led by former *gaitanistas,* including Jorge Gaitán's daughter, Gloria Gaitán, and her husband, Luis Emirio Valencia, allowed him to reach a broad range of social groups: professionals, union activists, and university students. Ricardo Otero, a classmate of two of the founders of the MOEC, Antonio Larrota and Federico Arango, died fighting alongside Pedro Brincos.

Hence, Pedro Brincos unquestionably demonstrated much clearer social motives than did the other *cuadrilla* leaders. He was a revolutionary. In the second half of 1961, in Turbo—a town in the northwestern corner of Antioquia, far from his birthplace—he had founded the Ejército Revolucionario de Colombia (Colombian Revolutionary Army; ERC). Though the movement was not successful, it served as the seed for the Maoist Ejército Popular de Liberación, founded in 1966. After this disappointment in the Urabá region, Pedro Brincos secretly traveled to Cuba, where, according to Ramsey (1981, 209), he was welcomed by Fidel Castro in the newspaper *Verde Olivo* as a revolutionary hero.

Thus, if in 1962 the congressional debates on public order centered on the terror unleashed by Sangrenegra, starting in 1963 the focus of those debates would shift to the danger represented by Pedro Brincos. In the classic language of the worker-peasant-student alliance, Issue 4 of *Cordillera Central,* distributed in northern Tolima, vividly describes the nature of Brincos's struggle:

Central Cordillera, July 1963.
We once again begin to observe in our fields and cities frequent incursions of politicos of every stripe who promise the peasants and all the people "heaven and earth" to lead them like "sheep to the watering trough" to the elections and legalize, in the "Totalitarian Parliament," exploitation, hunger, the penetration of the mercenary armies led by American missions, and the pillaging of our natural resources, such as petroleum, platinum, etc., by American companies. The peasants and all the people must understand that pacific means of taking political power are just illusions. . . . While the rich minorities accumulate and squander the wealth, the peasants see

how their daily wage allows them only to drink *agua dulce* [sugar-cane drink] with their families, since the wage received by a day laborer and renter is only enough to buy *atados de panela* [brown-sugar bars]. . . . The landowners have taken over most of the arable lands through violence and by ruining medium-sized and small land-owners. . . . The rich can defend their privileges with paid assassins: the Armed Forces of repression, which massacre peaceful and de-fenseless peasants whom they later call *bandoleros*. . . . All these facts clearly tell us to continue: "Unity and Organization for Armed Action!" Because of these circumstances, the peasants must orga-nize in their workplace or in their *vereda*, with the collaboration of the Revolutionary Guerrilla. . . .

Campesinos, workers, students, professionals, To the Fight! Guerrilla Command, Roberto González P., Ricardo Otero H. (Guz-mán 1968, 315–316)

Where the leaders appeared to have very few differences, at least in the final period, when the hacendados' contributions ceased to be vol-untary, was in the threatening, imperious tone of their *boletas*. The *cuadrillas'* very expansion eventually entailed higher operating ex-penses and therefore required higher contributions from the landown-ers, who now refused to pay or only did so with obvious reluctance. This forced the *bandoleros* to resort to expropriations, which brought new contradictions. Both Liberal and Conservative landowners would henceforth be victimized by the same treatment and were unable to ask for the army's protection, since military intervention usually ag-gravated rather than alleviated the threats to a *boleta* recipient's per-sonal safety.

Two *boletas*, one from the Liberal Desquite and the other from the revolutionary Pedro Brincos to the same (Liberal) landowner exem-plify this:

1. From Desquite:
    I address myself to you most attentively, to request that you, as a humane and Liberal man, and [since] everyone must recognize our situation, [give us] a little help, which I expect to have in my pos-session as soon as possible or on whatever date you indicate; other-wise, I prefer that you not help me and leave things in my hands.

    I also want to ask you to please remove the administrator of haci-enda [omitted by the authors], since I know that he may have told you that I had been on that hacienda and that I stole some weapons, things that, according to reports, I don't need, since I don't trade rifles for shotguns. In addition, I was [supposedly] doing it for money, well I am asking for [money], but I don't resort to such cynicism. So, to avoid problems, whether I get it from there or not, one day a lot of coffee will be stolen and [the administrator] will tell you I was behind the theft. The help I am demanding from you is that you send me a good Revolver, and ($1,000) one thousand pesos to buy clothes for the personnel, since the troops burned everything of ours and stole everything we had, and rather than stealing, as they do, I instead ask.

I need this to arrive in my hands on the 23rd day of this month. If it is not done [and I] don't receive anything, everything will be taken care of by me.

I don't want comments [or explanations].

Your friend

[Signed]   William Aranguren
            Capitán Desquite
            Commander.

March 14, 1962[15]

2. From Pedro Brincos:

The purpose of this is to remind you that we are waiting for your response to the note we sent you approximately five months ago.

We warn you that we need to know your decision about where you plan to position yourself. If you collaborate with the Revolutionary Guerrillas, we will treat you as a friend, otherwise, we will have to consider you an enemy and treat you as such.

Send us the answer with the carrier.

Sincerely,

Roberto González

Ricardo Otero

(The letter is stamped with a map of Colombia crossed by a rifle and the initials "FLN")[16]

Although the two notes contain fundamentally the same message, they make it clear that Pedro Brincos had a much higher cultural level than did Desquite. In that regard, the note transcribed below, from Sangrenegra to the *carabineros* (military police) stationed in Murillo, Líbano, is at the lower end of the scale. Still, like the first two notes, it expresses an animosity toward and a feeling of superiority over the army.

3. From Sangrenegra:

Carabineros of Murillo: greetings from your friend Sangrenegra who requests [your presence] between October 21 and 25 at the Requintaderos mountain summit for a test. Bring about 150 comrades with you and let's see if we can have a chat. I'll wait for you to test your courage and see how brave you are because it appears that where you can [fight] is in the town. I await you. Don't show fear or cowardice. Goodbye vulturous *pájaros*, farewell from your servant and friend, Sangre negra.

Long live red unity and the MRL and the campaigns it has waged. . . .

(Guzmán 1968, 409)

Regardless of any other consideration, one element common to the three letters is the unwavering support of the overwhelmingly Liberal peasants. For campesinos, joining a *cuadrilla* could be an opportunity to climb the economic and social ladder, or at least to attain some income stability. In the words of one of Desquite's followers:

I came to Murillo to work on a *finca* milking cows; it was then that Desquite came through with his *cuadrilla* and it was then that I was recruited. He suggested that I go with him, that instead of earning five pesos a day I go with him, since he was having a better time of it. So I went away with him and he told me that he was not eliminating any peasants but only fighting for his cause. . . .

Then we headed up to Las Rocas de Santa Teresa. . . . We stayed there two days, and five more joined the *cuadrilla* from among the workers who were on that farm at Las Rocas. (Sumario 5, cuaderno 3, 198)

Another member of the same *cuadrilla* said: "I lack sown fields because I sold the land I had. I haven't worked now for two weeks because there is nothing to do, since I used to work picking cotton or weeding those crops" (Sumario 4, 162). Here, as elsewhere, day laborers and unemployed seasonal workers were the main source for *banda* recruiting. However, both Desquite's and Tarzán's go-betweens were campesinos from the area surrounding Santa Teresa who administrated large coffee plantations and who shared proceeds from the harvests with the *cuadrillas*, acted as their messengers by delivering extortion notes and picking up payments from the landowners, and even held the *cuadrillas'* funds. Thus, one informer told the judicial authorities that the administrator of El Triángulo farm had taken Tarzán in and had "divided money from the sale of coffee with that *bandolero.*" He then listed the administrators in each *vereda* who had a similar relationship with Tarzán (Sumario 7, 24).

Starting in 1962, especially, this plainly campesino facet of banditry, and particularly the variant that emerged in Tolima during this period, led even some members of the repressive state security forces to examine the social roots of the phenomenon and to warn of its potential dangers. The *Revista de la Policía Nacional* (vol. 95 [September–October 1962]: 107–108), for example, published the following:

> The stages for La Violencia are in the countryside and it is in the countryside that a great danger stalks the nation because every injustice takes place there. It was not an absurd coincidence that La Violencia was born there, that it continues there, that it is worsening there. . . . Let us keep in mind that it is also no coincidence that no factory workers or employees of banks or industrial or commercial organizations are among the 7,000 *violentos* the government speaks of. All are people from the countryside, the offspring of need, of insecurity, and of abandonment. And let us remember that peasants have carried out every revolution, both in modern and in ancient times, as a natural reaction against hopeless situations.

The mythical image of *bandoleros* as symbols of rebellion against injustice even penetrated classrooms and upset the social and cultural values of campesino children. No one could explain the implications of this better than a rural schoolteacher:

> Children need myths—food for their imagination, sustenance for their curiosity, [as] they are just beginning to discover the world and its wonders. The wonder for the children of my school has been La Violencia. It has, in fact, provided the characters of their dreams or nightmares. Just as others choose, in comic strips or cowboy movies, their favorite character—Tarzan or Rin Tin Tin, for example— [here] the reality of La Violencia gives them their heroes and their victims. I have overheard children's conversations that have left me perplexed. For many, the names from La Violencia have replaced the nation's great leaders. (*El Campesino,* December 9, 1962)

An April 1963 seminar in Ibagué on education in areas affected by La Violencia looked for ways to offset children's idealization of *bandoleros.*

Its two central topics were students' sociological and psychic problems, and the challenges facing schoolteachers in areas affected by La Violencia (*El Cronista*, April 26, 1963).

The army was also closely following the evolution of the *bandolero-campesino* relationship. Specifically regarding Desquite, an army source, the *Revista del Ejército*, pointed to the following milestones:

1. On December 4, 1961, Desquite reportedly began "receiving contributions from some *finca* owners"—that is, occasional and, moreover, voluntary economic support from a limited number of rural landowners;

2. Six months later, on June 4, the same source reported: "It has been verified that the entire rural region around Líbano supports Desquite with taxes," which implied a surprising growth in his influence that could not simply be the result of systematic coercion, as the army had tried to make the public believe.

3. Within this rapidly changing scenario, just three months later, on August 30, the source wrote: "It has been verified that several *finca* owners of the region have received demands for taxes or contributions." Their payments had, then, become obligatory. The meaning of this depended on one's perspective. For large landholders, it was an unequivocal sign that the *bandoleros* were losing the struggle; for the campesinos, it showed that Desquite had begun to side unambiguously with them, irrespective of party boundaries, or at least *with* Liberal campesinos and *against* the hacendados of the same party.[17]

Shortly thereafter, in a flyer distributed throughout his stronghold, the *corregimiento* de Santa Teresa, Desquite proudly made the following claim:

> The people of these regions support me, not out of fear but because I have always concerned myself with the welfare of the regions, solving many of the peasants' problems. I have absolute trust in the people, they have even asked me not to abandon them. . . . My people are in the same situation as I am, they have also been brought to this by tremendously painful events . . . especially young people just beginning their lives. . . . With gratitude on behalf of the *guerrilleros* and my own people.
> [Signed] José William Aranguren.[18]

Nevertheless, if the preceding statements gave the impression that Desquite was evolving linearly, other events offset that notion and revealed, instead, the wavering relations between Desquite and both

the hacendados and the political bosses. Ambiguity and internal contradiction appeared to be the very substance of daily *bandolero* life.

Of the three leaders studied in this section, Desquite was the only
one who continued to enjoy a privileged relationship with the local
and regional political power brokers: indeed, he was their closest ally.
Two episodes, of which the army was fully apprised, show the effectiveness of that support: On August 20, 1962, "Desquite and influen-
tial people from the area of Líbano signed an [agreement] in which
Desquite promised to work toward peace in the region and to enter
into talks with the army command in exchange for amnesty and for
being allowed to work honestly." The agreement was ratified one month
later in a letter to the president of the Republic in which the residents
of the area gave the Patriotas Battalion thirty days to pacify the region,
after which they would commission Desquite to do so.[19]

If there was continuity, it was in the Liberal peasants' ever receptive
treatment of Desquite. The campesinos supported him primarily because, as noted above, *bandas* operated in politically homogeneous
areas against the minorities of the opposing political affiliation. In addition, at least until late 1963, they generally carried out punitive actions in areas other than those where they received protection, to ward
off or avenge *pájaro* incursions in those same areas. Thus, within their
strongholds, they were clearly considered protectors and recognized as
guerrilla fighters. As a guardian of his fellow Liberals, in August 1962,
Desquite sent a letter to the DAS head in Líbano warning that his
cuadrilla was ready to attack Pedro Chivara, blamed for the murder of
numerous Liberal campesinos in Líbano, if the army failed to do so.
But, the threat was merely intended to exert political pressure on the
authorities, since, as noted, rival *cuadrillas* never faced off directly.

In addition to their local political and social support, another factor
strongly aided the *cuadrillas'* actions and contributed to their invulnerability: topography. Since topography has mainly military implications, the best sources for understanding it are the army observations.
In its general description of the area, the army command stated:

> The terrain comprising the municipality of Líbano is uneven; [its]
> central part is covered by coffee, banana, and yucca plantations. In
> its eastern area lie the foothills of the Nevado del Ruiz, a cold, moun-
> tainous place, appropriate for the *cuadrillas* to take refuge after com-
> mitting crimes in other sectors or when pressured by the troops.
> The west is bordered by the municipalities of Armero and Venadillo,
> areas suitable for conducting guerrilla operations. The main water-

course is the Río Recio, which begins in the foothills of the Nevado del Ruiz and flows into the Río Magdalena and has a deep, irregular bed, which hinders the passage of troops and supplies. The coffee-growing regions are quite populous, unlike the cold mountainous area. (Comando del Ejército n.d., part 2, case 38, 172)

The report further specified that the Río Recio area, between Santa Teresa and San Fernando, has "bluffs that overlook the terrain, surrounded by forests, an excellent shelter for *antisociales*." Whereas Chispas's *cuadrilla* frequently traveled through the foothills of the Nevado del Ruiz on mules, the army would cross on foot, which took days at a time and required uncommon physical endurance because of the distance and the climate. The *cuadrillas* used German shepherds to detect troop movements, and, when unfamiliar with the terrain, also used human guides. These treacherous routes put the army at a disadvantage, since the altitude and year-round snow hampered radio contact and the deployment of helicopters for following the enemy. On occasion, the army also needed to use police from nearby villages. Both sides used caves and other hiding places that were large enough "for a platoon or for an entire *banda*" (ibid., 136).

These northern Tolima *cuadrillas* appear to have had a more sophisticated understanding of military issues. According to the army, the *antisociales* tended "to position themselves around existing houses close to mountains or ravines and to use tunnels to exit [these houses] in an emergency. These positions were organized in a circle, allowing for mutual support; the entry roads led straight to the central area, subjecting the troops to enemy fire from all sides" (ibid., 167 and 175). In addition to using dogs trained to detect troops, their scouts also used field binoculars and mirrors to alert each other of dangers. Unlike the densely populated Quindío, in northern Tolima the distance between towns and their inaccessibility allowed the *cuadrillas* to conduct large-scale holdups of motor vehicles—they once committed twenty such robberies on the Fresno-Manizales road.

Another distinctive characteristic was women's prominent, militant role in these *cuadrillas*. In Desquite's *cuadrilla*, for example, four women stood out, "two uniformed and armed in military fashion" (Sumario 4, 140). Rosalba Velásquez ("La Aviadora"), Desquite's lover, elicited the most admiration. She was described at the time as carrying a nine-month-old baby on her back and a rifle in her hand as she fought the army in Las Rocas. Her fabled life was the topic of Alirio Vélez Machado's novel *Sargento Matacho* (1962), originally published in installments by a local newspaper. The tradition of women's participation in both agricultural production and politics has been a historical constant in the area.

Two events definitively diminished the chances for *bandolerismo*'s survival in the region: (1) the removal of the military commanders in charge of "pacification," and (2) the granting of full power to Colonel José Joaquín Matallana to use whatever means necessary to counter the widespread conviction—more than simple suspicion—of the active complicity of the army, or at least of some of its sectors, with the *bandoleros*. As often occurs in long periods of internal warfare, members of the army became involved in arms trafficking with their adversaries and at times even embraced their cause. A witness in a trial against Tarzán testified as follows:

> The troops came by my house several times and would ask me about the *bandoleros*—if they had passed by or if I had seen them—and I would deny it, because they, that is, the *bandoleros*, threatened you that if you talked you would pay for it. Besides that, the armed forces had an agreement with them, because there in Taburete, no sooner would those from the army and those from the mountains run into each other than they would start drinking, and if you gave information, the army would disseminate it. I know for sure that in the house of [name omitted] in the *vereda* of La Aurora, the head of the DAS sent ammunition to Desquite, [and] when the army was deciding on expeditions, he sent letters telling him to go away from there because the expedition was coming. . . . In Santa Teresa a captain whose name I don't remember would often go up to the mountains and find people from the mountains [after being] notified, and he would say, "They were [killed] up there." So, if that's what the military authorities did, what [can you expect from someone] in the mountains, exposed to so many things? (Sumario 7, 362)

In another trial, the army was accused of responding to complicity in its ranks in Armero by merely transferring the captain in charge to Socorro, a Santander municipality. When the central government reversed its policy of relative tolerance toward regional political bosses, Colonel Matallana had to tackle various aspects of the situation: the need to instill morality and loyalty in mid-ranking army officers, the antagonism of the *gamonales*, and the ruthless punishment of the rural population that protected the *bandoleros*.

The second reason for the destabilization of the *bandolero* "empire" was President Guillermo León Valencia's audacious appointment of the leading *gamonal* and political boss of northern Tolima as governor. This initially neutralized the *bandoleros'* quasi-institutional foundations and subsequently brought about the governor's enthusiastic cooperation with the central government. The new governor was thus able to rid himself of the political competition of the *bandoleros*, whose military and political power presented more than a remote risk to *gamonales'* authority and maneuvering capacity, given the ambivalent objectives of the main *cuadrilla* leaders. A clear example of this challenge to the authority of local officials was a market day in February 1963 when Desquite took over the town of El Hatillo and gave a speech in the plaza proclaiming himself the civilian and military head of the region and inviting the populace to support him (*Revista del Ejército* 6, no. 26 [September 1966]: 161).

The MRL's regional bosses quickly filled the political vacuum left by the *gamonales* with links to the National Front; still, the MRL's status as an opposition movement made it much easier for the authorities to justify repression. In addition, the MRL quickly softened its stance, lost the revolutionary thrust it apparently had at the beginning, and began to reconcile with and finally reintegrate itself into the National Front. When these political realignments logically led many landowners to decrease or withdraw their voluntary support of the *bandoleros*, the *bandas* responded, as noted, by demanding even higher quotas and resorting to outright coercion against the wealthiest hacendados, whether coffee growers or cattle raisers.

Besieged by the army, politically vulnerable, and increasingly strapped financially, Desquite and Sangrenegra desperately took their actions to another theater. These actions also became increasingly brutal, as the *cuadrillas* resorted to plundering, to robbing humble farmhands, and, with a deeply negative impact on the morale and safety of communities in the countryside, to raping schoolteachers and the daughters and wives of peasants. Henceforth, one of their preferred areas became eastern Caldas, along the Tolima border. Every Colombian remembers Desquite's macabre atrocity in August 1963, at La Italia, a town on the Victoria-Marquetalia highway, where he killed forty people, including twenty-five public-works employees. All, merely because they were Conservatives, were bludgeoned to death and decapitated. Following the massacre, the area's mostly Conservative terrified peasants organized "self-defense committees" to avoid further incidents.

The army did not fail to exploit the disapproval caused by this violence. In the second half of 1963, various companies began a multifaceted offensive, including air support (Fajardo 1979, 202).[20] It strictly controlled taking foodstuffs from the city to the countryside; required safe-conduct passes for anyone traveling in the area; and, to maximize the efficiency of the repressive measures, unified the military commands, which established extra-departmental political-administrative jurisdictions. These measures were similar to those taken in Italy around 1863, during the pursuit of Michele Caruso, who, like the *bandoleros* here, cruelly castigated any peasant suspected of treason (Molfese [1964] 1979, 244). The Colombian army's new tack was to eliminate—not merely capture—the most important *banda* leaders, in an attempt to demoralize their followers. This led, in the end, to a situation similar to the one that Franco Molfese called the "informer industry" during Italy's Risorgimento. In September 1963, the Colombian government dropped flyers from helicopters over the rural areas of Líbano and broadcast radio spots attributing large numbers of misdeeds to the *cuadrilla* leaders and offering a 100,000-peso reward for each of them. This incentive was combined with an utterly disproportionate use of force by the government—supported precisely by many of the same individuals who in previous years had helped to create the situation authorities were now trying to overcome. One local newspaper, defying the army's continual threats against and harassment of its director, courageously wrote:

> This region has always been accused of covering up for *bandoleros*. However, it is illogical that this should now justify so much persecution, when the foremost authorities of law and order traveled arm-in-arm with Mr. Desquite and had the opportunity to hear his voice. The most eminent merchants and even members of religious communities had contact with the insurgents, with the full knowledge and awareness of the police. Hence, why are poor and humble peasants, who are subjected to disastrous visits by both sides, judged, even by individuals who have belonged to the irregular armed groups? (*Estrella Roja*, November 9, 1963)

Although the army's relentless offensive did force the *bandas* to constantly disperse and regroup, the *bandoleros'* response to the onslaught merely underscored their renewed tactical ability to defend themselves. Each time their definitive demise was announced, they would reemerge with greater strength than before, undermining the army's credibility and at times ridiculing it or creating an unquestionable impression that the army was powerless. This, in turn, led the army to resort to increasingly excessive shows of force. The draconian military-control measures of the Colombia Battalion, which had received emergency powers from President Valencia, began to target the defenseless civilian population. The restrictions included a 7 P.M. to 5 A.M. curfew; a prohibition on playing *tejo* (a popular game in the region in which players throw a coin into a can containing a firecracker); and the obligation to carry an identification card issued by the army. *Tejo* was banned because the *bandoleros* used gunpowder like radio repeaters, to announce the presence of troops. The requirement to carry identification cards, issued by Colonel Matallana, created an untenable situation for campesinos. In simple words, the spokesman for the ad hoc commission of peasants from Líbano explained to President Valencia the difficulties caused by the regulations:

> Your Excellency, let's imagine a modest peasant digging up yucca, far from his hut. The troops arrive; they demand his military identity card. He doesn't have it at that moment. The army takes him as a *bandolero* to the Armero farmhouse. Or, in another case, the *bandoleros* arrive. They present themselves as soldiers and ask a farmhand picking coffee to show his card. He presents it, and here is the most serious problem, because those armed men, everyone knows, naturally understand the meaning of that card and are aware that anyone possessing it has sworn to serve the army and to pursue *bandoleros*. Then, Your Excellency, it turns out that this peasant has a very hard time of it. Something else, if the cardholder does not come when he hears the army's alarm—a siren—for reasons beyond his control, he is then written up as a traitor to the armed forces, and what was said when [the campesinos] were rounded up by the thousands will be fulfilled. . . . "They shall be prosecuted by the War Council as simple deserters and they may even be shot since we merely follow the orders of the military hierarchy and there shall be no appeal to any authority in the Republic."
>
> I ask myself, Your Excellency, what would happen if one of the *violentos* were to decide to sound an alarm siren in an unprotected *vereda*, and innocent, defenseless peasants were to rush into it? (*Estrella Roja*, second half of November 1963)

Until now the campesinos had been ambivalent toward the *bandoleros*. However, they would henceforth side with the military because of what appears to have been a gross blunder by Sangrenegra and Desquite, equivalent to their own death sentence: in 1963, to neutralize voluntary or coerced army collaborators, they began conducting brutal retaliatory operations in the zone that had been their most reliable refuge, rural Líbano and especially Santa Teresa. When they most needed the solidarity and protection of the peasantry in their home bases, their actions made them seem to be butchers—although testimony from the area indicates that several operations that shocked the peasantry may have been staged by the army to create "negative propaganda"; still, this would not be known until the psychological effect had been achieved and, even then, only in limited circles, generally those close to the victims.

Pedro Brincos, accused by the Tolima governor and the Manizales press of being the "Communist inspiration" of the Tolima *guerrilleros* (*La Patria*, March 25 and September 17, 1963), was the first of the three *cuadrilla* leaders studied here to be targeted for military persecution. He was gunned down by the Colombia Battalion in La Isla, Lérida, along with an economics student from the Universidad Jorge Tadeo Lozano, on September 15, 1963.

Although by late 1963 the authorities claimed to have the broad support of the populace, one must not misunderstand the scope of that cooperation. The methods that the army continued to use largely belied this support or, at least, its allegedly voluntary nature. One description of the events in the oft-mentioned *corregimiento* of Santa Teresa, in early 1964, suffices:

> We ha[d] a premonition that something barbaric could occur to the people of these regions, especially to friends from Santa Teresa, a zone scourged by cruel brutality during every reactionary period. We knew, in addition, that, following the death of three individuals rumored to be soldiers of Sangrenegra's, it was Santa Teresa's turn for exile, persecution, and savagery. They [took] honest, hard-working people from their lands and places of work, put uniforms on them, and put them out in front, defenseless, to haphazardly patrol and serve as targets, as canon fodder, for all the bad things that could happen. . . .
>
> Finally, the army, under the command of Colonel Matallana, attacked the town of Santa Teresa and pulled people and merchants from their beds where they had been sleeping peacefully, broke the locks on stores and cantinas, and herded the entire town at that

hour of the night and threw them into the pastures of La Trina hacienda, where men, women, the elderly, and children, jumbled together, wept at the bitterness of the merciless government persecution.

Excellent people from Líbano came to help and gave them drugs, food, and blankets. The town of Santa Teresa, the most long-suffering of Tolima, has been left deserted. (*Estrella Roja*, second half of January 1964)

This was not, however, the first such occurrence. In December 1961, the army had carried out a census of the rural Líbano area, warning that it might slaughter the occupants of houses without the special official census sticker (Villegas and Rivas Moreno 1980, 31). The futility of these operations, at least in the short term, buttressed to a certain extent the persecuted *bandoleros'* image of ubiquity and invulnerability. Although peasant communities typically ascribe such attributes to their "heroes," even the authorities charged with capturing the *bandoleros* were not immune to their myths. In February 1964, one police agent told an editor of *La Patria*:

Imagine that at the beginning of the week, when Desquite was able to evade the encirclement we were preparing on the plains of Neira, he headed for the region of Guacaica, in the area of Maracas. There, between soldiers and police, nine hundred of us souls were hounding him. We did not leave an open space of more than 100 meters. And just think that he escaped through there. Of course he must be helped by the devil! (February 9, 1964)

Likewise, a month before, after ambushing Sangrenegra's *cuadrilla*, the army spoke of "the head of the *cuadrilla*'s almost inexplicable salvation, if we consider the destruction of other *bandoleros* caused by the explosion of grenades" (Comando del Ejército n.d., part 2, case 31, 94). By this time, the *cuadrillas* had broken up into groups of ten to thirteen, to elude the troops.

Several months before, in August 1963, Desquite had carried out another spectacular escape, described by Darío Fajardo (1979, 206) as follows:

El Tiempo reported on August 15 that military intelligence had located, through information from campesinos, Desquite's hiding place on Lumbí hill. . . . For several days the area was bombarded by the air force, to open the way for the advance of the infantry.

"The encirclement of Desquite is nine days old," wrote *El Tiempo* on August 8. "On Monday an area of two [square] kilometers was bombarded, although it is not known if any *bandoleros* were killed. The place where the *banda* is has approximately 100 [square] kilometers of jungle."

Next, the army announced it would "use a system implemented in the Korean War, which consists of hurling flames at the mountain with special weapons. With this special weapon for caves, we will force the *bandoleros* to come out of the tunnels where they are."

Fajardo continues:

> The pro-government press uttered something about the *bandoleros'* "cohorts" precisely at that time; their reporters were slipped an order to report how, while their heroic troops, armed with napalm, besieged Desquite's men, they were also forced to face "the silent complicity of fearful campesinos and, what is more serious, . . . the collaboration of people of a certain importance who still support the *bandoleros* in Marquetalia, La Victoria, El Hatillo, and many other places."

The operation against Lumbí hill was a fiasco. Desquite and the remaining survivors in his group broke through the encirclement and fled toward the Central Cordillera. In January 1964, "*El Tiempo* reproduced military information placing him in the Department of Caldas" (ibid.). A commercial almanac indicating the precise location of the siege against Desquite on Lumbí hill later circulated throughout the Líbano region.[21]

Nevertheless, by January 1964, the campesinos were showing signs of weariness—weariness with the army's harassment and weariness with the permanent fear of *bandoleros*, who also had to admit that their presence was not wanted in their old strongholds. Still, none of the three leaders would die in rural Líbano. All three were gunned down after being informed on. On March 17, 1964, after learning of Desquite's whereabouts from a civilian informer, the army and police sent a patrol to the El Perú hacienda, in Venadillo. An account in *La Patria* (March 20, 1964) after Desquite's death reported that expeditions were organized to search for the "booty" left by him somewhere in the Central Cordillera. Average Colombians found it inconceivable that his only belongings were a wristwatch and the 45 pesos found in his pocket. The army subsequently conducted an all-out propaganda campaign, which, it claimed, caused "the *banda*'s demoralization over the death of its leader not only in Tolima but throughout the country" (Comando del Ejército n.d., part 3, case 44, 39).

Only after Desquite's death did the press cautiously venture to show his other image, the image it had always concealed: "For numerous campesinos of northern Tolima, Desquite had become a myth. In this regard, it became known that many people had to contribute pecuniarily to him to have their lives 'insured' and they even firmly believed that their only protection came from the *bandoleros*" (*El Cronista*, March 19, 1964). From the central prison of Ibagué, where she had been detained for fifteen months, Desquite's last lover told a reporter:

> I met William on an outing to El Incendial, a farm near Líbano. We fell in love and from that day on I resolved to follow him, even if it meant sacrificing my life. In my house, which unfortunately I abandoned, I had everything I wanted, but one's heart does not obey even oneself. Several times I thought about giving up my intention out of fear, but I couldn't forget William, whom I loved so much. He was especially well-mannered and he showed he loved me. My [women] comrades, of whom there were more than twenty, all respected me because I was their commander's companion.
>
> When were you detained?
>
> Following the robbery at El Hatillo.
>
> Did you take part in it?
>
> No [emphatically]. They left me with the women at the hiding place. That was fifteen months ago and each day I asked God that his wish be fulfilled—that they not take him alive—and it was. (*El Cronista*, March 18, 1964)

Sangrenegra, for his part, after being wounded in an army ambush on January 25, 1964, fled from Líbano to escape the military siege. He headed for El Cairo, where he had spent his adolescence. With the remaining members of his *cuadrilla*, which had been decimated in northern Tolima, he passed through the municipalities of Génova, Calarcá, and Pijao, in Quindío, to coordinate his future attacks with Despiste's men, the remnants of Chispas's *cuadrilla* (Comando del Ejército n.d., part 3, case 50, 115). Sangrenegra and three companions eventually made it to Río Bonito, in El Cairo, by posing as rural police.

However, by this time news of their movements had reached the area, and the mayors of El Cairo and Versalles had initiated their own intense intelligence operation and psychological action to frighten the populace, persuading many to provide information to the police and army commands. One informer identified Sangrenegra because of his physical similarity to one of his brothers, who lived in the area. This, rather than the brother's collaboration with the army—as the official accounts claim—allowed Sangrenegra to be located and finally killed in combat as he attempted to flee to El Cairo. His body was tracked by bloodhounds and found at a considerable distance from the area of the fighting. The objects found on him included a map of the region, binoculars, a U.S.-made compass, and portable instruments to print the words "Jacinto Cruz Usma Rebel Forces of Northern Tolima," "SN" [Sangrenegra], and "Quindío Guerrilla Command" (Comando del Ejército n.d., part 3, case 48, 87; case 50, 115). These events took place from April 26 to 28, 1964. The following day, *La Patria*, which had described him as the cruelest bandit in the history of the country and possibly of the continent—the "Creole Attila"—ran the headline "The Tenebrous Empire of *Bandolerismo* is Collapsing." And it was. In northern Tolima only Tarzán remained, and he would be eliminated a few days later.

The army once again, for what appeared to be the final time, resorted to the familiar psychological tactics it used after a successful operation:

> For this purpose, the command of the Colombia Battalion planned meetings to take definitive control of the region. It also ordered the deployment of the Psychological Action Platoon, through a broad program of activities in the critical areas of the jurisdiction, to sow confusion among partisans of the *cuadrillas* and encourage [the populace] to inform on or turn in their scattered remnants. (Comando del Ejército n.d., part 3, case 49, 107)

The army jubilantly claimed that the armed forces had regained the full confidence of the civilian population. In an orgy of death, the bodies of Desquite, Sangrenegra, and Tarzán were transported by helicopter to Ibagué, Venadillo, and Líbano and put on display for the curious. In Líbano, schoolchildren were given the day off so they could learn a new lesson: the intimidation of the generation just beginning to grow up. Although thousands turned out to see the bodies, the army failed to understand the mixed emotions underlying these pilgrimages. For some, this was a celebration of the *bandoleros'* deaths; for others, it was the last tribute of admiration; but for all, it perhaps had something of both sentiments.

In August, when the army had established complete military control over the area, it forced frightened peasants to participate in the tragedy's final travesty: a contrived reception to honor the region's pacifiers, most notably, Colonel José Joaquín Matallana. In stark irony, the local *gamonal* who had supported the erection of the *"bandolero empire"*—to use *La Patria's* expression—was also present.

Last, the army also promoted a phonograph record decrying the *bandoleros'* "black legend," but this tack backfired: Campesinos would get drunk in urban and rural cantinas listening (and, reportedly, crying) to the record, and then leave, shouting "Viva Desquite," "Viva Sangrenegra," "Viva Tarzán." The record eventually had to be confiscated.

CHAPTER FOUR

Regional and Sociopolitical Diversity of Banditry 2: Extremes

Mercenary or Late Banditry and the Pájaros: *Departments of Quindío and Northern Valle*

In the coffee-growing region of Hoya del Quindío, near northern Valle, a type of mercenary banditry arose with characteristics different from those of the *cuadrillas* analyzed thus far. It is also called *late* banditry partly because of the period in which these *bandoleros* operated—it was still growing in 1963, when Chispas's *cuadrilla* and those in northern Tolima had begun to decline—and partly because of its fundamental characteristics, its distinct evolution from the *cuadrillas* that operated in the first period of the Violencia.

The stages late banditry operated on and the networks of relationships it established differ in various respects from the cases studied thus far, including the breadth of its urban contacts. In this sense, it even represents what we might call an "intermediary form" between cases such as Chispas, who operated exclusively in the countryside, and the *pájaros* in central Valle, who either acted only in urban centers or used these centers as bases for their forays into the countryside.

None of the late *bandoleros*—except, perhaps, Mosco, the founder of the *cuadrillas* in the area—evolved from being *guerrilleros* in the first stage of the Violencia to *bandoleros* in the final stage. Hence, they did not follow a path similar to that of Chispas, for example, who passed through every phase from political legitimacy to illegitimacy in his career as an insurgent. By contrast, the rebels in Hoya del Quindío, who did not begin their life "in the mountains" until 1960 and 1961, were immediately decried as *bandoleros*.

Both in the late *bandoleros'* personal trajectories and in their individual motivations for joining a *cuadrilla* there is a certain dissociation between them and the *bandoleros* of the previous stages of the Violencia. Late *bandoleros* were not directly motivated by the traumas of the first stage of the Violencia, such as a desire for retaliation, symbolized in the nicknames of, say, Desquite or Venganza. By contrast, immediate economic incentives, although not the only motivation, played heavily in many of these *cuadrillas'* actions. And economic motives were, in turn, closely linked to another characteristic element of late banditry: the role of the "intellectual author" (mastermind or plotter) who paid for certain "tasks" to be carried out. Urban politicians, whose sectarianism was rooted in the partisan confrontations of the first period, guided many of the *cuadrillas'* activities. In this respect, an element of continuity exists, then, between the different phases of *bandolerismo*—not as a mere side effect, but as one of its characteristic stages: the mercenary or *extortionary bandolerismo* of the final period of the Violencia.

Hoya del Quindío—later the stage for activities of two other *bandoleros*, Mosco and Zarpazo—witnessed violent confrontations between Liberals and Conservatives and, beginning in 1949, the exodus of Liberal families, especially from Quimbaya. A Conservative *banda* began to operate that year, traveling—similar to the *pájaros*, as discussed below—in "phantom" cars without license plates. With the help of the "signalers" of future victims, the occupants of these cars carried out their first robberies and murders in the nearby town of Montenegro. Even at that time, political sectarianism was much more an urban phenomenon than a rural one, not only because the intellectual authors lived in the cities but also because most attacks took place in urban areas.[1] These confrontations continued through the 1950s, except for a brief respite in 1953, when Rojas Pinillas's military government created exaggerated optimism regarding a possibility of peace, leading the *Diario del Quindío* to gloat that the region was a place of "harmony," an "arcadia" of peace, with "camaraderie everywhere." One year later, the pages of the same newspaper were again filled with accounts of massacres, and robbery and murder were again on the rise. In 1958, the department of Caldas's *secretario de gobierno* (secretary for political affairs) reported 880 deaths in ten months, and Montenegro stood out as one of the towns hardest hit by the violence (INCORA 1958, part 3; *La Patria*, July 22, 1958, and May 19, 1964). These events would later lead local Liberal *gamonales* not only to protect and harbor the *bandoleros* but also to take a more active role, paying handsomely for the execution of the bloody tasks they incited. Urban political influence, although waning, affected nearly all *cuadrilla* operations in the countryside and determined many specific aspects of their modus operandi.[2]

Their contacts with urban centers also allowed *cuadrillas* to extend their supply and logistical/support networks. Nevertheless, the *cuadrillas'* main base and the hub of their movements continued to be the countryside, where most of their targets were also located.

Last, the area's geography—with large coffee and livestock estates, a rolling landscape, and good highways—facilitated the integration of rural and urban areas, and lent itself to another typical element of late *bandolerismo:* frequent trips in public jeeps.

These elements—urban contacts, intellectual authors, payment for some "jobs," and the use of motor vehicles—brought late *bandolerismo* close to the modus operandi that had been associated with *pájaros* since the 1950s. Thus, it is important to define more clearly some aspects of the structure and operations of the *pájaros*, who were enmeshed in one form or another in all these regional episodes.

The *pájaros* were authentic "criminal wage earners," perpetrators of violent acts planned from offices, public posts, political directorates. This was the typical form of violence in Valle, which by the 1950s had attained a higher level of agricultural development and urbanization than had Colombia's other departments. So widespread had the wage system become in Valle that not even criminal activity escaped: for the commission of a crime, the equivalent of a wage was paid. The Violencia was thus planned as a business undertaking whose political and economic dividends had to be calculated in advance.

Forming private repressive organizations on the large haciendas and plantations was an old tradition among Valle's landholders; this, along with the peculiar partisan nature of the department's police force, completed the context within which the services of men such as León María Lozano ("El Cóndor") or "Pájaro Verde" (Green Bird) were contracted; although Pájaro Verde operated under the command of Cóndor, he belonged to a second generation of *pájaros* formed within the police ranks (Alvarez Gardeazábal 1974; Sumario 12).[3]

With these visible protagonists, the history of confrontations in Valle followed a somewhat different course from what it had in other areas. *Pájaro* bands were essentially paramilitary criminal associations with the threefold incentive of "sectarianism, money, and impunity" (*Tri-*

buna, July 22, 1955). Their simple organizational hierarchy was more transparent than that of *bandoleros;* they could operate more openly and defiantly because they had obvious institutional support (from public administration, the judiciary, prisons, secret services, etc.); and they received the complicity of the communities more because of intimidation than by agreement. The identity of the direct perpetrators was known, as was that of the *banda* leaders (who never directly carried out a "job"), and the names of the intellectual authors, who never appeared in public, could be surmised; nevertheless, an inexorable law of silence governed everything: the silence of accomplices in positions of authority and the silence of terrified victims.

The *pájaros* operated in urban areas, where they targeted selected victims whose heads would bring from two thousand to five thousand pesos, depending on their importance. On the rare occasions when the *pájaros* ventured into the countryside, they did so solely to sow widespread terror. For this type of operation they were not paid set fees; rather, their expenses were covered from the criminal organization's "general funds" or with the property pillaged from their victims (Sumario 11).

Geographically, *pájaros* and late *bandoleros* operated in contiguous areas, the blurred boundaries of which were located somewhere between Viejo Caldas and northern Valle. Typical areas for *pájaro* activities were Tuluá, Riofrío, and Trujillo, and the triangle formed by Versalles, El Dovio, and La Unión. The *pájaros* from Versalles and La Unión were supported by political bosses and the police, including some former lawmakers and coffee merchants. In 1953, with the fall of the last Liberal refuges in Zarzal and Betania, the *pájaros'* two most characteristic procedures spread throughout the region: the "paveo"[4] and the driving of "phantom" cars from which they would stage late-night raids, firing machine guns into the air or at people, buildings, or other targets to terrify the population. In the ensuing exodus from these areas, some Liberal families went to Cali, others headed for the northern Valle municipality of Obando, and still others settled throughout Quindío (authors' interviews, November 1978; *El Relator*, January and February 1958). This particular form of violence in the 1950s would largely determine the nature of *bandolero* retaliation in the 1960s.

In this same area that straddled the two departments—and more precisely between the *corregimiento* of San Isidro, in Valle, and Montenegro, Quimbaya, and Alcalá, in Hoya del Quindío—the *cuadrillas* of Mosco, Gata, Joselito, Tista Tabares, and Zarpazo gradually formed. These were all late *bandoleros* who, despite the similarities noted above, were also different from the "criminal wage earners," not only in their political affiliation but, more structurally, in their relationships with "those who ordered the jobs to be carried out."

Mosco, founder of these *cuadrillas*, first appeared in the area in 1959. His stay there would be short-lived, as he was captured in Armenia, disguised as a banana seller, just before taking a bus to Bogotá. His real name was Gustavo Espitia Valderrama; his nickname (Fly) came from "his clever way of operating, since he no sooner arrived in one place than he appeared in another." At the time of his arrest, the army had been hounding him for a month in Quindío, after killing four of his comrades and capturing five others. His decision to move to the region was also motivated, according to *La Patria* (August 30, 1959), by "the Valle government's bombardment with flyers of the place where he operated . . . [in which] the authorities offered the sum of three thousand pesos to whoever gave information [leading to] the criminal's capture. This sufficed for Mosco to fear that the people who knew him would turn him in." Nevertheless, fleeing did not prevent his capture, thanks to the collaboration of a reward-seeking informer.

Although Mosco was originally from La Tebaida, Quindío, his baptismal certificate had been issued in the rural Communist stronghold of Viotá, Cundinamarca, and he had purchased a forged identification card in Sevilla, Valle. As did so many other Liberal campesinos from the center of the country, in the early 1950s he moved to the Llanos Orientales. He later returned to Tolima, where, as he acknowledged, he joined the *cuadrillas* of Chispas, "Caballito" (Pony), and Mico. Until he arrived in Sevilla, where he worked on a farm owned by his companion's brother, Mosco's career had been similar to those of the *bandoleros* studied thus far.

In Sevilla he organized his own *cuadrilla*, with fifteen members from that town, including "Gasolina" (his second-in-command), "Pastuso" (from the southern city of Pasto, Nariño), "Malasombra" (Evil Shadow), "Paticorto" (Short Leg), "Puente Roto" (Broken Bridge), "El Señalador" (the Signaler), "El Moche" (the Mutilated), "Puñal de Chispas" (Chispas's Dagger), and several others, all with their respective nicknames. After Mosco was killed, Puente Roto and the famed "Capitán Cenizas" (Captain Ashes) would replace him in Valle, the former operating between Sevilla and Obando, to the north, and the latter, from

Sevilla to the southern end of the department. The principal support bases for Mosco's *cuadrilla* were the *veredas* of La Estrella and Canoas, in Sevilla, from where he frequently raided towns in neighboring Tuluá and Buga, including one well-known attack on the Conservative *corregimiento* of Nogales in mid-1958 that was one of the *cuadrilla's* first operations (Sumario 10; *La Patria*, August 27 and July 13, 1964). Within its home base, the *cuadrilla* set up camp on an expropriated farm and appointed an administrator of its liking. One peasant woman from the region described the *bandoleros'* arrival as follows:

> We left for the *vereda* of Canoas, but then we settled on a farm . . . so then Mosco liked [the farm], since he began to take everyone who made up his *banda*; as many as eighteen or twenty guys would meet there; they would come down from Cebollal to meet there at our house, because that was where they lived and there was more than enough meat because they would bring it by the sackful. When they had meetings to discuss the jobs they were going to carry out, since they were also overseen, that is, [the jobs] were initiated by Mr. [name omitted by the authors], who would come from the town to where we were. (Sumario 10, 148)

In Sevilla, the "jobs"—to use the woman's euphemism—were the *cuadrilla's* main activity, consisting of murders or land takeovers at the behest of urban sectarian politicians who almost always paid them. The sharecroppers or administrators of the coffee farms, whether they had been coerced by the *cuadrilla* or were simply friendly with it, served as intermediaries in these takeovers. One victim described the process leading up to the forced sale of his farm:

> I realized they were following me to kill me and that persecution came directly from this city and that it was based on political matters, because I am a Conservative and [my] property at El Retiro is in territories inhabited by people opposed to my opinion. . . . The situation began to turn very serious, and I saw that if I returned they would kill me. I left the farm with some sharecroppers—they, one Conservative and the other Liberal, seemed all right to me, since they were not known to have committed dishonest acts in the eight years in which they were my laborers. One day Señalador came and notified them they had to evacuate the farms immediately or they

would kill both of them . . . in light of that, I sent some other share-croppers there, Mr. [name omitted by the authors] and then another [brothers of a *cuadrilla* member] . . . no one bothered these individuals and they stayed there until I sold the farm . . . and they continue to work on the same farm. (Ibid., 157)

The same persons who planned the murders and land takeovers—the intellectual authors—also supplied weapons and ammunition and set aside considerable amounts of money to bribe prison guards when a *banda* member was jailed.

Thus, Mosco, who had been sent to Cali's Villanueva prison after being arrested in Armenia, was able to escape "through the main gate of the prison" on the morning of January 14, 1960.[5] After regaining his freedom, Mosco took greater precautions, reorganized his *cuadrilla*, and went to an area near Obando and Montenegro, where he could rely on the presence and support of several relatives (*La Patria*, May 22 and 23, 1961). Along with his old cohort from Sevilla, Puente Roto, he rebuilt his *cuadrilla* with new members: Zarpazo (Conrado Salazar García, an Obando native), "Tista" (Juan Bautista Tabares, from Santuario), "Pachito," "Elefante," and "Elefantico" (the Restrepo brothers), among others. The towns of Obando, La Victoria, Montenegro, and Quimbaya provided an ideal milieu for their activities. Moreover, they had three distinct sources of support, political protection, and economic sustenance there. At the forefront were the urban protectors and the intellectual authors. Testimony by *banda* members indicated that the Liberal committees in Cartago, Pereira, Obando, and Armenia were to send Mosco written orders, warn him when expeditions or patrols were en route to his home base, and obtain money for him.

Second, *cuadrilla* members received the support of their family members and from peasants—although even the people of the region had difficulty differentiating between sympathizers and forced harborers, as shown in the following statement:

The people in that *vereda* are all in cahoots with these *bandoleros*, because it turns out that [the *bandoleros*] come to the tavern to drink liquor and they get drunk there and shoot into the air and they ask anyone who comes by for their papers. When the papers are not in line with their demands, that is, if they are not from Obando, they rip them up and threaten them with death. When the troops arrive unexpectedly, these *cuadrilleros* go to any farm in the region, ask for a basket or a hat and go pick coffee or ask for a hoe and go weed, disguising themselves as laborers and shaking off the army, with the consent of the townspeople. And this is easy for them because each one of them carries several identification cards. The townspeople say, "What are [we] going to do?"—that if they don't do this, they will be killed. But almost all the people help them out of solidarity, because if they came to an agreement with the authorities they could exterminate them. . . . The *bandoleros* threaten the people saying that they [will] do what they did in Córdoba, [where] they tied up the husbands and men of the houses and in their presence raped the women and then [performed] the well-known *corte de franela*. (Sumario 13, 6 and 99)

Nevertheless, within the broad spectrum of expressions of *bandolerismo*, including the late variety, *bandoleros* played roles other than that of cruel murderers. They were protectors and benefactors of the region's farm laborers. In a message to President Valencia, an extension worker, in reporting on the poverty in Obando, noted, "everything indicates that the *bandolero* Tista Tabares . . . [killed by the army a month or so ago] and others who dominate the region have been helping many families, and hence they can count on the silence and information necessary for their movements" (INCORA 1964).

The third element of Mosco's economic infrastructure was obligatory contributions from all the coffee *fincas* in the region. All Liberals were required to give him one-third of their coffee harvest; Conservative *finca* owners who had hired Liberal administrators were required to give half their harvest. *Finca* administrators had generally become accomplices of the *cuadrillas*—sometimes out of fear, other times because they were close to the *cuadrillas* and had received a *coloca* (employment on a *finca*) directly from them, but usually because they had simply become aware of the economic advantages of complicity.

Administrators' new autonomy implied a profound change in their power relations with landowners, who were inevitably absent, especially Conservatives landowners. Administrators oversaw *fincas*, manipulated the sharecropping system to their advantage, and decided what to do with the harvests. Therefore, the "tax" demanded by the *cuadrillas* did not affect the administrator, who simply deducted it from the owner's share. In these conditions, taxes were always collected at the expense of the landowner.[6] Owners would wait in the city, often in vain, for the harvest to be delivered, frequently receiving nothing more than threats from administrators or sharecroppers who now worked for a new boss.

Some of these situations were brought to the attention of the Tribunals of Reconciliation and Equity, decreed in February 1960 to find a compromise between parties feuding about sales made under duress or for low prices, or over de facto seizures of property during the Violencia. One of the lawsuits heard by the tribunals—which were few, since the Tribunals operated in 1960 and 1961, when coming before them could still mean a death sentence—provides the following example:

> Subsequently two individuals came to my house here in Armenia to inform me that the farm was in their possession, since Mr. [name omitted] had given it to them, but the farm was in their possession without my consent. . . . [One of them] continued to harvest the crops on the farm, and occasionally he would send part of it to my house, always so that I wouldn't say anything. He took the harvest and continued to live there as if he were in his own house, doing whatever he wanted. (Sumario 20)

To which the plaintiff's legal representative added:

> It is a mystery to no one that in some regions of Quindío the owners of rural farms were compelled to hire administrators not to their liking, because of the Violencia that prevailed then and that did not allow them to choose from among several but [only] resignedly to accept the administrators whom the so-called "*vereda* bosses" arbitrarily imposed. (Sumario 20)[7]

Imposing taxes afforded the *cuadrillas* a financial situation that was, if not well-off, at least free of difficulties. One *cuadrilla* member said that he had only once seen Mosco "broke." Collecting funds was an important activity, since *cuadrillas* would, with a certain frequency, remain *encaletadas* (in hiding) for a week at a time while the leaders went from farm to farm "picking up coffee and receiving part of the coffee owed them" (Sumario 13, 40). The monies collected were placed in a "common fund" handled exclusively, and in typical *gamonal* fashion, by the *cuadrilla's* leader.

During harvest season, this sophisticated system, based on complicity and "peaceful extortion," allowed the *bandas* linked to Mosco to leave robbery to common highwaymen and less important *bandoleros*; the *bandas* simply took advantage of the existing "infrastructure" (*La Patria*, April 28, 1961, and September 30, 1964).[8]

> I also know of the "*Vereda* Bosses," that is, the persons in charge of picking up the money for the *cuadrilla* leaders; they have been picking up money since the time of Mosco, who named them . . . in the *veredas* of Cantores, Morro Azul, San Isidro, Riveralta, Miravalle, Marcopolis. . . . All those I named earlier collected money for Joselito, Gata, and Conrado Salazar, and now that the first two were killed by the army, they do so only for Conrado and his *cuadrilla*. (Sumario 14, 155)

The "*vereda* bosses" were part of a vast network of collaborators, protectors, drivers, and couriers who met the *cuadrilla*'s needs for support, information, and protection. The *cuadrilla* had at least fifty people in their "permanent service," some with chores as general as delivering messages, arms, munitions, clothing, and so on. However, there were also specialized jobs, such as driving the *cuadrilleros* from Montenegro to Puerto Samaria, past the La Vieja River, or transporting coffee from the *fincas* to merchants friendly with the *cuadrilla*, placing "orders" for coffee and extorting the hacendados, bringing foodstuffs from Cartago, buying green drill and sewing the *bandoleros'* uniforms, or making their yellow, blue, and red armbands—the colors of the national flag. A soldier in the Vencedores Battalion who had befriended them provided arms and munitions. Local politicians kept them apprised of national affairs: "Well-off people in Cartago and Montenegro would send us *El Tiempo, El Espectador, El País* [Colombia's leading newspapers], and the regional newspapers from Armenia and Cartago with the man who picks up the milk" (Sumario 14, 87–135; Buitrago Salazar n.d., 89).

This extended, peripheral network sharply differentiated these *cuadrillas* from those of, for example, Chispas and Desquite, which were more closed and authentically peasant-based. That they more frequently consulted news sources such as the print media also indicates a higher cultural level than Chispas's or Desquite's *cuadrillas*. The independence and urban integration of the late *bandoleros* were also facilitated by the area where they operated: flat, rolling terrain easily accessed by automobile, with large coffee and livestock estates owned by city dwellers. Although the peasants supported them, their most important backing came from hacienda administrators and sharecroppers who held a special position in the *cuadrillas'* economic network. Still, the late and mercenary *bandoleros* as a group never attained the popularity of a Chispas or a Desquite, nor did they inspire myths comparable to Capitán Venganza's or Efraín González's.

On May 20, 1961, after his *cuadrilla* had been infiltrated by a secret agent and all his movements detected, Mosco was gunned down in the *vereda* of Reviralta de Obando, at the spot where some months before he had carried out a massacre. After Mosco's death, Conrado Salazar (Zarpazo) took charge of the *cuadrilla*.

Zarpazo continued to recruit new *cuadrilla* members from among the local people, especially the unemployed. Unemployment appears to have been a major motivation for the late *bandoleros*, unlike those whose life of crime began with the traumas inflicted on their families in the first stage of the Violencia. All the late *bandoleros* were single men about 25 years old who worked as day laborers. The new *cuadrilleros* included Joselito and Gata (natives of the El Cuzco district, in the municipality of Montenegro), who soon after Mosco's death formed their own *bandas*, probably because of internal rivalries. Although the region's three *cuadrillas* operated independently, they communicated by courier. When necessary, one *cuadrilla* might ask another to send reinforcements. In addition, they were in contact with Celedonio Vargas's *bandas* in Sevilla, with Puente Roto's *banda* in northern Valle, and with some members of Chispas's dispersed *cuadrilla*, who continued to work in Quindío after their leader's death (Sumario 13, 57). Because the rolling terrain was more easily accessible by the army than had been the barren plains of the Central Cordillera where Chispas had taken refuge, and because of the concentration of troops in the region, the late *bandoleros* generally acted in small groups. Valencia Tovar, then commander of the Ayacucho Battalion, noted the different tactics used by the *bandas:*

> We cannot compare the situation in May 1959 with the present one. At that time, the Violencia took the form of organized *cuadrillas* that had to be fought by military means, at the same time as other, parallel steps [were carried out] to achieve peace with the peasant masses affected by the *violentos*. That stage passed. . . . Today violent action is carried out by groups that meet occasionally in the shadows, strike, and scatter. (*La Patria*, January 12, 1961)

However, behind the "occasional" meetings was a tightly structured organization. Conrado Salazar commanded twenty-four men, divided into three groups of between six and nine; each group was given a particular region to control and tax. The entire *cuadrilla* met every five days to plan attacks. A *cuadrilla* leader never took part in an attack: "he would give the order to kill and wait somewhere else for the results." Moreover, the *cuadrillas* used ingenious surveillance techniques: in addition to posting sentinels, they would give coded signals with flashlights when army troops approached; tie dogs at given locations, whose barking would announce the arrival of soldiers; and send couriers with messages whose coded numbers at first glance appeared to be a simple list of daily wages (Osorio 1966; Buitrago Salazar n.d.).

Key for the *cuadrillas* was the area near the La Vieja River, which separates the municipalities of Montenegro and Quimbaya from Obando and Cartago in Valle. Here there were shallow crossing points, and the riverbank concealed coves among the *guadua* (bamboo) plants. The *cuadrillas* also had many protectors, including some owners of large livestock ranches who gave them tacit support to avoid having their cattle stolen (Sumario 19, 149). They would emerge from these hideouts to commit robberies and massacres, the most notorious attacks being one in the Quimbayan district of El Jazmín, in June of 1962, with a death toll of twenty-one, and another in July 1963 in the El Laurel district, where four died. One of Gata's last actions was a robbery in Santa Rita, in the neighboring municipality of Circasia, in December 1964, in which nine persons died (*La Patria*, June 20, 1962, July 18, 1963, December 8, 1964).

Because the La Vieja River divides the departments of Valle and Quindío, and each army unit's movements were confined to the department where it had been assigned, the army found it extremely difficult to conduct effective operations in this border area. Whenever the *bandoleros* discovered that the army had concentrated troops in a given area to "pacify" it, they would simply cross to the neighboring department. In 1962, to end what the Caldas governor called the game of ping-pong, the Eighth Brigade was created, headquartered in Armenia, and given jurisdiction over Quindío, Risaralda, and northern Valle (INCORA 1963, 42).[9]

What were the objectives of the late *bandoleros*? At the time, different goals were suggested. One soldier who for some time had infiltrated Zarpazo's *cuadrilla* declared, "They don't even have any politics, since their aim is just to get money" (Osorio 1966, n.p.). Still, a relative of Eliécer Sepúlveda (Gata) observed: "For me . . . that was done sort of [based on their] opinions, more than anything. Of course, that *vereda* down there, Santa Rita, is very Conservative, and Eliécer and his comrades were Liberals. [Their purpose] wasn't to steal, at least during the month and a half I was with them" (Sumario 14, 155). This was perhaps how the peasants viewed the *cuadrilla*.

In fact, both views may have been right. The massacres were conducted in accordance with a certain political objective, but one that, although shared by the *cuadrilla*, was essentially a creation of the intellectual authors: the perpetrators were paid for their crimes. The convergence of the two criteria was clearly present in the account by Joselito, then a member of the *cuadrilla* of Zarpazo, who carried in his pocket a list of his intended victims during a massacre at the Española hacienda:

> Later on, we held up the Española hacienda, killing four people with machetes, all of them of Conservative affiliation; the list of the victims was given to Conrado Salazar (Zarpazo) by the same individual who delivered the money. . . . Conrado had all the workers called over, lined them up, and called roll. He had those who came forward tied up and we took them to a sugarcane plantation and he had them killed with machetes. (Sumario 14, 314 and 316)

The *cuadrilla* leaders distributed the considerable sums of money they received how and when they saw fit, making money a source of great expectation and of potential conflicts and rivalries. Two members of Gata's *banda* noted:

> Gata had received the amount of forty-five thousand pesos for the massacre and to receive said money Sepúlveda [Gata] and "Picardías" [Crafty] traveled to the municipality of Alcalá, [where] a pickup had arrived. . . . That same afternoon they appeared drunk in the district of El Gigante. They were all in a cellar when Sepúlveda arrived and distributed two hundred pesos to each of them and [said] that within two weeks he would give them 500 pesos more. (Ibid., 173)

Nevertheless, if remuneration was an important motive, *bandoleros* never established the type of clearly mercenary relationship that prevailed between patrons and *pájaros* in Valle's "criminal enterprises." They also maintained greater independence from urban collaborators than did the *pájaros*, at least economically, thanks to their system of collecting funds in the countryside. But the differences were not only organizational and political; the late *bandoleros* and the *pájaros*, one of the most important expressions of the Violencia in the 1950s, were Colombians of different generations.[10]

Late *bandoleros* were sworn enemies not only of *pájaros* and of Conservatives in general but also of anyone, including Liberals, who had come to terms with the National Front; thus they adhered to the MRL's guidelines, which appeared to provide the only rationale to justify their acts. A member of the "periphery" of Zarpazo's *cuadrilla* would pass himself off as a traveling salesman and photographer so as to collect the quotas earmarked for the "MRL's fund" and to distribute among the peasants the movement's identification card, with the corresponding photo. For peasants to refuse to take the card or to admit they had voted for the National Front in the preceding elections was sufficient for them to be murdered or threatened. Still, late *bandoleros* never indicated having assimilated political and social doctrines other than a vague and simple notion that they were fighting against a government that negotiated with Conservatives.

Unlike the official portrayals of them, they were not simply hired assassins who coldly calculated murder. They shared some characteristics of the peasant milieu with the more "social" *bandoleros*. Their actions were surrounded by an aura of magic, superstition, and candor. *Cuadrilla* leaders had special prayers to which they attributed the success of their robberies and confrontations with the army. One of these was the "prayer to become invisible," also known as the "Prayer of the Just Judge":

> Counting to three, I see you
> Counting to five, I tie you up
> Your blood I scatter
> And your heart I cut in two
> Christ, look at me
> And deliver me from all evil. . . .
> Here comes the enemy
> Oh, Just Judge:
> If he has eyes,
> May he not see me
> If he has hands,
> May they not touch me
> If he has weapons,
> May they do me no harm.
> Holy Cross of May

Go to my house,
Deliver me from evils
And from Satan
Amen.
(Buitrago Salazar n.d., 90; Sumario 19, 52)

The *bandoleros'* invisibility did not last long, however. In mid-1964 the first *cuadrilla* members began to fall, most during their visits to the red-light districts of Montenegro, Quimbaya, and Cartago. On September 17, 1964, Joselito was captured in Norcasia, Samaná, a *corregimiento* in northeastern Caldas, where he had taken refuge in a relative's house. Two days later, while being taken by the army to Quindío, the *ley de fuga* was applied in Montenegro—that is, he was extrajudicially executed.

Gata and three companions were finally killed in a two-hour confrontation with the army in the *corregimiento* of San Isidro, on February 27, 1965—a relatively late date, compared with the deaths of other *bandoleros* such as Chispas or those in northern Tolima (*La Patria*, June 9 and September 18, 19, 20, 1964, and February 17, 24, 27, 1965).

Only Zarpazo was able to evade the army's encirclement. His case was, perhaps, somewhat exceptional within late *bandolerismo* and compared with other cases in his area. He had begun to change ideologically, giving more social orientation to his struggle as different revolutionary groups influenced him. Two years later, on July 3, 1967, he was found in Villavicencio, Meta, having died under "unclear circumstances" (Sumario 18).

The demise of these late *bandoleros* resulted—more directly than was the case with other *bandoleros*—from the gradual withdrawal of economic support by their urban contacts, since peasants' voluntary contributions had never been essential for the expansion of these *cuadrillas*. These *bandoleros* also reacted differently to the loss of protection than had Chispas, Desquite, or Sangrenegra, who, in similar circumstances, had shifted nearly all the burden of their economic support to the region's peasants (which further contributed to their loss of peasant support). The *bandoleros* in central Quindío, however, developed, in a more widespread and systematic manner than had occurred anywhere else, a new source of funding: kidnapping wealthy hacendados.

Nevertheless, to completely turn on their former protectors, the *cuadrillas* would have had to totally transform their very structure, which depended partly on relatively open contacts—visible but never "seen"—as long as they received sufficient political backing. Once they had lost legitimacy, keeping this structure—as they, in fact, did—meant exposing themselves to a lethal vulnerability, since their internal workings and connections were known by former allies who were now real or potential enemies.

Peasant Myths and the Crossroads of Banditry

Capitán Venganza: Department of Risaralda

In western Caldas, the municipalities of Quinchía, Riosucio, Apía, and Santuario stood out for their long tradition of interparty confrontations. Particularly in towns where the numbers of Liberals and Conservatives were relatively equal, the Violencia had begun long before April 9, 1948, and had continued without interruption through the 1950s, despite several attempts by local political bosses to bring about peace. As early as 1947, events that would not be seen elsewhere until April 1948 were already taking place in this area: the organization of armed bands (in Apía, for example, Conservatives had a group known as the Bejucos [Lianas]) and the exodus of peasant families (*La Mañana*, July 3, 8, and September 16, 1947; October 3, 1949; *La Patria*, May 25 and October 3, 1949). As late as the mid-1950s, the police continued to carry out violence, such as that suffered by the hamlet of Irra, near the Cauca River:

> We remember the time that the Irra (Quinchía) police, in a ritual-like way, threw bodies into the river. Once they had been executed with a rifle or revolver they were taken to a wall along the Cauca River, where a construction project was under way. They were placed one on top of another, then [the police] threw them in the order that they had been placed on the wall.
>
> The criminal gendarmes apparently didn't comprehend the evil of their actions; they seemed to feel they had the right to do this by virtue of their official positions. However, very early the next day they were looking for possible witnesses to give a [fabricated] statement in the event they had to go to the investigation offices. The real witnesses already knew what awaited them if they went against the ferocious police: the same treatment as those victims who had been thrown into the river...
>
> This explains why, for nearly two years, starting October 8, 1956, none of the residents of Irra and Tapias, and not even the victims'

relatives, dared file a criminal complaint regarding the events dealt with in this trial. (Sumario 15)

The slaughter in Irra canyon is but one of the many political antecedents alluded to in the nickname of the region's most famous *bandolero:* Capitán Venganza (Captain Vengeance).

Capitán Venganza's home base comprised the districts of Naranjal, Botero, Moreto, Juan Tapado, Opiramá, and Irra, in the municipalities of Quinchía and Riosucio. This region, where Venganza had the broad support of peasants—mostly coffee-growing smallholders—was known as the "Independent Republic of Quinchía."

Bandolero autonomy in this territory was almost proverbial. Independence from those "above" and unconditional (Liberal) peasant support emerged as the distinctive traits of Capitán Venganza's *bandolero* realm. Thus, he had very little in common with late *bandoleros,* even though he also operated in the department of Caldas. His "Republic" was clearly rural and peasant-based; neither urban contacts, nor direct *gamonal* protection, nor payment for chores commissioned by intellectual authors had a decisive effect on his actions. Venganza's *cuadrilla* did, however, maintain close contact with other *bandolero* groups, most notably the "revolutionary" Pedro Brincos, who had come from Líbano in 1957 to organize campesinos in Quinchía—in fact, he led the first *cuadrilla* command in Santa Helena. When Pedro Brincos left the region, Capitán Venganza assumed the general command, setting up his headquarters in Opiramá. His contact with Pedro Brincos and other MOEC militants undoubtedly left a deep mark on Capitán Venganza's independent, social outlook, although he continued to be a Liberal. Although we do not know the extent to which he espoused revolutionary ideas, his organization left an imprint of social justice within the boundaries of his "Republic."

Capitán Venganza is estimated to have had one thousand men under his command in 1958, making his group of insurgents one of the largest in the last phase of the Violencia. His *"bandolero* army" normally divided into groups that would set up camp in strategic locations. The second- and third-in-command were "Capitán Aguila" and "Sargento García," the latter of whom set up his camp in the hamlet of Naranjal. When planning a "job," the leaders would request reinforcements from the other *cuadrillas.* The "Independent Republic" was a sort of liberated territory, and, as was only logical, this local autonomy, more than the robberies and killings, deeply troubled the regional politicians and new congressmen of President Lleras Camargo's ruling National Front. The Conservative opposition missed no opportunity to accuse the *bandolero* republic of giving a false image of peace in Colombian territory:

> The peasants between Bonafont and Irra have been deprived of their lands, which are in the possession of the *bandoleros*. Similarly, it has happened that the authorities in Quinchía and Irra lack the backing of the troops, so the *bandoleros* there have complete freedom. As a curious footnote, the only authority there for the farms is said to be the famous bandit Capitán Venganza. (*Anales del Congreso*, excerpts from a speech given by Senator de Angulo on May 6, 1959, 1555–1556)

> There is a garrison of twenty-five soldiers who don't patrol . . . a mayor who doesn't intervene . . . and a few days ago two police agents who were still there [were] unarmed, because they weren't allowed to bear arms . . . they were a threat to Venganza's forces. (*Anales del Congreso*, excerpts from a speech given by Senator Solórzano on May 12, 1959, 1603)

All recorded accounts and testimonies stress, however, that local peasants supported the *bandoleros*. One Conservative campesino, who had been jailed for two days by Liberal *bandoleros*, gave the following report: "In that *vereda* [Naranjal], the *bandoleros* are in charge. Neither the police, nor the mayor, nor anyone the criminals don't like comes there. They took over that region and all the families provide a safe haven . . . they distribute food to them . . . they fix up their clothes . . . they give them a place to sleep" (*La Patria*, April 9, 1958).

To support the *cuadrillas*, Venganza charged all the campesino families a monthly quota based on their income. The better-off peasants would pay one peso or more; those with a lower income would pay one peso or less, in a proportional and fair system. A coded receipt was issued, as if the "Republic" had an authentic "minister of finance" (*La Patria*, May 16, 1958; *Semana*, June 2, 1959). The highest taxes were, logically, imposed on the hacendados. Initially their contribution was set at 400 pesos, but during 1959, Venganza upped the amount to 800 pesos, pointing to the high cost of living. Not only the peasants—who were required to pay on Saturday (market day)—but all Venganza's "subjects" were taxed to support the "Independent State." Day laborers also paid one peso for each day they worked, and the *cuadrilla* instituted "teachers' Mondays," when it was the educators' turn to fill Venganza's coffers. Each Wednesday the "Republic's" treasurers had to submit their accounts to their leader.

Both the regional and national press, and later on the congressional debates, made much of a mysterious "concentration camp" in an unnamed location that no one ever saw but that horrified readers and radio listeners opposed to Capitán Venganza, who was reportedly punishing thieves and anyone else who disobeyed his orders (*Anales del Congreso*, excerpts from a speech given by Senator Solórzano on May 12, 1959, 1604).

Through tax collection and social control, Capitán Venganza received contributions from nearly all the rural classes that he "governed." He thus avoided relying solely on politicians and local *gamonales*. However, what gave him the most popularity and allowed him to protect his social image was the proportional taxation. He avoided overcharging small farmers and impoverished peasants, a trap the other *cuadrilla* leaders fell into at the end of their careers, accelerating the loss of their bases of support in the countryside.

Who was this Capitán Venganza? More than an avenger, as his nickname suggests, he was a defender of campesinos. Under his *cuadrilla's* protection, in 1958, two years after the fact, Irra's peasants dared to denounce the police massacres after Venganza had succeeded in having a politician friend of his appointed as police inspector (*La Patria*, May 14, 1959; March 21, 1961). His real name was Medardo Trejos, but he was also known by other names, and some confusion existed regarding his real identity. Because Venganza was, above all, a myth.

For the government, for the Conservative press, and, in general, for outsiders, he embodied the myth of the cruel, Communist bandit. Therefore, a group of journalists visiting Quinchía expected to find "first, a moral monster, and second, a wretch and renegade of Colombian society who, as such, lacks any influence on peasant consciousness, that is, 'popularity,' and whose name, consequently, elicits instantaneous public condemnation wherever it is mentioned" (*Semana*, June 2, 1959).

For the peasantry, he was a different kind of myth, a myth closer to the typical social bandit: generous and mysterious. The description given by Father Tamayo, who had been coadjutor of the Quinchía parish, clearly captures this side of Venganza, although he concludes by echoing the official accusations against him:

Venganza is just like everyone else. Nothing sets him apart, and therefore, because Venganza is like a twin brother of any indigenous person from Quinchía, no one knows or has ever seen Venganza. I came to this parish four years ago. . . . The peasants of the region . . . welcomed me kindly but basically told me, "No, Father, we respect you a lot, but here we do not need civil, ecclesiastical, or military authorities for the moment. We have no use for the mayor, or for the priest, or for the army, because we have Venganza. Venganza respects us, defends us, and loves us." Hence, Venganza had gone from a young 22-year-old Indian rebel to an agrarian institution, leaving no unfilled positions for competitors.

He is a *bandolero*. He rules through terror. He even has a concentration camp where he punishes with hard labor those who break his law. Venganza has promulgated his own criminal, civil, and tax code; he has organized a corps of tax collectors. People obey him and fear informing on him, given their impossibility of living without his protection. (*Semana*, June 2, 1959, 14)

Venganza's myth overtook not only political and church institutions but also the justice system. Though he was blamed for dozens of robberies and murders, not one file had been opened on him, as the governor of Caldas noted. Even the armed forces fell prey to the mythical bandit. Major Alvaro Valencia Tovar, commander of the Ayacucho Battalion, who led military operations in Caldas and had certain knowledge of peasant psychology, gives an even clearer account of this mysterious side of Venganza:

Early one morning I led a military expedition against Venganza's farm. Because Venganza is the owner of an hacienda, "El Poleal," about which the most chilling things were said, I thought I would find, based on the rumors, an impregnable fortress, an enormous, unassailable, guarded concentration camp, an arsenal. I began to be surprised when we crossed the farm's periphery without difficulty. At dawn, the troops emerged from the bushes in an encircling action and broke into the hacienda house: we found a few administrators who were asleep. . . .

Not a shot was fired. As we searched the rooms, the only things we found that could be confiscated were some weapons, muzzle-loaded shotguns for the most part, and machetes and edged weapons that in the countryside are considered work tools, and some checkbooks with receipts proving growers' economic contribution to the support of Capitán Venganza's "Sovereign State."

Of course, Capitán Venganza wasn't there. He is a spirit, he is a gas, a man made of smoke who vanishes as soon as one tries to touch him. He evaporates and slips out through the rugged mountain paths. Moreover, there is no interest in catching him. The authorities have nothing on him. If we exclude the protection tax, there is not a single piece of evidence against Capitán Venganza. Each time a robbery occurs or a murder is committed, rumor places the blame on Capitán Venganza, but until now it has been impossible to prove a [single] murder with facts or testimonies. (*Semana*, June 2, 1959, 14)

Despite his links to Pedro Brincos and professionals such as lawyers and doctors from Pereira who would later enter the MOEC, Venganza remained loyal to the Liberal Party. In 1957, he came to Irra to vote for the National Front in a plebiscite. A friend and comrade of his, Claudio Rojas, had been a candidate for mayor of Quinchía before being appointed police inspector in the same *corregimiento* of Irra, in 1958. In 1959, however, when Venganza was at the height of his prestige, his political conduct changed. The transfer of the army commander to the area aggravated problems, law-and-order problems. The "Independent Republic" also suffered internal problems. Men loyal to Venganza assassinated "Sargento García," second-in-command in the *bandolero* state, over "business matters"—that is, political rivalries and contradictions, which, although rooted in the past (García had been friends with Pedro Brincos since the latter led the first command in Quinchía), became more acute when García decided to deal with the government, accept the amnesty offer, and surrender (*La Patria*, May 16, 1958; *Anales del Congreso*, excerpts from a speech given by Senator Solórzano on May 12, 1959, 1604).

As commander-in-chief, Venganza had decided on a tough, independent, noncooperative stance; although the exact reason is not known, it probably was not much different from those that forced other *bandoleros* to return to armed struggle. Four months later, Venganza killed a *bandolero* named Gabriel Serna ("El Ovejo" [The Sheep]), a member of his *cuadrilla*, in retaliation for Serna's killing of a kidnapped traveling salesman without Venganza's authorization.

In the meantime, so powerless had the authorities become in the "Independent Republic" that the Caldas governor refused to authorize a trip that a Peace Commission had planned to Quinchía, because he could not guarantee the safety of the Conservative members of the mission (*Anales del Congreso*, May 12, 1959, 1604). Venganza was becoming a national problem. In the Senate, heated debates continued on the *bandolero* who defied all established authority. The most serious problem for the government may have been that no political officials or regional strongmen with whom an understanding might have been reached, such as those in other *bandolero* regions, were willing to assume responsibility for Venganza. The rhetoric of Senator Solórzano, addressing the minister of the interior, expresses this loss of control over the situation:

> How long is a wretch who seizes the authority's powers and who is capable of imposing his will, of collecting taxes, of settling disputes over boundaries, and of deciding on the life and the honor and the property of all the inhabitants of that martyred district going to exist within the Colombian state, within the department of Caldas? How long is the operation of a "*bandolero* state" within the constitutional state going to be permitted? (Ibid., 1603)

The authorities did not, however, know how to deal with Venganza. They had no files, no evidence of any kind on the crimes attributed to him; he had never personally confronted the army, and they were not even certain that he existed.

In 1960 Venganza showed the public that he did exist. He came out of hiding, and his name appeared third on a list of Liberal town councilors in Quinchía. The local mayor said Venganza had threatened to create disturbances if he was excluded from the list; moreover, he appears to have said that he was again working for the National Front (*La Patria*, March 27, 1960). He in fact won a seat on the town council, apparently on the Liberal Party's ticket.

Still, Venganza's life within the law was as mysterious as his life as a *bandolero*. In 1960, he again became an enigma because nobody knew about his plans. Could it be that the mythical *bandolero* who governed a "Sovereign State" found it impossible to conduct legal activities in a public institution that was part of the official state? Did military harassment make it impossible for him to fulfill his official duties? Whatever the case, in March 1961 reports indicated that Venganza had again taken up arms; he was blamed for a massacre in the *ve- reda* of Peralonso, in the municipality of Santuario, quite far from his geographic base. Two members of his *cuadrilla* were killed there: "Juancho el Vengador" (Juancho the Avenger) and "El Aventurero" (the Adventurer).

Nothing else is known of Capitán Venganza's activities in the mountains. Just as the social origin of this popular *bandolero* is unknown, the ultimate intentions of his twofold activities have also remained hidden. We know only that at 6:00 P.M., June 5, 1961, Venganza had his last drink in a cantina in a Quinchía *vereda*, where he had arrived alone on horseback. When he was surprised there by an army patrol demanding his surrender, Venganza put up no resistance. A short time later, the *bandolero* leader died on the highway—or perhaps, and more in line with the practices of that period, the sinister *ley de fuga* was carried out against him.

The press published contradictory reports in which Venganza had either tried to flee or, in the most carefully prepared version, released a day after the first accounts, had died in combat when his *cuadrilla* confronted an army patrol (*El Espectador*, June 6 [evening edition] and June 7 [morning edition], 1961; *La Patria*, June 7 and 8, 1961).

Capitán Venganza's myth has not died; he never completely became an anti-myth like those conjured up by the government and the armed forces regarding Chispas and Desquite or Sangrenegra, whose heads were displayed publicly to horrify the younger campesino generations. In Quinchía, by contrast, the memory of the social *bandolero* that Capitán Venganza had been for the region's farmhands lived on.

Within the different forms of political *bandolerismo*, the uniqueness of Capitán Venganza was that, although he had emerged within the political context of the two-party dispute, whose perspective he never completely abandoned, his social policies clearly surpassed those limits and sowed that seed of new social organization fleetingly expressed in the "Independent Republic of Quinchía."

The "Boys from the "Mountains": Similarities in Diversity

This chapter and the previous one have emphasized *bandolerismo's* regional differences. Perhaps, in conclusion, we should note some common elements within the differences described above.

First and foremost, in nearly all the cases studied herein we see an organic relationship between *bandolerismo* and the first period of the Violencia: soldiers of the 1950s rebel armies transformed into *banda* leaders in the 1960s, giving a first line of continuity; or political bosses whose local power was threatened in the initial phase and who sought to reassert their positions by using the paid sectarianism of disaffected campesinos constituted a second line of continuity, in this case, one from "above." In addition, all *cuadrilla* members were in some way "sons" of that Violencia. The Desquites and Venganzas who retaliated for attacks suffered either personally or by their families; who defended what was theirs, despite being trapped by merciless government policies; or who had been robbed of all their possessions and whose personalities had been formed amid the fear, frustration, and disintegration of the Violencia, aspired only to use the income they received through the *banda* to attain a certain financial stability, a certain degree of power, however illegitimate, and a means—the only one possible—of social mobility. The history of the regional profiles is, then, the very history of the Violencia.

In addition, *cuadrilla* members' social background as well as the *cuadrillas'* operations show basic commonalties. *Banda* leaders' smallholder origins are particularly evident, and the importance of day laborers, unemployed rural workers, or seasonal workers can also be seen in *cuadrilla* followers or foot soldiers. All the *cuadrilleros* were young, free of family commitments, and had little if any formal education, although they generally—at least in the case of the leaders—had completed their military service and thus had military experience. The sharecroppers and administrators provided the main logistical support and were the allies most interested in ensuring the perpetuation of the conditions that had allowed *bandolerismo* to survive. In their social makeup and in the outward links they established, the *cuadrillas* included nearly every sector of the peasantry: this was a typically rural phenomenon, despite its initial urban links based on political dependence. Another similarity among the different *cuadrillas* was not only the support they received from the peasants but their structure and their integration into the social milieu of the densely populated coffee-growing areas. If those men from the mountains considered themselves—as their nicknames frequently indicated—marginalized from society, they could, at any time, become simple day laborers who belonged to that society. Many of them even alternated between "part-time" *bandolerismo* and seasonal coffee picking. The complexity of the *cuadrillas'* internal organization, with their multiple specialized tasks; the vast support networks; the fluidity in moving between roles as authentic "soldiers" or militants of the organization, collaborators responsible for logistics or supplies, and simple providers of a safe haven; the *cuadrillas'* participation in the market through the sale of stolen or seized coffee—all these elements expressed their specific, advanced integration into rural society as a whole.

Also, as an integral part of the more widespread political and social discontent, the great majority of the cases studied herein reveal an obvious inclination to identify with various expressions of opposition to the National Front: Efraín González with ANAPO; Pedro Brincos with the MOEC; and the remaining *bandoleros* with the MRL. This was, naturally, one factor that put them at the center of political debate in the 1960s, as shown in the next chapter.

Finally, the *cuadrilla* leaders' claims to greater independence appear to have been followed not by a general strengthening of their political capacity but by their growing disintegration and their irreversible isolation from the sociopolitical forces that had constituted their initial support. When the anti-myth appeared on the stage, the erstwhile hero was made into a monster, a terrorist, an *antisocial*, a deranged individual. The real deterioration of their public image made them appear to their former allies as simple proponents of social turmoil, unworthy of the mission allegedly entrusted to them; and with the loss of *gamonal* legitimization, not only did the impunity and logistic support "from above" (that had done so much to help construct the myths of invulnerability, ubiquity, and generosity) disappear but so did the mechanisms that had ensured *bandolerismo's* integration into the nation's politics. In Hobsbawm's words: "Bandits now belong to just one social category: that of the poor and oppressed."

Perhaps the best description of this world of contradictions surrounding the enigmatic *bandoleros* is the elegy left by poet and writer Gonzalo Arango on the grave of José William Aranguren, Capitán Desquite:

> Yes. Just a rose, but not one of blood. Very red, as he liked. Red, Liberal, and murderous. Because he was a malefactor, a poet of death, a surrealist: he made crime into a fine art. He killed. He got even. He was killed. His name was Desquite.
>
> He was killed because he was a bandit and had to die. Undoubtedly he deserved to die, but no more than do the bandits in power.
>
> In seeing his bullet-riddled body in the newspapers, one discovered in that face a decency, an authenticity: that of the perfect bandit: thin, nervous, deluded, a mystique of terror. That is, the dignity of the *bandolero* who could be only that: a *bandolero*. But he was

one with all his soul, with all the ferocity of his enigmatic soul, of his devastating Satanism.

Having no ideal, he could be but a murderer who kills for the sake of killing. Destroying was his creative mission. But this bandit appeared not to be one. I mean, there was a whisper of delicacy, of cleanliness in his body. I do not doubt that on another soil, a soil other than the sinister one of his country, this *bandolero* could have been a missionary or an authentic revolutionary.

The destiny of certain men who took the wrong path, who lost their chance to lead history, has always seemed tragic to me.

Desquite was one of those: he was one of the Colombians who was worth the most: 160,000 pesos. Others sell themselves for less, they deliver themselves for a vote. Desquite did not sell out. What he was worth, they paid to the informer after his death. That wild beast did not fit in any cage. A psychiatrist would say that he suffered from the Herostratus complex: his hatred was destructive, irrational, godless, wild, and he had to die like a wild beast: cornered.

Even after his death, the soldiers feared approaching him, afraid of his ghosts. His red legend had made him fearful, invincible. . . .

He had become a *guerrillero* when he was barely more than a child: not to kill but so that they wouldn't kill him, to defend his right to live, which in his time was the only human cause left to defend: Life!

Henceforth, this man, or rather, this child would have no law other than murder. His country, his government made him into a murderer, gave him the psychology of a murderer. He would continue to kill because it was the only thing he knew how to do: kill to live. (Not live to kill.) They taught him only this bitter and deadly lesson, and he would make it a philosophy applicable to all the acts of his existence. Terror became his nature and we all know that it is not easy to fight Destiny. Crime was his Cause. He would be able to think only in terms of blood. . . .

Within his strange, criminal philosophy, this man recognized no fault other than allowing himself to be killed by his enemy: all of society. . . .

Was he guilty? Yes. Because he was free to choose murder and he chose it.

But he was also innocent insofar as murder chose him.

Thus, in one of the eight holes they shot in the bandit's body, I place my rose of blood. One of those shots killed an innocent man who had no possibility to be one. The other seven killed the murderer that he was. . . .

The soldiers who killed him in fulfillment of their duty captured a weapon of his with an inscription on the butt engraved with the blade of a knife. It said only: This is my life.

No man's life had ever been so mortal. I ask on his grave, dug on the mountain:

Is there not some way that Colombia, rather than killing its sons, will make them worthy of living?

If Colombia is unable to answer this question, I predict a tragedy: Desquite will rise from the dead, and the land will again be watered with blood, pain, and tears. (*La Nueva Prensa,* April 14, 1964)

The widows of
La Violencia.

The mules that in peacetime had transported coffee now
carried the bodies of campesinos.

Guadalupe Salcedo,
symbol of resistance
in the 1950s.

The "insurgent" army of the Llanos Orientales, waiting to surrender.

Guadalupe Salcedo (*right*), the most important leader of the Liberal *guerrilleros*, and General Duarte Blum, Commander of the Army, discussing the surrender; Llanos Orientales, 1953.

In front, Efraín González, the most important Conservative *bandolero*; behind him, his bodyguards and a priest sympathizer.

Teófilo Rojas (Chispas), the most prominent Liberal *bandolero* in the coffee region.

Teniente Roosevelt, one of the youngest members of Chispas's *cuadrilla*.

An entire army against one man: Efraín González, entrenched in a Bogotá neighborhood (July 1965).

Efraín González's bombed and bullet-ridden hiding place in the south of Bogotá.

Capitán Desquite, *bandolero* leader in northern Tolima.

Pedro Brincos, the most revolutionary *bandolero* in northern Tolima, in prison.

Sangrenegra (*left*) and Tarzán (*right*): two of the bloodiest *bandoleros* of the last phase of La Violencia.

Two women *bandoleras* (photo found on Almanegra).

Capitán Venganza, the mythical *bandolero* from the coffee-growing region of Risaralda.

The controversial photo of General Gustavo Rojas Pinilla (President, 1953–1957, *second from left*), with a political leader from Valle and the infamous "King of the *pájaros*," Jesús María Lozano (*left*).

GANESE UD. LA SUMA DE
$ 120.000.00

Como recompensa al particular o particulares
que entreguen o faciliten la captura de ·

TEOFILO ROJAS
- A CHISPAS -

Gobernación de Caldas $ 50.000

Gobernación del Tolima $ 30.000

TOTAL $ 80.000

Y a quienes entreguen o faciliten la captura de

EFRAIN GONZALEZ

Gobernación de Caldas $ 40.000

TEOFILO ROJAS
(a. Chispas)

NOTA: las informaciones dadas por usted serán
mantenidas bajo la más rigurosa y es-
tricta reserva y no serán dadas a cono-
cer por ningún motivo.

Contribuya usted a afianzar la seguridad social y su propia seguridad de-
nunciando sin ningún temor los antisociales.

En esta forma le prestará usted el me-
jor servicio a la sociedad y podrá ganar-
se la apreciable suma de
CIENTO VEINTE MIL PESOS.

EFRAIN GONZALEZ

The state creates the "informer industry" through posters offering rewards for information on the *bandolero* leaders.

USTED

PUEDE SER

OTRA VICTIMA DE

JACINTO CRUZ USMA

SANGRE NEGRA

Y SU CUADRILLA DE MALECHORES

Sangrenegra's body, displayed in public near the offices of the Fourth Brigade, in Ibagué.

Sangrenegra's body being transported to different areas of Tolima for public display.

CHAPTER FIVE

The National Dimension: Political Debates

The preceding chapters analyzed *bandolerismo*'s different regional processes, its forms, its rate of evolution, and the political and social linkages that determined its development, as well as the causes of its disintegration.

Within an overview of *bandolerismo*, this chapter will examine the different ways in which these regional processes informed the overall development of La Violencia. To be sure, there is often correspondence between the meaning and the importance given, both regionally and nationally, to some of the character types studied here. Nationally, however, more importance has sometimes been given to certain qualitative manifestations of *bandolerismo* than to its quantitative expressions (the size of the *cuadrillas*, the number of victims attributed to them, etc.). Pedro Brincos, for example, was viewed with more apprehension in government ministries and national political directorates than he was in his theater of operations.

To examine these contrasts in greater detail, we have researched a source that covers the key period of this study (1958–1965) and that until now had not been tapped for this purpose: the congressional debates. Among its many roles, Congress was the stage for the political currents, trends, and contradictions that emerged within the dominant classes. It was a forum not only for regional political interests, key to explaining *bandolerismo*, but also for government spokespersons, for the agents of centralizing forces, and for the representatives of the hegemonic factions explicitly committed to ending the divisive effects of La Violencia in general and of *bandolerismo* in particular. The following discussion examines those debates in some detail.

First, we must note that the central problems faced by the military junta that replaced Rojas Pinillas's ousted regime in mid-1957 appeared, initially, to come down to two: the general problem of "law and order," which fundamentally meant eradicating the gangs of *pájaros*, or paid assassins, and the economic and social recovery of the areas completely or partially destroyed in over ten years of "blood and fire," to use the tragically celebrated expression of José Antonio Montalvo, *ministro de gobierno* (minister of the interior) under Ospina Pérez.

The greater complexity of the task at hand was tacitly acknowledged by the creation of the "National Committee to Investigate the Causes of La Violencia," made up of political leaders, members of the military, and priests, including Germán Guzmán from the Líbano parish. A few years later, Guzmán, along with Eduardo Umaña Luna and Orlando Fals Borda, published the first and best-known study on La Violencia.

A man relatively removed from the traditional virulence of bipartisan confrontation and who served as the oligarchy's "political stand-in" in its times of greatest need—former President Echandía—accepted the governorship of his native department, Tolima, in 1958. In doing so, he risked his prestige for what was declared a crucial objective: establishing, at least outwardly and in the department where the wounds were the hardest to heal, a climate of dialogue and reconciliation. This was indispensable for legitimizing the National Front that Alberto Lleras and Laureano Gómez had formed in the Spanish resorts of Benidorm and Sitges in 1956 and 1957, and which would take over in July 1958.

Nevertheless, the assessment of the status of La Violencia made by the head of the military junta, Major General Gabriel París, and presented to the first National Front Congress, which had convened in July 1958, was not particularly encouraging. The report stated:

> The present government has spared no effort in its determination to eradicate La Violencia. It has issued harsh orders to the authorities to establish a fail-safe encirclement around the *violentos*; it has sent a considerable part of the police forces to reestablish order in the affected areas; it has created commissions charged with finding the underlying, determinant causes of the events and to formulate appropriate recommendations; it has increased the number of judges [and] removed several authorities; it has given fiscal assistance to the departments, and economic assistance to the devastated areas; and it has continuously sent its ministers to study and solve the

problems within its grasp, convinced as it is that preferential importance must be given to law and order. In this area it has received the valuable collaboration of former President Echandía, who with praiseworthy patriotism has practically lived in Tolima and has been with the governor of that department [Manuel Coronado, governor before Echandía], visiting every place and thoroughly examining the distinct aspects of the situation.

Still, the junta found it impossible to conceal the other side of the coin:

The government wishes to emphasize to the senators and representatives the seriousness revealed by a *prolongation of La Violencia* in certain areas of the nation's territory in which *it has become endemic*, and in which the indefatigable steps taken by the government and the political directorates have not been effective in averting it. La Violencia continues to scourge the fields, sacrificing promising lives and offering *dismal perspectives for consolidating national harmony. (Anales del Congreso*, Presidential address to Congress, July 24, 1958, 37; our emphasis)

As imprecise as they may have been, the data on the number of persons killed were sufficiently eloquent and indicative, as indicated in Table 2. These five departments continued under an uninterrupted state of siege until January 1, 1962. The chronological breakdown of nationwide Violencia-related deaths between 1957 and 1962 is shown in Table 3. At the very least, these figures indicate that the first National Front

TABLE 2. *Violencia-Related Deaths for Four Departments (January 1– June 30, 1958)*

Department	Conserv-atives	Lib-erals	Un-known	Mili-tary	Total	Percent-age
Tolima	289	487	266	32	1,074	43.4
Valle	244	225	219	2	690	27.9
Viejo Caldas	93	74	399	0	566	22.8
Huila	14	20	17	1	52	2.1
Total	644	812	986	35	2,477	100.0

Source: Guillermo Amaya Ramírez, *Memoria del Ministerio de Gobierno al Congreso de 1959,* cited in Ramsey (1981, 278).

TABLE 3. *Total Violencia-Related Deaths per Year, 1957–1962*

Year	Total Deaths
1957	2,877
1958	3,796
1959	2,550
1960	2,557
1961	3,173
1962	2,370

Source: Oquist (1978, 332).

government had failed to "pacify" and that Dr. Echandía's famous quip that "in Tolima and Huila you can go fishing at night" spoke of his cynicism more than it reflected reality. The National Front instead ushered in a new period of La Violencia in which democrats could at least be consoled by the freedom to publicly debate the causes of its prolongation and the number of victims left along the roadsides.

The congressional debates would revolve around two questions: How could the endemic nature of La Violencia be explained and what steps should be taken to stop it? The central geographic point of reference would be the area comprising the departments of Tolima, Valle, and Viejo Caldas, which are the focus of this study. Of the 18,481 deaths fortunate enough to be tallied between 1958 and 1966, a high proportion (13,873, or 75%) occurred in these departments, while the remaining 25 percent were distributed throughout seven other departments (Oquist 1978, 323).

The first extra-party explanation for the persistence of the phenomenon was readily available: the thesis that La Violencia was a legacy of the dictatorship (1953–1957), an explanation that was advocated vigorously, particularly by the *laureanista* faction of the Conservative Party, during the sensational trial of Rojas Pinilla from mid-1958 to mid-1959. During this period, the trial captured the attention not only of the debates but also of the public in general. Real or imaginary plots hatched by Rojas Pinillas's followers provided a recurrent excuse for reestablishing the state of siege and adopting harsh repression. The most significant accusation against the ousted general concerned his links to and protection of León María Lozano, alias "El Cóndor," who had been the kingpin of the *pájaros* and the epitome of terror in the ten preceding years.[1] In any event, the thesis that attempted to reduce

La Violencia to a fatal "legacy of the dictatorship," in exclusive reference to Rojas Pinilla and not to Laureano Gómez, imposed a cloak of silence regarding the more than 150,000 bodies that had turned up between 1948 and 1953. Never before had the need to forget been so emphasized, and it involved the National Front's complicity, at the very moment of its birth, vis-à-vis the period that was supposedly being left behind. However, this expunging of memory was also needed for another reason: the National Front's purported democracy and liberty could only be erected on the foundation of an arbitrarily circumscribed past. In addition, as time would show, its ideology of "peace" only masked a new phase in the war.

Between Amnesty and Repression

The first signs of a break in the fragile truce stemmed from the application of the amnesty rules.[2] This was a debate between two clearly defined political options: either repressing or establishing channels to integrate into society the most prominent figures of the forces that had clashed in the preceding period of La Violencia. Nevertheless, during the process, a degree of complementarity between these two positions was sought—that is, between the state's repressive security forces and its ideological machinery.

The heated debates that began in March 1959 centered primarily on Pedro Brincos, Chispas, and Capitán Venganza, in that order. With Pedro Brincos, the inquiry stemmed from his release by a Manizales judge who found no grounds on which to try him; with Chispas, it concerned the accusation that he had massacred Conservative campesinos in Rovira while under the protection of temporary suspension of criminal proceedings against him; and the debate on Capitán Venganza focused on the government's inability to eliminate what Santander Senator Hernando Sorzano González called the "*bandolero* state" in the region of Quinchía (*Anales del Congreso*, May 6 and May 13, June 8 and 11, 1959; 1190–1191, 1266, 1553–1562, 1598–1605).

The Conservative legislators promoting the debates accused Interior Minister Guillermo Amaya Rodríguez of excessive tolerance and clemency toward people they deemed incorrigible. La Violencia—they now began to say—was Liberal, and accusations were made that in some areas, such as Cauca, Liberal identification cards were being demanded and thus constituted safe-conducts or even "life-insurance" policies. Massive numbers of Conservative peasants, unable to produce these cards, were being murdered, claimed Senator Alvaro Angulo (*Anales del Congreso*, June 2, 1959, 1502).

And, most ominous, said the senator, the army had been informed that the perpetrators of those massacres were *bandoleros* from Tolima and Caldas, "where some of them had already received money and special protection from the government to cease [committing] those misdeeds," and that the government had failed to block the strategic roads of the Central Cordillera and cut off the supply of salt and other necessities; there was no sign of a decision to jointly use artillery and aviation to conduct an all-out onslaught against the outlaws; and Conservative peasants were being disarmed and were even being tried by the War Council for having weapons for purely defensive purposes. Furthermore, it made no sense to build highways and health clinics "if they were only going to serve to transport bodies and heal wounds, since until now no displaced person has succeeded in returning to his plot or *vereda*, among other reasons, because the *bandoleros* claim that the rehabilitation is for them" (*Anales del Congreso*, June 2, 1959, 1503). To illustrate the armed forces' negligence in the fight against this situation, Senator Angulo gave the following personal account:

When I was in Belalcázar, municipality of Cauca, [which is] seriously affected by La Violencia, during the plebiscite campaign, I encountered the following fact: to go to Belalcázar, it was necessary to cross the Páez River at the Guetando bridge. I was driving my private pickup, alone, taking National Front political propaganda. I was stopped by a lieutenant who was with several soldiers; he didn't ask me to identify myself, nor did he see what I was carrying, which was very voluminous, a lot of National Front propaganda. He simply stopped me and let me continue. When I arrived in Belalcázar, I informed the officer in charge of the troops that I felt that the necessary steps were not being taken, that they should have searched me to determine if I was carrying weapons or munitions to an area seriously affected by La Violencia. The officer, of the Regular Army of Colombia, answered that he had nothing to do with that post in Guetando, because that post belonged to others. The others [were] the other army, the army of subversion, the army of the *bandoleros*. The Army of Colombia troops invited me to meet Major Marulanda, of the other army, the army of subversion, and the Regular Army of Colombia arranged for me to meet Major Marulanda at the Simbola bridge, about two kilometers from the town. But as the troops of the Regular Army—noncommissioned officers and soldiers—talked, they didn't refer to "Major Marulanda, leader of the *bandoleros,*" but rather to "our Major Marulanda." This was how they referred to a *bandolero* leader, and "our Colonel Arboleda"—another colonel of the army of subversion. With that use of the possessive, [which is reserved for] the hierarchy of the Armed Forces of the Regular Army of Colombia, our troops referred to officers of the *bandolero* army. (Ibid.)

The argument of the Conservatives—both those who claimed to be independent and those who described themselves as belonging to the National Front—came down to the following assertion: the Liberal Party was failing to honor the bipartisan agreement and the National Front's policy of reconciliation, while theoretically positive, in practice encouraged a resurgence of La Violencia. The statements made by Senator Sorzano González reflected the same viewpoint. Sorzano González maintained that in Tolima, Caldas, and Cauca known *bandoleros* had been named mayors and police inspectors, in a clear reference to Governor Rafael Parga Cortés, while in Santander the green light had been given for the murder of Conservative peasants. He denounced that the amnestied Chispas had purchased a *finca* with 100,000 pesos from the rehabilitation fund and had been seen, prior to the Rovira massacre, "piloting a plane!" notwithstanding which nothing had been done to prevent the tragedy of the resurgence of violence. He also claimed that the amnesty decrees fostered impunity and had allowed Pedro Brincos and Capitán Venganza to create a *bandolero* republic in Quinchía (*Anales del Congreso*, June 11, 1959, 1598–1604).

These debates naturally affected government policy. On May 25, 1959, the government issued a decree practically annulling the decree issued November 28 of the preceding year, which had suspended criminal proceedings for political crimes committed prior to October 15, 1958, in the five departments still under the state of siege (Caldas, Cauca, Huila, Tolima, and Valle del Cauca). The May 1959 decree was an important victory for hard-liners.[3]

In a July 1959 address to Congress, President Lleras Camargo responded to his critics. First, he recalled the warning he had issued when taking power the preceding year: "I said then: 'Above all, we need to examine what our role should be regarding the disturbance of law and order by the constant phenomena of violence.' I will state in advance that I don't believe it will suddenly disappear and the country should prepare for an intense pacification campaign of unforeseeable duration" (*Anales del Congreso*, July 25, 1959, 1734).

Then, regarding the true scope of the so-called amnesty decrees and their relation to the tasks carried out by the Special Commission for the Rehabilitation of the Areas Affected by La Violencia, created in September 1958 and made up of the ministers of the interior, justice, finance, war, public health, national education, and public works, he stated:

I begin with the unequivocal acknowledgment that no Colombian, or, in any event, very few, has nothing to regret for directly or indirectly contributing to this great catastrophe. I accept that it is not possible that hundreds of thousands of compatriots have converted to *bandolerismo* and the brutal guerrilla life simply for pleasure or a sudden perversion of the people's Christian sentiments. For this reason, I understood that repression without reasonable prudence or an opportunity for peaceful citizens to recover would only deepen and extend the evil. And at the same time, I recognized that a total, unqualified, and blind amnesty could only give a free hand to people who can no longer change their ways and who must be handed over to justice and isolated from society. For that reason, we have not enforced the provisions of Article 121 of said amnesty, even though popular [thinking] and political ill will have tried to blame us for what we most painstakingly tried to avoid. Suspending criminal procedures for certain crimes that may have been committed amid the confusion and error of that brutal period is not amnesty. It is, moreover, limited and discriminate, and can only be obtained by request and through the verification by the authorities that it is being sought with an honest intention of rehabilitation. It continues to be a sort of monitored freedom, conditioned on the behavior of the beneficiary in response to this exceptional pardon. [Criminal] procedures do not have a statute of limitations and may be resumed at any time, at the first shortcoming of the person benefiting from the pardon. At the same time, we have facilitated the return of many of these individuals to honest and productive work, so they will not feel impelled by an untrusting and hard society, or by the total loss of their possessions, to return to the mountains and again take up arms. One example of this [policy] has been the downpayment on public works given mainly to open roads to the regions where guerrillas and bandits are concentrated and where the authorities had no access for many years. These projects are carried out with more laborers than the mechanized projects in peaceful regions. We assumed, and have been proven right, that as they plant [their crops] and before the first harvests are ready or the *fincas* have been restored, those people will have salaries, doctors, support, tools, and credit permitting their rehabilitation, if they truly want it. (*Anales del Congreso*, July 25, 1959, 1735)

Debates of this type continued for the entire second half of 1959, during which the Conservatives repeatedly attacked by pointing out extreme cases, or cases they claimed to be such, and questioning any economic support for victims of the first phase of La Violencia. This phase continued to be seen as a simple problem of law and order and not as a symptom of a profound social crisis. Significantly, for example, since 1958 an agrarian-reform bill, apparently unrelated to the region affected by La Violencia, had been on legislators' desks. Many senators and representatives, after long and weighty discourses on La Violencia, felt obliged to "change topics" when it came time to debate agrarian reform. There were few voices such as that of José Antonio Montalvo, the man of "blood and fire," who offered different diagnoses, even if his comments were alarmist:

We should ask if the social phenomenon we are examining today is a simple case of the masses' collective criminality or if it is instead a social revolution. . . . When those *bandolero* masses succeed in contacting the working masses in the city, this oligarchic gathering constituted by those of us who are here, this political power organized by us, the ruling classes, whom the needy classes are beginning to consider their antagonists, will be powerless to stop the revolution. (*Anales del Congreso*, September 11, 1959, 2579)

Although a Bogotá senator living relatively far from the events could hold this position, the provincial *gamonales* clung much more obstinately to blindly partisan positions, in part because their ability to survive as political leaders depended on doing so. In September 1959, a Conservative representative from what was then the *intendencia* of Meta, Justo Vega Lizarazo, undoubtedly very annoyed by the memory of the guerrilla groups in the Llano region, submitted a bill that purported to end amnesty once and for all. Article One of the bill stated, "as of [the time] this law takes effect, the system that has been adopted in Colombia based on the personal rehabilitation of the civilian criminals known as *guerrilleros* or *bandoleros* with money from the Nation is hereby prohibited, and the amnesty for the same class of criminals is likewise hereby prohibited, in order for impunity to disappear from Colombia" (*Anales del Congreso*, October 5, 1959, 3179; *Proyecto de Ley No. 428*, submitted September 22, 1959).

Contrary to what we might expect, the debates were not simply rhetoric. Their effects were at times felt in the most far-flung corners of the country. Thus, the news stories that appeared in early January 1960, pointing to a new correlation of forces and a new tack, must be examined with this context in mind. Three prominent former *guerrilleros* who had availed themselves of the amnesty decrees were killed in cold blood by government forces or their proxies: Silvestre Bermúdez (Mayor Mediavida), in the municipality of Prado, Tolima; Hermógenes Vargas (General Vencedor), in El Limón, within the municipality of Chaparral; and Jacobo Prías Alape ("Charronegro" [Black Horseman]), in the far southern end of the same department of Tolima (Fajardo 1979, 177–178). The new decade, the decade that would be governed by the "ideology of peace," was thus ushered in.

The March 1960 elections introduced important changes in the political makeup of Congress. The defeat of the *laureanista*, or doctrinarian, Conservatives who had been among the architects of the National Front forced the National Front's Liberals to look for new partners to preserve the coalition's legitimacy. Another important change was the vigorous irruption—claiming seventeen seats—of a dissident, anti–National Front faction within the Liberal Party: the MRL, led by Alfonso López Michelsen, on whose ticket former *guerrilleros* as prestigious as Juan de la Cruz Varela and Rafael Rangel Gómez would hold seats in the lower house.

This meant that the political struggle would be much more complex, since the opposition to the National Front was growing and its decisions clearly would be hindered, but also because the struggle between different factions would move to the forefront in the interparty rivalry. Moreover, the local or regional influence that might be exercised by armed groups, whether called *guerrilleros* or *bandoleros*, in controlling votes and political loyalties, now appeared decisive. Political splintering clearly encouraged the expansion or resurgence of *bandolerismo*.

Liberal *bandolerismo* would be combated by Conservative *bandolerismo*. This was the beginning of Efraín González's era in Santander, particularly in Vélez. The overall situation was basically the same as that described in an exchange of messages—it is not known if in jest or in earnest, but nonetheless revealing—attributed to two top officials in Tolima:

> Ibagué, 27. Civilian-military mayor of Cunday, I ask you to inform without delay how political parity operates [in] your jurisdiction. Echandía, Governor.

To which the mayor reportedly responded:

> Governor Echandía, Ibagué. Parity in my jurisdiction operates in following manner: two dead Conservatives, two dead Liberals. Respectfully, Civilian and Military Mayor.
> (*Anales del Congreso*, June 8, 1959, 1561)

The MRL was a coalition of forces opposed to the National Front for a variety of reasons. Its entrance into Congress introduced a new aspect to the phenomenon: La Violencia as a social problem. Two types of positions would now be superimposed on the debates: those that reduced the issue to a clearly partisan matter of law and order, and those that deemed law and order inseparable from the socioeconomic context. The latter perspective had been proposed from several angles. The government had issued a decree in early 1960 creating the so-called Tribunals of Reconciliation and Equity to hear disputes regarding the forced sale of land during the entire period of La Violencia; in August 1969, numerous peasants from Rovira, Tolima, had proposed the creation of a Peasant Ministry to deal with problems faced by the victims of La Violencia (*Anales del Congreso*, August 23, 1960, 318); and, finally, the debates on the agrarian problem were linked much more clearly to social conflicts generated in the shadow of the partisan conflict. Although to acknowledge that social ingredient in La Violencia before 1958 seemed acceptable, to do so after the establishment of the National Front was very difficult. The predominant tendency, both among Conservatives in general and among National Front Liberals, was to explain it as the product not of the internal dynamics of the process but as a reflection of outside influences. Thus, just as the "legacy of dictatorship" had explained the continuing violence from 1957 to 1959, now a factor external not only to the parties but also to the country was said to have determined its new evolution: The Cuban Revolution, seen by the disaffected in Colombia and other Latin American countries as a fresh, homegrown experience compared to the bureaucratic Soviet model, became the favorite excuse for avoiding an objective analysis of the most troubling transformations and justified the new systems for repression. La Violencia was now sponsored by "foreign powers" and "foreign ideologies," supplanting the opposing party, which was now described on both sides as an "occasional, fraternal adversary" (*Anales del Congreso*, March 21, 1961, 1057).

Following the same reasoning, ultrareactionary Tolima Senator Diego Tovar Concha, one of the champions of the campaign against any agrarian reform who specialized in conjuring up arms contraband, subversive propaganda, and all sorts of foreign invasions, backed up his theses by pointing to the publication in the Havana newspaper *El Mundo* of an article in which Capitán Chispas and other *bandoleros* were "the promoters of a new and future democracy against oligarchies" (*Anales del Congreso*, March 16, 1961, 987).

The MRL contested these arguments by pointing out that the persistence and even the expansion of La Violencia demonstrated the National Front's failure and the need to rethink the political rules through democratization and a reform of the exclusionary nature of the norms approved through the 1958 plebiscite. Valle del Cauca Representative Alfonso Barberena summarized the MRL's diagnosis of the situation in the following manner:

> We have maintained that La Violencia, which began as a political phenomenon, has now turned into a tremendous class struggle . . . anyone who wishes to combat La Violencia must begin from the standpoint of the fundamental reform that Colombia is demanding, which is agrarian reform. (*Anales del Congreso*, January 25, 1961, 181)

Moreover, although amnesty and rehabilitation, which had dominated national discourse from 1958 to 1960, would periodically resurface in subsequent years, the central point of debate would be state-sponsored repression. "How should La Violencia be fought effectively?" was the question to which a satisfactory answer began to be sought.

Some, such as Senator Gutiérrez Anzola, felt that, given the complicity of regional political leaders and public officials with the *bandoleros*, the state had proven itself increasingly powerless to stop La Violencia. This led him to suggest "adopting the system employed in Mexico, consisting of arming people to defend themselves against miscreants" (*Anales del Congreso*, January 25, 1961, 181). Although two top army officers supported this proposal, other lawmakers considered it a "shirking by the government forces" of their duties (*Anales del Congreso*, February 8, 1961, 403). A third group of legislators, including a Conservative representative from Tolima, José Ramírez Castaño, insisted less on the army's ineffectiveness, idleness, or complicity than on the counterproductiveness of the brutal mechanisms of repression, including the summary "merciless" shooting of *bandoleros* "of a certain political affiliation":

> The systems being put into practice by the police and army forces have created a social malaise, because they are systems of repression that do not fit within the country's republican and legal tradition. The emergency decrees and measures issued to apply in the departments subject to the state of siege do not exist in the most barbaric and despotic countries of the world; they are an ignominy; they do no honor to the National Front government. (*Anales del Congreso*, January 25, 1961, 181–183)

Liberal Valle Representative Carlos Holmes Trujillo had other reasons for feeling that the methods of repression and prevention being practiced were ineffective. He pointed to the following limitations: the army was generally slow in sending punitive expeditions in response to violence; communication with distant regions was difficult; the armed forces were unfamiliar, or only partially familiar, with the terrain where they operated, as well as with the human and social environment of those same areas. He proposed establishing a system of permanent surveillance, particularly in highly vulnerable areas with "political minorities," and creating the "farm worker guard, specially trained and under official responsibility, made up of men of goodwill who would be responsible, if necessary, for defending their own lives, their own lands, and their own families" (*Anales del Congreso*, February 14, 1961, 507). More than a substitute for military action, "peasant self-defense" was seen as a complement to the rising repression. Still, the same congressman warned of the danger that the armed peasants, after defeating the *bandoleros*, might begin their own revolutionary episode in the country (ibid., 403).

Alongside peasant self-defense, two closely linked issues began to be debated: rewards for capturing or killing *bandoleros*, and the death penalty. Both were already being practiced, but the attempt to legalize them now through the congressional debates was telling. Leaders of both parties were increasingly troubled by several facts. Rather than waning, La Violencia was spreading at a dizzying pace through Quindío and northern Valle and was plunging several municipalities in Antioquia into mourning as well. Enforcing justice was a dead issue because of the difficulty in obtaining witness testimonies and the impossibility that juries, subjected to constant threats of retaliation, could exercise their legal duties. Men were being illegally hired, said one Conservative senator, "for one thousand pesos a month [and] recruited to join the *bandolero* gangs," most notably in Pereira. In sum, a strident voice of alarm was being sounded, as summarized in the complaints of Conservative legislators from Valle, headed by Cornelio Reyes, that armed *bandas* "almost completely" dominated the Central Cordillera "to such an extent that they have imposed a special tax on landholders, consisting of an obligation to pay large sums of money set by [the *guerrilleros*], or deliver to them part of their harvests and cattle" (*Anales del Congreso*, April 19, 1961, 1387). Insistent claims were also made more or less continually that "*bandoleros* demand proof of membership in certain political movements, proof without which the inhabitants of the area are subjected to all sorts of outrages" (*Anales del Congreso*, April 26, 1962, 1467). All these points were the focus of the debates held in March and April 1961 and served as the backdrop for proposals to institute the death penalty. The respective bill was submitted to the Chamber of Representatives on May 30, 1961, with the following text:

> Article One of One. Congress may impose the death penalty for the following crimes: murder in the open or by a *cuadrilla* of malefactors, murder during the commission of nighttime robbery within [town limits], and heinous crimes. In no event shall said penalty be applied for political crimes.

The death penalty had long obsessed the bill's author, Marino Jaramillo Echeverri. Four years before, in 1957, prior to the plebiscite that brought the National Front to power, as Caldas's secretary for political affairs, Jaramillo had suggested that the military junta include the issue of the death penalty in the plebiscite.[4] At that time, the proposal was categorically opposed by part of the Liberal press and some Conservative newspapers that spoke out in favor of the "inviolability" of human life.[5]

The most unprecedented aspect of the debate being revived in 1961 was Jaramillo's attempt to deceive the public regarding his proposal.

Jaramillo acknowledged that the military authorities already practiced the death penalty, through the *ley de fuga;* that civilian authorities such as governors were instigating "paid murder" by publishing rewards; and that encouraging peasant self-defense, as was being done, was tantamount to practicing the death penalty. Nonetheless, he argued that legalizing capital punishment would restrict the practice by transferring to the state, and specifically to the judicial branch, the power to carry out the death penalty, thus preventing private parties from doing so and reducing its application. Despite his reasoning, all Colombia understood that such an institutionalization would only expand the practice and give it legal backing (*Anales del Congreso*, June 23, 1961, 2238).

So clear was this that, two months later, Representative Vega Lizarazo, a spokesman for landowners in the Llanos Orientales and for his class in general, proposed a measure equivalent to the death penalty not only for "heinous crimes" but also for simple cattle rustling, that is, for crimes against *latifundista* property and the integrity of cattle herds. His bill can only be interpreted as an attempt to arm the cattle owners and workers "so they may defend their lives, that of their peers, and their own properties against the attacks of *bandoleros* and cattle thieves, who since November 25, 1949, have engaged Colombia in a war to the death" (*Anales del Congreso*, September 8, 1961, 3451).

The lower house was unable to consider the two bills during that legislative period, but the death-penalty bill was resubmitted in the regular session that began in July. In the meantime, during a special session in April 1962, the Chamber of Representatives, at the executive's request, hastily began to debate a bill to allow governors to offer "rewards" for *bandoleros*. The purpose was to revive a legislative decree (issued under the state of siege) that had ceased being applied when the state of emergency was completely lifted in January of that year. During the first debate on the bill in the upper house's First Committee, Senator Juan Antonio Murillo, although he felt that passage was inevitable, expressed reservations that clearly set forth the implications of such an emergency measure:

> Need has brought us to this, to admit a break in authority, a break in the centralized, powerful state, which is responsible for fighting crime. The informer system, paying for informing on criminals, was a system used when society was very backward, when the state had

not concentrated its power. . . . Naturally, the state has agents in charge of discovering, of investigating, and it also has agents who are judges entrusted with doing justice. What is the role of detectives? What is the role of the police? To capture criminals and bring them to justice. When we authorize private parties to carry out these duties, we must be admitting that the Colombian state is ineffective and that it has been unable to carry out that specific duty. (*Anales del Congreso*, April 12, 1961, 412)

The zeal to repress the *bandoleros* was increasingly accompanied by an undeniable sense of powerlessness. In early September, the war minister, General Ruiz Novoa, gave unilateral authorization for peasants to arm themselves, once the safe-conduct formality had been completed. Representative Alberto Bermúdez unflinchingly responded, telling Ruiz Novoa, "The people in the region are incredulous: in Quindío, I assure you, there are 420,000 inhabitants who don't believe in Colombian institutions because they are convinced that they don't work, that they don't protect them" (*Anales del Congreso*, April 12, 1962, 412). He proposed completely transforming the military and police security forces and the general way of looking at the problem. He noted that the present Violencia could no longer be explained by pointing to La Violencia that occurred ten, fifteen, or twenty years before, that is, violence for the sake of violence, and that entirely new questions needed to be asked:

Why does an individual set out to work twenty-four hours a day to pursue his peers, even though that is such a painstaking task? Why do they not prefer to live a normal life? Why is it that for them being members of guerrilla *cuadrillas* is more promising? . . . Why is Chispas's *cuadrilla* made up of 14- and 18-year-old children; why, instead of continuing to go to confession and communion on the First Friday of each month, are those children heeding what we have heard about here—Castro, the terrible Bolshevik revolution? (*Anales del Congreso*, December 24, 1962, 2703–2704)

He next asked why peasants and other Colombians were hostile toward the state, toward authority, toward the army, toward the police, toward judges—questions that he answered by concluding:

[T]hey are right to think like that because this state has been very cruel to those people. Do you believe, members of the Chamber of

Representatives, that it is possible, with impunity, to apprehend fifty peasants, take them to be investigated by a judge or an army officer, keep them detained for two or four months, and then tell them: "Go home; nothing has happened here." That traumatizes people. (Ibid.)

One year before, Senator Sorzano González had used the same reasoning to explain Efraín González's actions in Santander. After complaining at length about the impunity enjoyed by Carlos Bernal, a Liberal *bandolero* charged with containing Efraín González (which clearly indicated which side had the senator's loyalty), reciting long lists of army abuses against Conservative peasants, and recalling Efraín González's painful youth, Sorzano noted:

Because the press covered it and it received much attention, everyone is familiar with the attempt to capture [him] at his parents' house, their deaths, the burning of the house, and this individual's spectacular escape. As of that moment, Efraín González became the region's hero. That was because he vowed to put himself at the service of the region's Conservatives . . . I understand this individual's formation, to a certain extent comparable to that which fostered the rise of feudalism in Europe. In Europe, at that time, the influence of the Caesars, the control of the Imperial Government, had ceased to be felt. There was no authority to administer justice. Peasants were enfeoffed and gave a part of their property and swore loyalty to an audacious, violent, and powerful lord who guaranteed their lives and the integrity of their harvests. That system was born from the lack of primary authority. . . . The Conservatives of that region, simple peasants who were threatened, whose houses, whose haciendas were threatened, decided to create a fiefdom. Yes, the army complains that there is no collaboration from those people in the region. They [acted] because of the crisis of authority at the time, and this man is a Robin Hood, a legend who half protects them, through retaliation, which is reprehensible and which I condemn, but in a certain way he guarantees their survival. (*Anales del Congreso*, September 21, 1961, 3659)

A few months later, Senator Jaramillo felt that conditions were right for a surreptitious revival of his perennial issue: the death penalty. On September 4, 1962, he submitted a bill providing that anyone summoned by judicial or other authorities for "unresolved charges" regarding acts of violence and who failed to appear within ninety days after the law took effect would be considered a *bandolero* and therefore a dangerous fugitive, subject to pursuit by public or private parties. Article 7 of the bill read: "Establish the presumption of legitimate defense in favor of anyone who kills *bandoleros*. This presumption is not subject to rebutting evidence." Lest the public think this was a new form of war, the officials entrusted with overseeing the respective trials were to be called "peace prosecutors" (*Anales del Congreso*; Proyecto de Ley no. 243, submitted September 4, 1962). As noted by Representative Francisco Zuleta Holguín, the measure would have made it possible to do in an enemy or collect a reward simply by claiming that someone was a *bandolero* (*Anales del Congreso*, September 24, 1962, 2723–2724).

The congressional obstacles to all the proposals for solving the state crisis finally led Senator Eduardo Lemaitre to submit a bill calling for a referendum on the death penalty and life imprisonment for "murder committed by groups of criminals [*cuadrillas*]" (*Anales del Congreso*, September 3, 1962, 962–963). Although the proposals were shelved, they showed the mood in Congress.

Political Dissidents and Rural Unrest

As noted above, the 1960 Congress was in no way homogeneous; rather, it was extremely splintered, as were the parties both nationally and regionally. Within these multiple forces, the MRL, which appears to have been the most cohesive of the forces opposed to the National Front, had to carry the burden of presenting structural diagnoses and solutions, thereby neutralizing the purely repressive responses. The MRL, as its leader, Alfonso López Michelsen, would later state, was like a "red [leftist] flag" stretched out alongside dissent. At that time, no one asked if López was a simple channel for that dissent or when he would negotiate it away. He claimed and appeared to be a simple spokesman for a certain democratic tradition within the Liberal Party that tolerated an alliance with other expressions of the opposition, including the Communist Party.

With a straightforward program, summed up in the slogan Health, Education, Housing, Land (Salud, Educación, Techo, Tierra; SETT), and by questioning the National Front's democratic credentials because it had barred open party competition, the MRL was able to unite disparate stakeholders who had come together for merely short-term needs.

The view that only structural transformations could effectively solve La Violencia; the belief that a democratic agrarian reform was a necessary response to peasant insurgency; and the conviction that relentlessly broadening the executive's special powers tended to harm the majority of the populace to the benefit of a voracious minority—all these positions were formidable obstacles to official policy, which can be summarized by Minister of the Interior Lleras Camargo's statement that the dilemma regarding *bandolerismo* came down to either "capturing or shooting" the *bandoleros* (*Anales del Congreso*, May 10, 1961, 1611).

Under these circumstances, *bandolerismo* found a tacit ally in the MRL, which was willing to milk that support for any and all electoral gains, and this alliance led to the highly controversial issuance of MRL identification cards in numerous rural areas. However, a sizable majority of the National Front's *gamonales* began to distance themselves from their former *bandolero* allies, relying instead on the electoral advantages afforded by the institutional, economic, and military power of the ruling-coalition factions.

By 1962, most of the *bandolero*-controlled areas supported the MRL, with minimal Conservative exceptions (Efraín González) or Liberal ones (Dumur Aljure, in the Llanos). The expansion of both groups, as well as their demise, would largely occur simultaneously: they both reached their peak in 1962, and in 1967 they were both definitely liquidated and disbanded.

In 1960, the MRL obtained 341,521 votes and seventeen seats in Congress; in 1962, it more than doubled its congressional representation (twelve seats in the Senate, thirty-three in the Chamber of Representatives) with 625,630 votes, or 23 percent of the total. In 1964, its support fell to 381,847 votes and it was divided into "hard" and "soft" factions. At the same time, ANAPO tripled its strength. In coming years this contrast would reflect a characteristic gap between urban opposition movements and fundamentally rural ones.

In any event, *bandolerismo* and the MRL both existed within the opposition-integration dialectic, although they were moving in opposite directions: *bandolerismo* was becoming relatively more radicalized, or was at least proclaiming its autonomy, while the MRL was clearly becoming institutionalized.

Outright charges of MRL complicity increased noticeably. The accusations were based on cases such as that raised by Interior Minister Fernando Londoño y Londoño regarding a speech by an MRL cadre at the burial in Cartago (Valle) of a *bandolero* for whose capture a reward had been offered and on whose body the national flag had been placed (*Anales del Congreso*, April 12, 1962, 418). Although the MRL's political leaders censured the identification-card campaigns carried out in its name in the provinces, accusations such as these were very costly for the opposition in human lives, especially before and after the 1962 elections.[6]

However, the results of those elections, that is, the 625,000 MRL votes, forced the new president, Guillermo Valencia, to adopt a new tack regarding the opposition: negotiation. Valencia offered Juan José Turbay, a prominent MRL member of Congress, a post as minister of mines. Turbay accepted, and his fellow MRL members welcomed the step as a fundamental correction of National Front policies.

The premise now being proposed was that the MRL had not been formed to oppose the National Front, per se, but to counteract the distorted interpretation of it. This was a remarkable political victory for the new president and would lead to the immediate splintering of the MRL and to its break with the Communist Party and all independent leftist forces represented in Congress by Gerardo Molina.[7]

This wavering of both the government and the opposition paved the way for the key member of the new administration, Minister of War General Alberto Ruiz Novoa, to design the military strategy for the coming years. In a speech before the Senate on August 22, 1962—the most complete treatise ever heard there on La Violencia—he listed the causes and solutions of the conflict, in the following order:

1. Political causes that, although considered by top congressional leaders to have been surpassed at the national level, still had to be dealt with head on in other areas of influence. He outlined the specific method to be used:

> I would like to request a concrete declaration, expressly identifying [the culprits], by the departmental and municipal directorates condemning Sangrenegra, Almanegra, Desquite, or Efraín González, Carlos Bernal or Chispas, or Tirofijo, El Diablo, El Mico, and Raya. And any others [whose] names [would be] quaint if they weren't tragic and who signify the permanent scourge of Colombian territory. (*Anales del Congreso*, September 4, 1962, 979)

2. Economic causes stemming from the permanent "usufruct" of *fincas* over which the owners had no control. The extremely unequal

and widely known distribution agreed upon between administrators and *cuadrillas* in Quindío was: 50 percent for the *cuadrilla*, 30 percent for the administrator, and 20 percent for the landowner. And this was the best option. Ruiz Novoa also noted the link between paid *cuadrillas* and persons who ordered the killing of the legitimate owners and occupants of a piece of land so as to appropriate it, purchase it at a low price from the heirs or widows, or keep the harvests. To curb this practice, the minister of war proposed regulations on real estate transactions.

3. Social causes, most notably unemployment in regions such as northern Cauca, northern Valle, and Quindío (seasonal unemployment of coffee pickers in the latter two), which had created an "authentic market for crime" or, perhaps, in the case of women, encouraged prostitution. Educating and rehabilitating young people, the "offspring of La Violencia," and creating employment were among the measures proposed by Novoa to deal with the social causes.

4. The state's weakness and its dearth of resources, which translated into low salaries for everyone employed by the "repressive machinery" (judges, police, the military). This was, in turn, a main cause of impunity. The state's inability to respond to demands for social-welfare programs, schools, and roads in many rural areas created an authority vacuum for the peasants that was often filled by *bandoleros*. To solve the state's budgetary shortfall and its inability to resolve problems, Ruiz Novoa proposed a special tax to pay for the fight against La Violencia.

5. Colombian society's acquiescence to La Violencia; that is, its complacency regarding the deaths of 300,000 persons during this period, whose bodies, if "placed side by side, would cover the road from the Plaza de Bolívar to the Puente de Boyacá, 150 kilometers of bodies that would join the two most significant landmarks of Colombian freedom and democracy"; its indifference to the deaths of 35 army officers, 129 noncommissioned officers, and 1,135 soldiers, as well as 9 police officers, 73 noncommissioned police officers, and 779 agents in the last years of the fight against La Violencia, and the 17,000 deaths between 1957 and 1962; and its indifference to the 256 Colombians "sentenced to death each month." Ruiz Novoa added: "Because of this we can understand the answer given by that peasant who, when asked what he thought of the death penalty, hastened to answer: 'I think they should do away with it'" (*Anales del Congreso*, September 4, 1962, 980). The minister of war saw additional evidence of the internalization and

chronic nature of La Violencia projected through cultural expressions such as literature or the awarding of the first national painting prize to Alejandro Obregón's stark *La Violencia*.

6. Ruiz Novoa also pointed to "pure" *bandolerismo*, made up of children or adolescents who had no alternative for survival but to join the *cuadrilla*, as a specific cause of La Violencia, for which he proposed a definitive solution: "end[ing] it with public force."

7. Finally, of all the causes and difficulties he listed, the principal and most intractable was collective complicity, that is, campesinos' solidarity with the *bandoleros*: "Despite the permanent repudiations by the directorates and the most distinguished political leaders, this solidarity continues like a deep sea in campesino regions where the *bandolero*, as noted by the minister of justice, is considered a sort of hero" (*Anales del Congreso*, September 4, 1962, 981). Removing this obstacle was the precise intent of the civil and psychological efforts. In Ruiz Novoa's words:

> [T]his psychological type of action is intended to destroy the guerrilla-warfare phenomenon valued by Mao Tse Tung, perhaps the leading exponent on the topic, as an indispensable [element] for the success of this type of campaign when he says that guerrillas should move "between the people and the region where they operate like fish in water." This psychological action tries to remove the water and destroy the fish. (Ibid.)

Significantly, it was the MRL, through Senators Jaime Isaza Cadavid and Alvaro Uribe Rueda, that took the initiative in responding to the minister of war's views of the political protection still received by *bandoleros*. The next day it submitted to the upper house a proposal exactly in accordance with the minister's request:

> The Senate of the Republic, heeding the request of the minister of war in his speech yesterday, most energetically condemns the *bandolero* activity that has been conducted in the country. And especially the conduct of *antisociales* who appear, according to the minister's statement, as leaders of *cuadrillas* of miscreants: Sangrenegra, El Diablo (Agustín Bonilla), Tres Espadas, Tirofijo, El Mico, Chispas, Efraín González, and others, and exhorts the directorates of the various sectors of Colombian society to make similar pronouncements. Consequently, we summon the ministers of the interior, justice, and war to join the debate that will be held in re-

sponse to this proposal. (*Anales del Congreso,* August 28, 876; September 6, 1011; September 19, 1168; September 25, 1255; September 28; October 2, 1962)

The recommendation led to discussions of little import—for example, whether the Senate hierarchy was qualified to name the perpetrators of La Violencia; if the simple addition of Christian names to the lists of aliases protected the Senate's dignity and prestige; whether a specific listing such as the one being debated might give those in question the publicity they sought and lead the press and the Senate to "increase their prominence." The following week, the MRL's directorate for Antioquia disseminated its condemnation in line with the war minister's exhortation to municipal directorates. Although the first item on the war minister's list had been formally fulfilled, in practice the events of the early days of the National Front would be repeated: while the national directorates issued condemnations, many regional leaders were obliged to give some support or tacit protection to *bandoleros,* who had the real political control of some areas. Nonetheless, even this simple, formal condemnation legitimized the impending genocide.

However, to return to the war minister's plan and, in general, to the new government, once the executive branch had achieved the relative political isolation of the *bandoleros,* it proceeded to the plan's other points and requested special powers to issue unrestricted laws covering La Violencia, turning Congress into a mere political club. These authorizations covered topics as diverse as modifying criminal legislation and revamping the entire judicial branch; reorganizing the military and police structure (the army, police, DAS, prison system); placing municipalities belonging to one or more departments in critical areas under a single political authority; creating, organizing, or extending educational and health-care services for the victims of La Violencia, as well as carrying out road and public-works projects to prepare for "pacification"; and financing all these measures by creating a "national peace quota" (under the perennial guise of "peace"!). The peace quota was to take the form of a 20 percent tax on income, supplementary revenue, and absenteeism, and a possible 250-million peso loan from the central bank (*Anales del Congreso,* September 12, 1092, and October 16, 1962).

At this time the effectiveness of this new, multifaceted offensive was difficult to predict, but there was a general sense of distrust and despair. The *bandoleros* responded to each official communiqué of victory, to each governors' meeting announcing the final battle, with massacres that neutralized the government's triumphalism. A clear indication of the bewilderment was the heated debate on the use of military uniforms. As noted in Chapter 3, *bandoleros'* systematic use of military garb had created such confusion that one representative said that in Quindío a "uniform is the same as fear." The war minister was particularly annoyed when a congressman questioned him in the following terms:

> I would like to ask General Ruiz Novoa whether the street account of the formula suggested by the foreign relations minister, Doctor Montalvo, is true—that the only logical formula for ending La Violencia is the following: that the police and army dress up as civilians and kill anyone they find in uniform. [He then repeated:] This is a street account. (*Anales del Congreso*, November 9, 1924– 1926, and December 14, 1962)

In sum, at the end of 1962, the large *bandas* continued intact; as late as May 1963, there was talk in Congress of two republics existing in Valle—in one, only Conservatives could enter, and the other, *lopista* (for supporters of López Michelsen and the MRL), where neither Conservatives nor pro-government Liberals could enter. However, the MRL's change of course had fundamentally reformulated the problem. The struggle could now be described as a conflict not between parties but between the *bandoleros* and the government.

Political Marginalization and Radicalization

Chispas's death in early 1963 (January 22, to be exact) was hailed as the first major government victory and the product of the realignment of forces and of the political isolation that had begun to beset the *bandoleros*. Henceforth, attention centered on the prominent leaders in northern Tolima: Desquite, Sangrenegra, and Pedro Brincos. The MRL representative from Tolima, Saúl Pineda, graphically described the situation: "What occurs is this: in Tolima, the political director-ates have completely lost control of the forces that operate in the countryside; this is a kite that has come loose from the string of the person flying it" (*Anales del Congreso*, February 9, 1963, 241). In the same debate, Fermín Ospina Torres, a sectarian Conservative representative and ally of Laureano Gómez and Alvaro Leyva, pointed to numerous examples of kidnappings and extortions, showing that the situation was becoming increasingly stultifying for Conservatives and even some Liberals, and he sounded an alarm: Pedro Brincos, Sangrenegra, and Desquite were preparing more than 3,000 troops for a revolution in Tolima (*Anales del Congreso*, January 23, 1963, 97). In February, a group of lawmakers suggested—unsuccessfully, because the proposal was rejected—creating bipartisan committees to study public order and the causes and sources of *bandolerismo* in Quindío, Vélez, Líbano, Cartago, and Neiva, then considered the nerve centers of the problem. It was then that Desquite famously took over the town of El Hatillo, as noted above, proclaiming himself civil and military leader of northern Tolima. Members of Congress said he used "inexplicable and unacceptable instruments" that demonstrated "the inefficacy of the departmental government and of the army and police forces in liquidating the criminal *bandas* that scourge the country" (*Anales del Congreso*, February 12, 265, and February 14, 1963, 299).

The national debates were rehashed at the regional level. For example, the most sectarian Conservatives insisted that the departmental authorities, beginning with Governor Jaramillo Salazar, repeatedly demonstrated a lack of will to eliminate the *bandoleros*. They pointed to what they considered outrageous cases, such as the party offered to Desquite at a *finca* near Líbano with the approval of "society, the clergy, and the authorities" (*Anales del Congreso*, March 17, 1963). However, MRL representatives such as Saúl Pineda felt that prolonging the hostilities between the army and the peasants would be futile and that the only way to bring about peace was by withdrawing the army and police from Tolima (*Anales del Congreso*, April 26, 1963, 909). The same lawmakers synthesized the two opposing diagnoses in a special session of the Chamber of Representatives on January 22, 1963:

I do not believe that, as Representative Fermín Ospina says, a Communist-type agrarian revolution is being conceived, guided by remote control by Brazilian leader Julião or Doctor Fidel Castro.

The campesinos are undoubtedly fighting to have land to work on someday, security for their old age, education for their children, and hospital[s] for their illnesses, not by obeying instructions from other countries but rather by heeding their own impulses and the national demands themselves.

In reality, the people of Líbano have not gone away, as Representative Fermín Ospina says, because the Communist revolution of which he speaks has come to the main plaza, but rather, because the economic and social foundations of this municipality were destroyed by La Violencia and it is impossible to work there. (*Anales del Congreso*, May 18, 1963, 1088)

That the profound economic crisis that wracked the country had led to discontent and malaise was something that even Minister of War General Ruiz Novoa was willing to concede. He was also the first to proclaim that force alone could not eliminate discontent. But neither he nor his like-minded peers could accept that discontent had begun to follow a revolutionary path. Thus in May he devoted an entire speech before the Senate to warning of the dangers of the new evolution of La Violencia, which he deemed to be personified in Pedro Brincos. To prove his point, he read an instructive document signed by Pedro Brincos and Ricardo Otero H. on behalf of the National Liberation Front, which he claimed was being distributed in Tolima:

> Our guerrillas bring together, on a single battlefront, all the organizations, such as peasant leagues, workers' and employees' unions, that struggle to liberate our Colombian people, peasants, workers, students, and professionals, regardless of their sex, religion, or political tendency. We know that workers will be able to enjoy political power only by tearing down the huge wall they have always come up against: the armed forces of repression. This will be achieved by forming a national liberation army, whose most simple forms are revolutionary guerrillas, who will collaborate closely with workers from the cities. Otherwise, we will continue to grope in the dark, because we cannot form the liberation army in the cities, but rather, only in our fields, as much as the dogmatic [members of the opposition] insist on the contrary.
>
> We maintain this position in weighing our country's conditions, such as its low industrial development, its working class divided by the CTC [Confederación de Trabajadores de Colombia] and UTC [Unión de Trabajadores de Colombia], worker federations whose leadership is in the hands of corrupt individuals and who receive advice from union representatives from the United States Embassy, and who, in addition, must deal with the ferocious persecution against the unions.
>
> By contrast, most of our people are located in the countryside, [where] they suffer the most inhumane exploitation and famine. At the same time, our peasants have received the most training and experience during these fifteen years of La Violencia, provoked by the Liberal and Conservatives directorates.

The revolutionary guerrillas will create the conditions for the emergence of the organization and the leadership of our revolution by constituting the most cognizant armed vanguard. Thus, the most urgent task is to organize our campesinos, which will be a hard, painstaking task and may only be achieved with the help of guns. This is not a *guerrillista* attitude but an interpretation of reality.

Through organizing, our campesinos will acquire political knowledge so that they may go about doing away with the partisan struggles and join together to defiantly resist their worst enemy, the rich *hacendado*.

They will be able to better avoid the infiltration of spies in the *veredas*, and they will thoroughly understand the tactics of deceit used by the government through the civic-military brigades and the community-action meetings.

Organizing will bring all the peasants and their families to identify with the revolutionary guerrillas, since the latter will respect them and see that their properties, spouses, children, and lives are respected, but they will treat informers or stool-pigeons or those who raise calumnies against the revolutionary guerrillas without mercy, because the bases of operations must be cleared of obstacles to armed struggle.

The violence initiated by the governments of Ospina Pérez, Laureano Gómez, Urdaneta, and Rojas Pinilla, under the slogan of blood and fire and scorched earth, ruined hundreds and thousands of peasants. When they abandoned their properties or sold them below the assessed value, the rich got richer and others also got rich.

This period left many widows and orphans, many of whom rose up in arms and linked up with groups lacking organization and orientation, which often led them to act improperly, sometimes out of a desire for revenge, other times out of despair. Last, La Violencia gave rise to bad habits in many campesinos, such as inviting revolutionary guerrillas to pillage, which is wrong.

This entire, serious situation will have to change when workers win their rights through arms. We now have an example in Latin America. Peasants, workers, students, professionals support us. Victory or death. (*Anales del Congreso*, June 22, 1963, 1439)

The minister who prided himself for studying Communist literature and doctrine to combat them observed that Pedro Brincos's document showed a clear assimilation of the ideas of Chinese strategists who, unlike orthodox Marxists, felt that the principal stage for revolution-ary struggle in underdeveloped countries should be the countryside. Thereafter, even the most recalcitrant Conservatives increasingly stressed the social effects of La Violencia. For instance, the sectarian *laureanista* senator from Tolima, Jaime Pava Navarro, pointed out, "We are seeing how in Tolima the *hacendados* and growers have to pay more in taxes to the *bandoleros* than they have to pay to the le-gitimately constituted government through collections by the Trea-sury" (*Anales del Congreso*, June 10, 1963, 1617).

Nevertheless, political recriminations continued to play an impor-tant role in the debates, although by now they reflected a past that was being left behind. The history of *bandolero-gamonal* relations was reaching its denouement. The overall development of that process can be seen in the governorship of Alfonso Jaramillo Salazar, regarding whose term in office one representative noted, "To be governor of Tolima one has to have good relations with the former *guerrilleros* and the present *bandoleros*" (*Anales del Congreso*, July 12, 1963, 1659). This governor—the most prominent pro-government Liberal political boss in northern Tolima—had run virtually unopposed for his seat in the Chamber of Representatives in both 1958 and 1960. Although he was an adamant *frentenacionalista*, he continued to acknowledge the legitimacy of men such as Desquite and Sangrenegra, who returned the favor by influencing a considerable portion of the electorate. This was in the beginning. This relationship changed substantially during the next two years, following the irruption of the MRL and Jaramillo Salazar's decision to continue acting as a loyal agent of the central government, which implied a minimal collaboration with its "pacifi-cation" effort. Although Jaramillo again won a legislative seat in 1962, he lost in Líbano, his electoral fiefdom—an indication that *ban-dolerismo* in the region, which had reached the pinnacle of its power, was now siding with the MRL. A second moment in the political evo-lution had arrived. However, when the government rewarded Jaramillo for his loyalty by naming him governor of the department, he attempted to protect or recover his electoral base and to reach a negotiated solu-tion with Desquite by offering him amnesty.[8] Desquite rejected the offer, and it caused a confrontation between the governor and the com-mander of the Sixth Brigade. The dispute was temporarily resolved in Jaramillo's favor, but in the end it strengthened the position of the army, which advocated a military solution. Nevertheless, by late 1962, there was much uncertainty about what path to take. When the mayor of Santa Isabel, near Líbano, told the governor that Pedro Brincos had received guerrilla-warfare training in Cuba and was settling in Líbano as well as selling "revolutionary bonds," Jaramillo retorted, according to sectarian Conservative Senator Pava Navarro, that "Pedrito was not creating problems for him [Jaramillo], [since] he had returned to a peaceful life" (*Anales del Congreso*, July 6, 1277, and June 12, 1963, 1659).

In mid-1963, however, in what might be considered the third decisive moment, the military and civilian authorities (including the governor) and the police distributed 70,000 flyers with the photographs of the principal *banda* leaders in the region and rewards of up to 100,000 pesos for the capture of each of them. For Pedro Brincos, now accused of having a well-organized "school for *bandoleros*" near Líbano, where inhabitants of the surrounding municipalities received "guerrilla-warfare classes," the governor offered 50,000 pesos (*Anales del Congreso*, June 6, 1963, 1277). The final onslaught was under way.

To recapitulate, this analysis of the congressional debates reflects the general evolution of *bandolerismo* and its three basic contradictions:

1. The contradiction that led to the two-faceted strategy of *legitimacy* and *illegitimacy*. The regional and even national political forces that had created the very space where *bandolerismo* developed on a massive scale were expressed in those congressional debates. However, the debates also defined the evolution of the state policies to annihilate *bandolerismo*—within, naturally, certain objective limits on the state's actions. The state, which was too weak economically and politically to respond to the social crisis of which *bandolerismo* was an effect, increasingly reformed and perfected its mechanisms of repression and developed a sophisticated ideology to legitimate its punitive actions. As shown, every imaginable form of repression was implemented or proposed in the name of peace.

2. The contradictions between the *electoral advantages* expected from the expansion of *bandolerismo* and the risk that said expansion effectively entailed. The leading cadres of the dissenting forces such as the MRL understood that the growth, either in their shadow or with their encouragement, of the *bandolero* groups made them increasingly difficult to control politically and, especially, made it difficult to control the social and economic effects wrought by *bandolerismo*. Under these circumstances, the early promoters or political allies preferred

to acquiesce to the National Front's co-optation and integration tactics, in a process similar to the *transformismo* that was followed by democratic opposition parties in Gramsci's Italy.

3. The contradictory effect of the combined strategy of politically isolating *bandolerismo* and repressing it. Although the political isolation resulting from *transformismo* created the conditions for the military siege, these two factors also produced a new situation: *Bandolerismo*—now with urban political linkages—emerged as a much more clearly peasant phenomenon, and, as an expression of the social malaise of the peasantry, it alarmed and terrified the dominant classes, who feared that it might lead to a social revolution.

In the name of the fight against Communism, the final offensive began, and it became an authentic war of counterinsurgency. Congress merely applauded and waited.

CHAPTER SIX

The Fall of the Bandolero Empire

*Against bandoleros and rebellious and inhumane individuals,
the only solution is efficacious fire arms.*
—Major General Ayerbe Chaux, 1966

"The Tenebrous Empire of *Bandolerismo* Is Collapsing" read the headline of the Manizales daily *La Patria* in April 1964 after Sangrenegra's death. And, indeed, from 1963 to 1965, the inevitable cycle of the decline and definitive defeat of the key persons examined in this study ran its course. A mere glimpse at these events is telling: Chispas died in January 1963, Melco in March, Capitán Ceniza in May, and Pedro Brincos in September; Desquite and Sangrenegra in March and April 1964, followed quickly by Tarzán and then Joselito in September. Gata's turn would come in February 1965 and Efraín González's in June. The death of Zarpazo, who was gunned down two years later, was, to a certain extent, overdue. And, in the *"bandolero* state" of Capitán Venganza, whose untimely death in 1961 had not obliterated his mythical presence among the peasantry, the national government also gradually restored its sovereignty.

Now leaderless, the *cuadrillas* quickly disbanded and many lieutenants or lower-ranking *bandoleros*, facing a much more energetic army offensive, were killed or captured. Police statistics in 1964 listed 312 *bandoleros* killed, including 138 in Tolima, 67 in Caldas, and 62 in Valle. Of the 337 prisoners reported by the same source, most were also from the center of the country: 128 from Valle, 75 from Tolima, and 65 from Caldas. During the first half of 1965, the number of *bandoleros* killed fell to 88, indicating not a reduction in the repression but the retreat of the organized *bandas* and their overall setbacks (Policía Nacional de Colombia 1964; *La Patria*, July 5, 1965).

As noted in Chapter 4, starting in 1962, the loss of legitimacy by the National Front and then by the MRL led directly to the *bandoleros'* political isolation. In August 1962, the minister of justice defined the situation in the following, threatening, terms: "The *bandoleros* should know that they are now alone and that the government will be implacable in its punishment" (*La Patria*, August 17, 1962). In this context, the continued existence or the demise of *bandolerismo* would depend on the course of the *bandoleros'* relationship both with army repression and with peasant bases of support.

First, a close look at repression is warranted. In the National Front's first three years, the official strategy against *bandolerismo* had tended to favor, at least in formal discourse, political measures over punitive action. Within this framework, the government issued the amnesty decree, created the National Commission to Investigate the Causes of La Violencia,[1] formed the Rehabilitation Department, and institutionalized social welfare and community development agencies, such as the Equipos Polivalentes (Versatile Teams) and Acción Communal (Community Action), intended not only to channel government resources but also to convey to the peasantry the official ideology of "peace."

With the passing of the legal amnesty deadline (July 26, 1959) and the subsequent renewal of La Violencia on a large scale, voices that opposed implementing a "social" strategy and that advocated fighting "violence with violence" began to speak out more openly, both in and out of Congress. Representatives of civil institutions, such as Caldas Governor Javier Ramírez Cardona, the growers associations, and even the interior minister repeatedly called for a purely military response. Nevertheless, instructors at the Escuela Superior de Guerra (war college) began to doubt, at least internally, the efficacy of the tactics being used, as some of its analysts acknowledged:

> Military action with regular troops against *bandoleros* has failed and has been very costly for the country. . . . [This] has diminished the prestige of the armed forces and helps increase the [size] of the *bandolero* forces. . . . In places where the struggle has political motives, the performance of the armed forces is very controversial and complex. . . . Abuses and even serious crimes were committed by members of the armed forces [while carrying out] law enforcement actions, contributing to an increase in La Violencia because the peasants' honor and property were harmed. (Escuela Superior de Guerra n.d., 8–9)

Growers organizations—for example, that of the coffee growers—impatiently called for new repressive policies. Faced with the ineffectiveness of the fight against *bandolerismo* in their areas, participants in the Twenty-second National Congress of Coffee Growers went so far as to "suggest that the national government find systems different from those now employed to gain the peasants' confidence and cooperation in the struggle against the violence that is razing especially the country's coffee-growing regions" (*Revista Cafetera* 1964, 31–33). To this end, they recommended organizing the defense of campesinos and establishing counterinsurgency methods, an authentic military plan to which the Federation of Coffee Growers offered its support. Their recommendations included

[1] Organizing councils of persons of goodwill, clearly honorable, and removed from political struggle in the municipalities, *corregimientos*, and *veredas* to serve as a source of information for the armed services during their patrols, on their incursions into the countryside, etc.

[2] Requesting that investigating judges go more quickly to crime scenes and have enough assistants. For these assistants, preference should be given to a corps of detectives of peasant origin able to go to the fields [disguised] as agricultural workers.

[3] Establishing effective sanctions for the officers and noncommissioned officers of the armed forces who carry out raids on peasant homes at night or take patently inconsiderate measures against them. (*Revista Cafetera* 1964)

Within the framework of an overall reorganization plan and a new strategy, the combination of these critical tendencies in and out of the military led the army to gradually absorb clearly political and social duties that normally would have been the responsibility of the state's civilian institutions. This was, naturally, intended to allow the military to better fulfill its repressive duties.

This all-encompassing strategy was designed for a multifaceted war that would combine military, social, economic, ideological, and psychological elements, *all of which were to be controlled by the army*. It was not fully implemented until 1963, when the *bandoleros'* network of political protection—one of the elements the army found hardest to overcome—had clearly been weakened. This was the moment to introduce a modern version of the program used by the *carabinieri* in southern Italy: attacking civilian peasants, "systematically extending repression to other [nonbandit] sectors, in order to strike more effectively against the hidden supports that constituted the true force of banditry" (Molfese [1964] 1979, 171, 185, 189)—that is, to destroy what General Ruiz Novoa, then commander of the army, had denounced as an "authentic state of collective complicity" (*La Patria*, May 1, 1961). The comprehensive campaign was to be carried out through the following actions:

1. Purely technical-military measures, such as increasing the number of soldiers, radio transmitters, and vehicles; creating the Eighth Brigade (in 1962), headquartered in Armenia and with interdepartmental jurisdiction, to overcome the difficulties of pursuing *bandoleros* caused by political and geographic boundaries; establishing small, versatile combat units, suitable for counterinsurgency operations.

2. The systematic development of counterinsurgency programs, for which the Colombia Battalion was reorganized and remade into the airborne Infantry Battalion, and the Administrative Security Department (Departamento Administrativo de Seguridad [DAS]) was created, replacing the overpoliticized and ineffective SIC (Ramsey 1981, 294–295).

The new counterinsurgency tactics included infiltrating *cuadrillas* (especially successful against "late" *bandolerismo*) and relying on various types of informers, from the relatives of victims to former *bandoleros* who had accepted amnesty and had been completely won over by the army. This, in turn, often stoked the wrath of the Conservative press, which held that the rehabilitated outlaws had "been rewarded for their previous conduct with a government post and salary" (*La Patria*, January 16, 1960).

3. Military action against *bandoleros* combined with a complex, often contradictory program against the civilian population. This meant relentless harassment and massive arrests, for example, in Córdoba (Quindío) and Santa Teresa (Líbano), and so-called civic action, along with pitched psychological warfare, solely to change the positive image of *bandoleros* and the negative opinion of the army so often held by campesinos. Flyers dropped from helicopters over Quindío and northern Tolima contained this message, for example: "The army treats citizens correctly. At no time does it resort to vulgar words. This is the best way to distinguish the army from the *bandoleros*" (*La Patria*, December 23, 1962).[2]

The army had successfully combined different approaches and flexible tactics without losing sight of the military framework for its actions—a policy advocated by one of the army's clearest exponents, Coronel Valencia Tovar, commander of the Ayacucho Battalion, who made several statements between 1959 and 1961 similar to the following ones:

> I have never advocated solutions involving force for any type of problem. To face conflicts with a violent approach seems a mistake to me. . . . I have preached [among the peasants] the advantages of peaceful relationships, but at the same time I have combined [this] with energetic military action . . . this is the only way to eradicate the [tendency]—very frequent among campesinos—to consider *guerrilleros* their protectors, when all legitimate authorities go into a crisis. *We must remove any campesino notions regarding the usefulness of the guerrillas.* (*Semana*, June 7, 1959, 14; our emphasis)
>
> [I]t is logical that military action intended to confront a problem as complex as that of La Violencia must change according to circumstances to avoid becoming a routine that will subsequently be ineffective. Nevertheless . . . , such changes can have no other purpose than that of facing the problem with a military intention of solving it. (*La Patria*, January 12, 1961)

The coupling of repression with social action stemmed, however, not only from internal pressure to improve the military's tarnished image but also from a new policy of the United States Army, which wanted steps taken to contain "subversion" in Latin America. The Kennedy administration's new doctrine viewed counterinsurgency programs and civic action as complements to traditional military training (Ramsey 1981, 296). Kennedy's visit to Colombia in 1961, the creation of the Alliance for Progress, and Agency for International Development funding reinforced the initial thrust of the "civic" programs (ibid., 300–301).

Under the command of a new generation of military officers trained at American bases in Panama, a systematic campaign of "civic-military" and psychological action was being undertaken, along with an enormous escalation in purely military action to weaken the *bandoleros'* bases of peasant support. The implementation of this strategy also revealed a characteristic ambivalence: whereas internally the army conducted analyses that studied and applied the principles of guerrilla warfare, externally it carried out massive propaganda operations that portrayed the rebels exclusively as aberrant common criminals.[3]

In August 1962, the apostle of civic action in Colombia, General Ruiz Novoa, explained to the Senate his views on the problems of and solutions to La Violencia. The general was influenced by the new ideas in the well-known "Lebret Report," written by a French priest and economist who advocated having the military perform civil and socio-economic duties in developing countries. In 1962 Ruiz Novoa devised the LASO (Latin America Security Operation) Plan, which, after several postponements, was carried out in one of the army's bloodiest actions, the 1964 "Marquetalia Operation."[4]

This controversial civic-action program was organized under the responsibility of a special department of the army's general staff, the E-5, and it exacted a high human and economic cost. Poorly disguising its repressive purpose, the program irritated the peasants by monitoring their daily comings and goings. The core of the program initially consisted of teams of engineers, doctors, agronomists, literacy instructors, and photographers; civic-military coordination committees; and officers and noncommissioned officers to supervise schools. Especially in territories controlled by the Sixth Brigade (Ibagué) and the Eighth Brigade (Armenia), sundry psychological campaigns were carried out using pamphlets, radio spots, flyers, conferences, etc. In particular, the Eighth Brigade's civic-military committees set out to "study the most urgent needs of each area" so as to win the confidence of the peasant population, and "they succeeded in, among other things, conducting a census of *fincas* and workers to control the rural population, watch over its activities, and learn the [political] tendencies and degree to which each individual can be trusted" (Octava Brigada 1965, 46–47).

Next, permanent workers were issued identification cards, consequently exposing migrant and unemployed rural workers to the risk of being considered "from outside the region," that is, *bandoleros*. Similar measures, carried out with the close cooperation of the Federation of Coffee Growers, produced the same result in southern Tolima, where peasants who failed to show a "cédula cafetera" (coffee-worker identification card) were likely to be treated as criminals (*Tribuna*, March 26, 1959), or in Líbano, where all farmworkers were required to carry an identification card. In Viejo Caldas, even wearing a *ruana* (woolen cape)—the "disguise used by *bandoleros*"—was banned, and in Tolima, peasants were forbidden to use flashlights or play *tejo* and were forced to keep dogs penned up because, as Colonel Matallana told the *El*

Espectador newspaper, "our experiences in the region demonstrate that dogs are trained to warn only of the presence of troops, not of *bandoleros*" (*Anales del Congreso*, October 8, 1963, 3476). In Tolima, the army took charge of organizing *fincas*, taking on the key role of naming or removing hacienda administrators (ibid., November 12, 1962, 3011; February 10, 1964, 478). The army even proposed reviewing property transactions at notary public offices to detect persons who had profited exorbitantly from purchasing undervalued land; the plan was never put into practice, however, for obvious reasons stemming from the pressure exerted by the new landowners.

One plan enthusiastically promoted by the large landowners and their associations, such as the SAC (Sociedad de Agricultores de Colombia) and Fedecafé, was peasant self-defense. It was continually debated in Congress, the national press, and growers' publications from 1961 to 1964, and it was resurrected in Quindío every year during the coffee harvest. The topic shifted from private conversations to the public arena in February 1961, when a meeting of governors, brigade commanders, and the ministers of war and the interior agreed on measures to, among other things, allow law-abiding peasants to purchase duly registered arms to defend their lives and property. In May, the governor of Caldas authorized not only permits to bear arms but also arms sales at an army warehouse in Pereira to *finca* owners presenting a recommendation from the commander of the area where they lived. A statement following the meeting noted that "the purpose is not to indiscriminately arm anyone and everyone but rather farm and hacienda owners; however, a person may be authorized several arms so as to deliver them to his employees" (*La Patria*, May 11, 1961). This measure, which inevitably revived memories of the private police forces hired by Valle landholders, led the magazine *Semana* (May 29, 1961) to warn that "La Violencia in the Caldas countryside has the pleonastic traits [described in] the popular saying 'the fight is carried out by fighting.'"

In 1962, when the army began to organize the self-defense of peasant communities, the SAC sent a message to the government suggesting that "arms be distributed to the campesinos through the SAC, its local chapters, and the Coffee Grower Committees" (*La Patria*, February 13, 1962; Ramsey 1981, 301). Although in Quindío self-defense units were concentrated on large haciendas, in Tolima, after the creation of "Campesino Defense Leagues" and the introduction of radiophones to communicate either with the Eighth Brigade or, more significantly, with the Coffee Grower Cooperatives (*Diario del Quindío*, July 18, 1961, and August 4, 1964), all vehicles traveling on the main highways in the northern part of the department were required to carry arms. Colonel Matallana defended this, arguing that it was necessary "to oblige civilians to defend themselves or at least require that they not give up their lives in the pitiful and cowardly way that a large number of citizens who obeyed the orders of small groups of poorly armed criminals have done when made to get out of their vehicles, form long lines, or shut themselves in a room to later come one by one and bow their head for it to be cut off with a hatchet or machete" (*El Cronista*, January 7, 1964). The only step taken to counteract the dangers of these policies—for example, that weapons of self-defense might be turned into instruments of retaliation—was to prohibit self-defense units from acting outside their areas of jurisdiction: "That means that self-defense [units] may not, either collectively or individually, carry out incursions or punitive invasions into other areas, which translates into the categorical affirmation that armed persons outside of their area are to be deemed *bandoleros* or outlaws" (*Revista de las Fuerzas Armadas* 1965, 184).

Through this host of measures, the army gradually wove a complex network of positive and negative relations with the peasantry: rewards and punishments; weapons for campesinos deemed trustworthy, and detention and jail for those considered sympathizers; monetary compensation for those who turned informer; and harassment, searches, extortion, and torture for those accused of complicity each time the *bandoleros* escaped military raids. Peasant support of the *bandoleros* had thus been brought to a dead end.

The flip side of this process was the relationship between *bandoleros* and their bases of support. Peasant solidarity had been based on their identification, during the first phase of La Violencia, with vague ideals of democracy and freedom or simply with legitimate defense from and retaliation for government persecution. The *cuadrillas de bandoleros*—as the *bandoleros* were now called, although they were either offshoots of the *guerrilleros* from the first period or their legitimate heirs, now being demonized by the National Front—again wanted to be acknowledged as protectors or avengers, but under much more difficult circumstances, since their struggle was no longer against a dictatorship but against a system with a façade of democracy. When their growing autonomy threatened the very *gamonales* who had encouraged them, they increasingly ceased to be political *bandoleros*, and their sectarianism began to contradict the social veneer of their actions. Only rarely were they able to overcome this contradiction, which led to inevitable results: the hacendados ceased to view them as simple allies or as the armed expression of their political rivals and definitively joined the army in declaring them enemies of all principles, especially their most cherished principle: private property. And as the *bandoleros* became divorced from the local and regional power structure, their fate was increasingly determined by what Hobsbawm calls "this special relationship between peasant and bandit that also turns the latter into a social" bandit.

This relationship explains why the purpose of the last phase of military action was mainly to break the social linkage between peasants and "protectors." It also made clear *bandoleros'* limited political and ideological ability to understand the new situation and to react appropriately to it. Undoubtedly, desertion, the army's purchase of informers, offers of impunity to prisoners on trial in exchange for precise information on *bandolero* bases of operations and movements, harassment of "peripheral" areas or bases of support, in addition to purely military action, weakened *bandoleros'* offensive capability and their ability to elude their pursuers. Nevertheless, the decisive moment in their liquidation was less military than political, and it was brought about by their inability to adjust to the changing struggle. When *bandoleros* most needed campesino sympathy and support, their actions led campesinos to gradually cease to view them as an expression of their despair and poverty or as their natural allies against the army's oppression.

The many urgent problems the *bandoleros* faced and were unprepared to solve included determining when, for example, informers acted voluntarily and when they were coerced through torture or intimidation; understanding why the peasants might tire of paying never-ending taxes and how to find funding alternatives that would alleviate the onerous burdens placed on the campesinos; knowing how to evaluate information; and learning how to neutralize the effects of propaganda, psychological warfare, and the abuses of isolated groups that sought to selfishly take advantage of the turmoil.

Although kidnapping and extortion provided some extra income—depending on the importance each *cuadrilla* gave that activity—once the *bandoleros* could no longer count on the economic support of their one-time patrons, they shifted almost the entire burden for their daily needs to the campesinos. Moreover, small splinter groups that had bro-

ken away from the large *bandas* often carried out indiscriminate robberies, and the *cuadrillas'* appeals to campesino families were increasingly based on terror rather than a commitment to a "cause." Nevertheless, even when "finance policies," such as those of Pedro Brincos,
stemmed from a different criterion, the peasants could not help but
feel that their economic support would continue perpetually. The shift
from collecting taxes at gay, enthusiastic bazaars in *veredas* to charg-
ing individual quotas was less than successful, perhaps because a large
gap still separated the level of political awareness and commitment of
some leaders from that of the peasant grassroots.

In any event, as the economic relationship became coercive, in the
precarious balance between admiration and fear—which classic studies say is so characteristic of peasant support for bandits—the scales
tended to tilt toward the latter. The conflicting sentiments turned to
frank rejection when, out of despair, the *bandoleros* committed a decisive mistake: harassing and indiscriminately punishing the very areas
that had provided them refuge. Retaliations against real or presumed
traitors in their former bases of support, accompanied by sexual violence—which has a profound impact in rural areas—intensified the
very reaction they intended to neutralize: betrayal, a growing reluctance to take the *bandoleros* in, a refusal to provide information on
troop movements. Indeed, many campesinos now viewed *bandoleros*
as murderers, plunderers, and blind, cruel avengers. An appropriate
climate had been created for the efficacious implementation of psychological warfare and for the emergence of the informer industry.

The course of events had put *bandoleros* face to face with a range of
options: break with two-party rule; devise a new strategy toward the
army; become a revolutionary guerrilla movement by clearly siding
with the peasantry; blindly strike out in all directions; initiate a disor-
derly, chaotic withdrawal; defy death with a certain fatalism; or join
with the enemy against their former comrades. But those who might
have weighed the different possibilities with the most clarity, such as
Chispas and Pedro Brincos, were the main targets of military persecution and were killed. Most of the remaining *bandoleros* were not ideologically or politically prepared to understand the complexity of the
situation, and they chose the worst option: extending their harassment
to the peasants, their most loyal protectors.

In these conditions, to dismiss the *bandoleros* as simple right-wing
agents or army allies, as the Communist Party did (*Voz Proletaria*,
January 23, 1964), precisely when the final attack against them was

being launched, was to demonstrate a complete and utter inability to understand the knot of contradictions they were dealing with.

The uncertainty of the dominant classes regarding the course of the *bandolero* struggle; *bandoleros'* breaks or rifts with the old partisan models; their rejection of any express commitment that would have limited their actions; their fear of seeing their immense local or regional power at the service of a new cause—all these factors, along with their underlying ambiguity, emerged as an unacceptable challenge by *bandoleros* to the established powers. For this reason, the dissident factions of the two parties and the *gamonales* negotiated and agreed—based on the power that *bandolerismo* had given them—to join the national political system, and from the government offices and ministries they planned the great crusade of extermination.[5] This also explained the apparently enigmatic and contradictory attitude of the peasants, who, after having contributed to the *bandoleros'* demise, mourned them. The death of men such as Chispas, Desquite, and Efraín González left the campesinos with a profound sense of abandonment and defeat, not because of who these *bandoleros* were but because after their deaths, the campesinos felt there would be no power to represent their desired changes and aspirations.

Social *bandoleros*, except perhaps in the idealized memory of campesinos in their former areas of support, had also been vanquished as mythical characters. In their stead, the anti-myth, so often instilled by the military during the psychological-warfare campaign, gradually prevailed in public opinion. Hence, a process opposite that of the Brazilian Cangaço took place. The mythical *cangaceiro* gradually lost the image of the perfect social bandit and became the nationalist symbol of Creole virtues and the incarnation of desires for national independence, in the context of massive foreign immigration and the expansion of imperialist control over Latin America's economy, culture, and politics. In Colombia, by contrast, *bandoleros*, at least until now, have personified the inhumane and cruel monster or, at best, the "offspring of La Violencia"—frustrated, disoriented, and manipulated by local political leaders. This has been the image accepted by the public—an expression, naturally, of the unequal correlation of forces between the representatives of the new political centralization and the—for now—defeated peasantry.

In this rise and fall of political *bandoleros* and their faltering evolution toward a more social role is a sense of the impossibility, despite exceptions, not only of a massive transformation of *bandolerismo* into a revolutionary movement but also, in its historic characterization, of pigeonholing all *bandoleros* into clearly defined options. They were neither the paradigm of contemporary revolutionary movements, nor right-wing agents, nor simple, merciless criminals. They were truly captives with nowhere to go!

Epilogue

Bandolerismo as a mass phenomenon may be seen as the dominant expression of a phase in the crisis of the relationships between the state, political parties, social movements, and armed actors. In mid-twentieth-century Colombia, this particular phase reached its full expression during the years of political turbulence and rupture in social cohesion known simply as La Violencia.

This premise reveals the profoundly political nature of Colombian *bandolerismo*. It certainly allows us to identify common patterns clearly observable in many other regions, and simultaneously to explore its unique characteristics. In addition to geographic conditions and social circumstances that contribute to the expansion of *bandolerismo*, a trend accepted by all scholars on the topic is that *bandolerismo*'s most prominent moments are associated with periods of fragile legitimacy or weakness of the state and in particular of its armed and judicial agencies. By contrast, *bandolerismo* declines in periods characterized by a growing centralization of state power and an extension of its legitimacy, as well as its coercive and modernizing presence in the most remote areas, its more effective channels of communications, and its means of exacting punishment. Without any idealization, *bandolerismo* may thus exist within a broad range of situations, all of which were present in the Colombian case. At times it projected itself as an instrument of people linked to powerful politicians, hacendados, and landowners who hoped to hold on to their privileges; at other times, it expressed itself as a force subordinated to regional and local powers caught up in internal struggles as well as resistance to central authorities. In addition, in the absence of parties and organized social movements, *bandolerismo* might operate as an autonomous force or as the materialization of informal powers that flourished in the shadow of a vast institutional crisis, which is precisely what the long, bloody period of La Violencia left. Colombian *bandolerismo* was, above all, the product of this network of political relations. But *bandolerismo* can also be characterized as one of the multiple forms of popular reaction to the state's incapacity to provide basic services to many regions and social classes. From this standpoint, mid-twentieth-century Colombian *bandolerismo* converged with present-day forms of rebellion, since motivations very similar to those put forth for *bandolerismo* are offered today to explain both the expansion of guerrilla groups, particularly in colonization areas, and the outbreak of multiple forms of urban organized crime in recent decades.

Viewing the Spanish edition of this book in retrospect, we feel it is important to return to some central topics and note the essential links with some elements of the subsequent political dynamics. First, we will look at the formation, structure, and nature of the *bandas* as a way in which the marginalized were able to insert themselves in the world; second, we will examine the controversial and recurring theme of the oscillation between reality and mythology in *bandolerismo;* third, we will discuss the changing gender relations and gender symbology between the armed conflicts of the 1960s and those of the end of the millennium. Finally, we will note the most salient continuities and discontinuities between *bandoleros* and the still-active and more-powerful-than-ever rural guerrilla groups, as well as the urban *bandas* that have flourished in the marginalized areas of the large cities from the 1980s through the dawn of the twenty-first century.

Bandas *and Their Multiple Roles*

Bandas were more than simple criminal associations, as they are defined in criminal codes. They were internally heterogeneous groups in which protectors and avengers, altruists and opportunists, bosses and underlings, organizers and executors coexisted. In them, multiple social relations and multiple approaches to action converged, while tension between individual preferences and collective needs was played out continuously. It was as if the entire outside world were inside the *banda*. The different tasks performed by María Bonita, the idealized companion of the king of the Brazilian bandits, Lampião, pathetically illustrate this: As María Isaura Pereira de Queiroz succinctly describes, "She would sew, embroider, cook, sing, dance, get pregnant, and give birth" (1992, 12). *Banda* life, then, reproduced life in society and even— it has been suggested—its external hierarchies, gender relationships, and chains of authority. Therefore, for a campesino, entering a *banda* simply meant substituting one set of bosses and relationships of domination for another. Likewise, and paradoxically, *bandoleros* can be seen as nomads who never left their own communities because they took them with them. Taking this a little further, perhaps *bandas* were not, despite all appearances to the contrary, an escape from existing society but a way of resigning oneself to it, or even "offensively (as opposed to defensively) adapting" to it. Clearly, *bandoleros* go to the "mountains" to remain in the society that is disintegrating around them.

Bandas did not perform exclusively military functions, and they can be characterized, first, as *a way of living or surviving* that ensured stable income; that reproduced values, beliefs, customs, dress, and cultural codes; and that even practiced a naïve religiosity not much different from that of their contemporaries outside the *bandas*. In the late twentieth century, it was also possible to observe that same unswerving religiosity in the leading drug-trafficking capos and in the world of hired assassins and youth gangs in Medellín. In sum, an authentic *bandolero subculture* was structured with rudimentary but draconian regulations, relative territorial stability, and links to the community. Entering a *banda*, like entering a convent, the army, or a Masonic lodge, required initiation rites and periodic updating, which also revealed its members' margin of autonomy. In any event, one joined a *banda* to stay in it. The outside world was full of enemies. To leave the *banda* was extremely dangerous, not only because of the vulnerability it brought on the exiting member, but also because it could be interpreted as a betrayal to those who remained. In general, *banda* members died in active service.

Second, *bandas* were a form of both *marginalization* and *self-exclusion*. *Bandoleros'* desire to remain separate and at a distance from society was often seen in their preference for declaring themselves civil and military leaders of a given zone and translating their strength into visible territorial controls. The Colombian *bandolero* Desquite did this in early 1963 in northern Tolima, as did Lampião, who, with memorable insolence, even proposed to a governor that the two divvy up an entire province. This was, undoubtedly, explicable as a demonstration to those in power, but it might also have concealed a feeling of power-lessness. Indeed, in these cases, those with power did not seek a nego-tiated solution with *bandoleros* or a way to incorporate them into state duties as police, soldiers, secret agents, or guardians of the interests of the large landowners, but rather attempted to carry the extermination campaign to its ultimate consequences. In the same vein, in addition to the attempts to attain autonomy and the territorialization of their spheres of influence, another expression of *bandas'* self-marginalization or self-exile was the emergence of the regular practice of controlling, sabotaging, and destroying the channels of communication. This was a way to preserve the cultivated image of the inaccessibility of their regions; however, from the standpoint we are stressing here, it allowed them to evade and to defend the boundaries of their own confinement. And if these manifestations are insufficient, we could add the follow-ing signs of that deliberate isolation: the implementation in their ar-eas of an extra-institutional tax and justice system and, most signifi-cant, the changing of their names, the discarding of the signs of their identity, which they replaced with names of animals, comparable, as noted by Billy Jaynes Chandler (1978), to a "rebaptism," the symbol of a new life. The norm of conduct by which *bandolero* leaders estab-lished pacts with regional caciques, as well as with the devil, was not divorced from this same objective. Last, *bandoleros'* marginalization, their nonbelonging to the rest of society, became brutally clear when sociologists and criminologists claimed they had peculiar cranial and facial measurements, as had occurred in Brazil and Peru in the 1920s–1930s.

From another standpoint, a third manner of approaching the *ban-dolero* phenomenon is suggested by Queiroz (1979) when she refers to *bandas* as a sort of "fraternal association" or "secular brotherhood."[1] Thus, *bandas* are seen not only as a way of withdrawing but also as a *form of sociability*, to use the conceptualization made popular by French historian Maurice Aghulon. The various narratives on daily life in the *bandas* lead to the conclusion that they operated as an alter-native space (overwhelmingly masculine) for meetings, recreation, music, dance, ballads, and spending "free time." *Bandas* could be par-ticularly useful in tasks such as cultivating protectors and allies, mak-ing new friends, overcoming isolation to face the most urgent daily needs, gaining the recognition of those in power (even if this was a negative recognition), or building their own power. *Bandoleros* knew of the precariousness of their "trade," but they preferred to exercise transitory power rather than live a routine life. None of this negates a fourth perspective, that of *bandas* as a *form of illegality*. The association with practices accepted by society or reputed by it as criminal, such as killing, kidnapping, robbery, extortion, abduction, burning houses, overrunning villages, and all the operations implied in carrying out these activities, from logistics planning to armed confrontation, was not exclusive to *bandas*, but it was part of their essence. *Bandoleros* appear to have found the world of legality incompatible with the world of justice. And, as we might expect, the practices listed above gradually became habits they found increasingly difficult to abandon, even when they wanted to, because *bandoleros* ended up residing on the frontier between legality and illegality, between life and death.

Beyond the Reality-Myth Dichotomy

The second area that the study of *bandolerismo* brings us to, despite the diverse actions covered by the concept, is that of political myths and symbols. As the reader has surely noticed, this book combines historical narration with mythical biography of *bandoleros*—or superimposes one upon the other—to such an extent that the distinction between the two tends to become blurred. The image of the *bandolero* is not the same in a police report as it is in an account by a campesino, in the testimony of a *banda* participant as in the appraisal by an hacendado, in the viewpoint of a contemporary chronicler as in the vision of an intellectual analyzing from a distance, in the playful memory of a child as in the observations of an adult, in the adventurous remembrance of a fugitive as in the sober reconstruction of a prisoner. In the account offered in this text, none of those versions claims superiority over the others because, in the final analysis, there is not one real history but many real histories, constellations of coexisting, complementary, or contradictory images of a single character or phenomenon.

Moreover—and this is the other side of the coin—these accounts are joined by the many faces of the myth. Because in this and any other study on *bandoleros*, myth leads to at least two basic alternatives. The first is the idealized myth, which was, of course, widely disseminated within the peasant areas where *bandoleros* operated. Recall the regional impact of a figure such as Capitán Venganza, whose very existence was doubted but whose actions were spoken about by everyone, including the army that pursued him. *Bandoleros* were ascribed an enormous capacity to return to a sort of natural state, to turn into a plantain plant and other types of trees, or into chimerical figures, such as Chispas riding a quasi-immaterial white horse, seen but impossible to catch. They were also ascribed a magical ability that allowed them to survive, to "reincarnate," and to transcend their own death. Some were "killed" several times. They embodied myths confused with legends from regional folklore of indigenous origin, such as "Patasola" (One Leg), who protected the forests and devoured the predators of nature, or "Mohán," in Tolima, who watched over rivers and drowned those who swam in his dominions without his consent. *Bandoleros* were, from this standpoint, the guardians of the topography, including the campesinos who lived there. Records of the real and the imaginary, in this case, are juxtaposed and reinforce each other. Idealization also had currency within certain intellectual circles (journalists, writers, movie directors) that attempted to see *bandoleros* as symbols of freedom and hidden forces for the oppressed and downtrodden. Hence, the *bandolero* myth was structured not as a nostalgic myth, a myth of the return to the past, but a myth to compensate for the harsh daily reality of our dependent and marginalized countries and, to some extent, as a transhistoric myth of the future of Latin American society, which could lead to millennialism or the armed pursuit of utopia. This occurred in Brazil with Lampião, who, stripped of his historical existence, has been cast as a "hero of the Third World." This idealization also includes a power to watch over future society, such as that which poet Gonzalo Arango attributed to Colombian *bandoleros* when he predicted that Desquite would "resurrect" if Colombian society failed to transform itself.

Simultaneously—and this is the second alternative—what might be called the demonization of *bandoleros* emerged, predominantly in the Communist intelligentsia, which saw *bandoleros* as the personification of backwardness and oppression, and invariably as the hidden hand of the landowners. These countermyths such as Sangrenegra—whose name, "Black Blood," says everything—occupied, significantly, the same areas or areas contiguous to those of the "revolutionary *bandolero*" Pedro Brincos, who served as a bridge to some of the modern-day guerrilla groups.

In sum, no definitive bipolarity exists between myth and reality, not only because reality is multiform but also because, in a strict sense, myth, with its own structures and transformation principles, is an integral and active part of reality. Therefore, we must not prioritize one level above others: they all form part of the same political landscape.

Bandoleros are historical reality in permanent mutation and a symbol available for multiple uses, according to pre-established objectives. Largely in this recognized coexistence, or "war of images," lies the interest that the phenomenon continues to elicit in Colombia today.

From this standpoint, we will examine the evolution and the role of *bandolerismo* in light of the historical formation and construction of the symbol. These reflections introduce us to the analysis of the transformation processes of oral traditions and of the perceptions of academics. Alternatively, what we are positing here, in general terms, is that the history of *bandolerismo* must lead to a study of political imageries, to a history of intellectuals, and, furthermore, to the cultural history of a nation.

Bandolerismo, *Gender, and Violence*

In symbolic spaces of armed confrontation—the ongoing encounter between life and death—the markers of one's own identity and of others' identity acquire extraordinary force. They condense the cultural representations of the complex web of relationships in which aggressors and victims perform. The characteristics for differentiating the enemy from those who are "our own" are taken to almost inconceivable extremes to justify eliminating the enemy. Gender, as one of the principal elements of the societal structure, is always present in these representations, although "gender violence" assumes different intensities and manifestations if, for example, we compare the *bandolerismo* of the 1950s and 1960s with the contemporary forms of conflict.[2]

In the twentieth century, a new dimension of armed conflict emerged, distinguishing it from the nineteenth-century civil wars that were predominantly confrontations between male armies that produced male casualties. During La Violencia, the civilian population became more involved and for the first time victims were systematically distributed between both sexes. The massacres perpetrated by *bandoleros* against entire peasant families involved women, although not simply as just other victims, but rather in representation of the enemy's whole collectivity. Their violent death and, frequently, their rape, torture, and mutilation when pregnant, exacerbated this symbolism, as summarized in a single expression coined during the period: "leave not even the seed." Thus, women were seen exclusively as mothers, as present or potential procreators of hated rivals.

Rape was frequent and expressed not only the male desire to dominate the opposite gender, but also, as in many other wars, the supreme humiliation of and scorn for enemies and their group, by violating what might be considered the most constitutive or intimate aspect of their identity: sexuality and procreation. Rape also aimed to sow terror and ensure silence—not the silence of solidarity or complacency but that of simple self-protection. "They said they were doing all this to us so that we would not talk, because of being so ashamed, and to show what they were capable of," said one young woman (quoted in Hobsbawm [1969] 1981, 135). These motives were, nonetheless, secondary compared with those that shaped the symbolic domination of the adversary. Hence, when insurgent groups raped women outside of this context, driven by sexual appetite or a desire to show their power, that is, when they applied the practice not to enemy women but to those of their own area or community of support, they were signing their own death sentence. This was what occurred during the last phase of La Violencia. That individuals such as Desquite or Sangrenegra resorted to these practices at the end of their lifespan in the mountains eroded the peasant population's identification with them. Rape was tolerated not as a simple individual act of perversion but, paradoxically, as a systematic practice, justified by the war and applicable only to a given segment of the population.

But women were not merely victims of La Violencia. They were also active participants in the broad support networks that supplied the rabble with the necessities for survival: they sewed uniforms out of drill and armbands with the nation's flag; supplied food; acted as nurses, scouts, informers, and spies—all roles essential for the war, although they did not challenge the traditional gender division of labor in peasant society. Some transgressed the traditional boundaries and took up arms—such as Desquite's companion, Rosalba Velásquez—although this almost invariably occurred under the guidance of their companions. Clearly, the few women combatants would normally abandon military and even political and organizational duties when they had their first child: "Women with children are like dead mules," the insurgents of Sumapaz would say (Aprile-Gniset 1991, 257). Motherhood, then, seems to be a pivotal moment for gender relationships in their adaptation to, or rupture with, the conditions of war.

In sum, from a gender perspective on the expressions of violence during that period, women were raped to break the enemy community's morale; and they were killed not because of their role in the dance of death, since they were not protagonists in it, but, paradoxically, because they generated life.

La Violencia is not, then, a simple historical antecedent of present-day political conflicts: its insertion into the most intimate aspects of the campesino family generated the conditions for its reproduction in the personal histories of many of our contemporaries. The *sons and daughters of La Violencia* made violence an inevitable evil, a way of life. References to that traumatic past, in rural and urban milieus as well as in the home, appear frequently in narratives of the present-day armed conflict. In these narratives we can detect continuities with and reproductions of, but also differences in, gender symbology.

At present, motherhood and feminine sexuality remain problematic issues in the everyday management of the war. However, the tensions they generate today are not so much related to the symbolic definition of the enemy or the violence practiced against "the Other," as to the gender relationships within the armed groups themselves. Motherhood does not appear to play a role as a *motive for extermination.* We sense a change here not only in the social representations of women—who are increasingly social and political *actors*—but also in the cultural dimensions of war. In the present-day dynamics of the internal armed conflict, multiple processes of de-ideologization take place, and acts of terror and retaliation are increasingly deprived of motivations based on political belonging or identification. Now they have become highly instrumental, and often they have little to do with specific forms of social protest. The enemy's cultural, political, and social identity tends to lose importance compared with other determinant factors: socio-economic condition, the effective support for one or another side, or simple momentary geographic location. In this same context, the slogan "exterminate the Other all the way to the seed" disappears and gives way to strategies of population and territorial conquest, or of the forced displacement of inhabitants to seize their lands. To attack motherhood as the reproducer of enemy lives, or to offend a community's sexual honor, has ceased to make sense as a war practice.

The present conflict has had the effect, among others, of diversifying gender representations. One of these is the combative *guerrillera* who elicits contradictory reactions: admiration, in some cases, because of her emulation of men in the war profession, and rejection, because of her break with traditional images of femininity. Another representation is that of women as victims of the conflict, the bearers of the rights of a civilian population removed from the armed conflict. Even representations in which femininity dominates are difficult to reconcile with the horrors of the war. For this reason, in today's "indiscriminate" massacres—those involving women, children, and the elderly—the perpetrators rarely take public credit for their actions. The perpetrators' silence somehow expresses the reluctance to define women as part of the armed conflict on an equal footing with men, as well as a certain caution regarding the public's sensitivity to the most flagrant violations of International Humanitarian Law. Nonetheless, rape as the maximum exercise of power over "the Other" continues—although perhaps more veiled—in military acts. Denunciations are scarce and dispersed, but they go from the south of the country to the Atlantic coast and involve all the armed actors. Our conclusion must be that, in contrast with the *bandolerismo* period, in present-day war practices, "gender violence" constitutes an underground pattern rarely acknowledged publicly.

From La Violencia to Las Violencias: Where Are We Heading?

In many ways, La Violencia, which was once believed to have been put behind us with the death of the last *bandolero* in the mid-1960s, continues to influence the various expressions of the present conflict. To begin with, present-day guerrillas, which are now real armies with resources, an ideology, and organizational structures that make their political and military potential undeniable, share a common origin—La Violencia of the 1950s—with the *bandoleros* studied in this book. In the 1960s, these guerrilla groups succeeded in inserting themselves, discursively and politically, in the liberation struggles being waged elsewhere in Latin America and in Africa and Asia. Nevertheless, one negative legacy of the bipartisan violence of the 1950s continues to plague them today: their absolute contempt for the rules of war set forth in International Humanitarian Law. The more power the present-day guerrilla groups have acquired, the more they have resorted to strategies of terror—massacring, destroying villages, burning vehicles on highways—against the civilian population they assume to be accomplices of or tolerant of the state and its allies; and the more resources they have acquired, the more widespread and indiscriminate has been their use of repugnant fund-raising methods such as kidnapping—recently through the massive "retention" of highway travelers (called "miracle catches"). So widespread is this practice that more than half the kidnappings in the world today take place in Colombia.

The situation would be less serious if the expansion of the guerrillas were not concomitant with, and frequently stoked by, the resources, arms, and international connections of drug traffickers, who have found comparative advantages to operating in Colombia because of its complex and propitious geography, the quality of its soil, its strategic location for international markets, and its accumulated tolerance of illegal activity. The fortunes created by these activities, perceived as alternative forms of social mobility in a closed society, gave vast power to new groups, such as the Escobar family in Medellín and the Rodríguez family in Cali. Likewise, drug money irrigated politics at every level, penetrated new fronts of social life, and, most important for the purposes of this text, gave an unexpected boon to insurgents, to counterinsurgents, and, in general, to all forms of organized crime. For the first time, the most extreme expression of organized crime, terrorism, also affected the political and social elites of the large urban centers. The proliferation of Mafia-type criminal organizations paved the way for an authentic crime-related market, the open selling of protection and security, and a notorious de-ideologization of the struggle for power in which the fight to the death even alternates with repeated cases of the various armed actors switching roles and sides.

The *bandas* that have emerged in support of or protected by the drug business are governed by a hierarchy among them, and they often compete for territory or spoils. Despite some superficial similarities, they perform duties different from those of the rural *bandas* of La Violencia studied in this book, which had clearly defined territories and boundaries. Moreover, in Medellín, where these *bandas* attained the strongest footing, they were not exclusively at the service of drug traffickers. *Bandas* frequently found legitimation for their actions in unemployment, the state's abdication from its duties, police violence, and white-collar crime. One of their characteristics is precisely a diversity in their makeup and functions. There were neighborhood-protection *bandas*, community self-defense *bandas*, and even *bandas* with organizational ties to insurgents through the so-called militias, which were more structured and politicized than the *bandas*. However, we must stress that the first typical drug-trafficking *bandas*, the hired assassins, did not ask questions about political objectives or the identity of their victims. The only factor that mattered—and in this they were a replica of the *pájaros* of La Violencia—was being paid for their "jobs," in the framework of an authentic system of death by contract.

In any event, the overlapping forms of violence of the final decades of the twentieth century overwhelmed the state's judicial and repressive agencies. Starting in the 1980s, first in Antioquia and Córdoba and then in other regions of the country, the other extralegal army, the army of self-defense or paramilitary units, emerged, many times with the state's complacency or because of the desperation of landowners and increasingly of the urban and rural middle classes. The operational capacity of these self-defense units resembled, but surpassed, that of the Rondas Campesinas (campesino "self-defense" patrols) in Peru and the Civil Patrols in Guatemala.

We should note, last, that the relative economic prosperity that had accompanied these multiple forms of violence, and that had also characterized the critical period of the 1950s, began to diminish and then entered an outright crisis in the late 1990s. The crisis allowed many of the sectors most affected by neoliberal policies to once again give the guerrilla groups a certain role as societal spokespersons. Still, for many, the guerrilla groups are also responsible for a crisis that has caused social breakdown, with a solution increasingly beyond the reach of Colombian authorities.

It is surely possible to have a less pessimistic and conservative vision of the crisis and to assume that at some point it will usher in a great cultural and social transformation. But at the close of the twentieth century, events and public perception require, for the moment, a different view: that La Violencia of the 1950s was poorly resolved; that the state was overwhelmed by the dimensions of the multifaceted armed conflict at the end of the century; and that there is no clear remedy on the horizon for the exclusion, want, and social demands accumulated since the assassination of popular leader Jorge Eliécer Gaitán in 1948. At the dawn of the twenty-first century, the conditions appear ripe, as has so often been predicted, for Desquites to continue to reproduce indefinitely in Colombian society.

—Gonzalo Sánchez G.
Donny Meertens
Bogotá, May 2000

Notes

Introduction

1. See Chapter 3 for a discussion on the difference between *bandas* and *cuadrillas*.

2. Parts of our work were discussed at the Primer Seminario Nacional de Investigadores–Colombia Siglo XX, held in April 1981 at the Universidad del Valle, in Cali; at the Tercer Congreso de Historia de Colombia, held in November 1981 at the Universidad de Antioquia (Medellín); and at the Primer Simposio Nacional sobre la Violencia en Colombia, held at the Universidad Pedagógica y Tecnológica de Colombia at Chiquinquirá (Boyacá), in June 1982. In somewhat different form, Chapter 2 was presented as a paper at the Symposium "Rupturas del Desarrollo–América Latina en los años 80," organized by the Berliner Institut für Vergleichende Sozialforschung, in May 1982.

1. Bandits and Society

1. *Ley de fuga*, literally "flight law," is used in Spain and Latin America to refer to the practice of executing a prisoner and then claiming he was trying to escape.

2. By Bernaldo de Quirós, also see *El espartaquismo agrario andaluz* ([1919] 1973), and *El bandolerismo en España y México* (1959).

3. López Albújar's *Los caballeros del delito* (1936) was based on a survey of prosecutors and investigating judges conducted in 1932 by José Varallanos, a student at the Universidad de San Marcos, to gather information for his undergraduate thesis. Varallanos's work was published in 1937 as *Los bandoleros en el Perú*.

4. More detailed references to these relationships can be found in Womack (1969), Chesneaux (1973), Devalle (1977), and Longworth (1978).

5. Originally published in French as *Os cangaceiros, les bandits d'honneur brésiliens* (1968). In Portuguese, it was published as *Os cangaceiros* (1977).

6. The most important recent text on Brazilian banditry—one to which we did not have access for the first version of this book—is Chandler (1978). Also see Matta Machado ([1969] 1978), Queiroz (1975, 495–516), Shaker (1975), Lewin (1979b, 157–204), and Pang (1981–1982, 1–23). Gonzalo Sánchez explored the topic in the prologue to the Spanish edition of María Isaura Pereira de Queiroz's *Os cangaceiros: La epopeya bandolera del Nordeste del Brasil* (1992).

7. Also see Blok (1975).

8. Peter Singleman, in an essay on the *cangaceiros* in northeastern Brazil (1975–1976), puts forth a similar proposal. He says that the *Cangaço* survived as an endemic expression in the Sertão, not because it had peasant support but because of its links with large *fazendeiros* and politicians in cities. Hence, the *cangaceiro* was integrated into the dominant sociopolitical structure. If *cangaceiros* had elements of social banditry, they were rooted in both the poverty and social injustice that led them to take the path of the *Cangaço* and in the myth that would later make them the heroes of popular protest.

9. The traits of a similar transformation were developed in the banditry of southern Italy starting in 1861, that is, in the wake of the war for national unification, when the hitherto latent problem of lands usurped by *galantuomini* became the core of bandits' struggle against the agrarian bourgeoisie (see Molfese [1964] 1979, 120).

2. La Violencia: Context for Political Banditry in Colombia

1. Pecaut's 1979 work is the best overview of the period in question.

2. For a more in-depth description of these events, see Sánchez (1982).

3. For further reading on this period, see Sánchez (1976b), Arrubla et al. (1978), Oquist (1978), and Fajardo (1981).

4. Political banditry, given its institutional or quasi-institutional ties, tends to express itself on a much more massive scale than does social banditry. Italy's Risorgimento is particularly illustrative: in the struggle of the House of Bourbon and the Papal States against the Unitá current—a configuration of competing royal powers—the *brigantaggio* (brigands), acting as the armed wing of the former, came to constitute authentic regular armies. For example, at the height of their power, they had 3,000 men in Crocco and Borjes and controlled vast regions (Molfese [1964] 1979, 103).

5. Whereas the *cangaceiros* were considered independent, *capangas* were at the service of a landowner (for which reason they were called "meek *cangaceiros*" in the nineteenth century); in practice, however, the distinction was rather tenuous or occasional, as noted by Singleman (1975–1976, 59–82), and it varied in accordance with the fortune of their protectors.

6. *El Espectador*, May 11, 1965. The same attitude, at the local level, can be seen in *Estrella Roja*, November 6, 1962.

7. See Hobsbawm ([1969] 1981), particularly "The Avengers" (58).

8. On Aljure's evolution, see Maullin (1968).

9. Coffee production dropped from 125,000 *cargas* before the Violencia to 25,000 in 1957 (*Tribuna*, December 14, 1957; Ruiz 1972).

10. This percentage comes from the Ministerio de Trabajo (1956, 207, 343, 344).

11. The authors subsequently dealt with this topic in Gonzalo Sánchez (1991) and Meertens (1997).

12. This disparity was repeatedly decried in the regional press. See, for example, *Tribuna*, March 3 and April 1, 1954.

3. Regional and Sociopolitical Diversity of Banditry 1: Transitions

1. See also the magazine article "Vida, muerte e intimidades de Efraín González" in *Sistema* 12 (July 1, 1965).

2. A pejorative term for Liberals.

3. For the complete text of this and the following quotations from Chispas's account, see Guzmán (1968, 294–300).

4. *Chulavitas* were originally the Conservative police from the region of Chulavo, in the municipality of Uvita, Boyacá, who gained national fame as the most irrepressible police of the first stage of the Violencia; by extension, the term was later used to denote all sectarian police during this period.

5. A *corte de franela*—literally, "cut in the undershirt"—refers to cutting the ligaments and tendons that hold the head in place; *picada de tamal*, or "chopping into a *tamal*," meant to chop up a victim's body.

6. Sumario 2, cuaderno 5, 10–31; also see *El Tiempo*, January 23, 1963.

7. This was, in fact, a more general problem: conflict between the Liberal and the Communist guerrilla groups—the *"limpios"* and the *"comunes,"* respectively—in southern Tolima from 1950 to 1953. The causes of this recurrent rivalry—still insufficiently clarified—are very complex, since relatively remote factors were at play, such as the confrontation between *gaitanismo* and the Communist Party, as well as various proximate factors that would become discernible over the course of the struggle, including disagreements regarding tactical proposals for resistance and self-defense, which were considered, at least initially, exclusionary, in addition to the sectarianism and "authoritarian and reckless" leadership of the Communist Party (see Partido Comunista de Colombia n.d., 95).

Another factor, naturally, was the excessive dependence of Liberal guerrilla leaders on local merchants, landowners, and traditional political bosses. These antagonisms, which, among other things, undermined the possibility of a joint armed effort between southern Tolima and the Llanos Orientales, were so intense that Leopoldo García ("Capitán Peligro") boasted: "[I]n 1952, after I had fought more against *comunes* than *chulavitas*, the guerrilla group promoted me to the rank of captain" (Guzmán 1968, 291). Mariachi's assassination in the 1970s was presumably linked to a settling of scores stemming from this old rivalry.

8. As can be gleaned from Jaime Arocha's account (1979, 154), Chispas had been traveling back and forth between Tolima and Quindío since 1955.

9. *La Nueva Prensa* (May 3, 1963, 26); also see Arocha (1979, 158).

10. The famous Spanish bandits "Pernales" and "Vivillo," who plied their trade at the beginning of the twentieth century in the region of Estepa, Andalusia, have been described as follows: "They did not kill anyone from Estepa nor did they steal from its native sons. Their field of operations was the bordering provinces and villages. Estepa [was their] headquarters, their ha-

ven." In that region they even had the protection of nearly all the local authorities and the powerful, who called them "boys" and not "bandits" (Hernández Girbal 1970, 138). And for Luis Pardo, the legendary bandit from the Peruvian department of Ancash, the world of the poor and the wealthy also had well-defined spatial boundaries: "Around these places, sir, I don't rob anyone because they are poor and they don't have anything to steal; and if I were to take something from these poor people, I would be a rogue. Listen closely, sir, I steal especially from the rich in other places to give to the poor, but to do that I have to go far, where there are people with money" (Carrillo Ramírez 1976, esp. 118–119 and 145). Because he abided by that norm, posterity has aggrandized his persona, as can be seen in ballads, songs, plays, movies, and novels from his native country.

11. Personal information.

12. Although this and other statements cannot be directly attributed to the barely literate Chispas, they do undoubtedly reflect the influences and orientations that defined his political outlook in each of his most important moments.

13. In our opinion, the best source on Efraín González is the 1980 cinematographic script-book "Efraín," by Dunav Kuzmanich (director of *Canaguaro*), Javier Orozco, and Jairo Obando.

14. Parra (notebook covering March 11, 1951, to May 1, 1953).

15. Source: Recipient's personal file. Original syntax respected.

16. Source: Recipient's personal file.

17. The preceding quotes are taken from *Revista del Ejército* (vol. 6, no. 26 [September 1966]: 161).

18. Ibid.

19. Ibid.

20. In this respect, Desquite complained that "President Kennedy, rather than sending money for the poor, had sent helicopters and arms to kill the masses" (*El Tiempo*, August 23, 1963, cited by Fajardo).

21. Personal information.

4. Regional and Sociopolitical Diversity of Banditry 2: Extremes

1. *La Mañana*, August 18 and September 30, 1949; authors' interviews in Armenia, October 1978.

2. The presence of "intellectual authors," who would have "jobs" carried out, explains much of the cruelty against victims' bodies. Mutilation had a special significance: the killers had to deliver "material proof" to receive payment. We find a good illustration of this principle in a homicide *sumario* in Chinchiná, in which the suspect stated: "I cut the ear off Alfonso's body to take it to Mr. and Mr. [names omitted by the authors] as proof that the crime had been perpetrated; afterward, the ear remained in my possession and I buried it. They paid me in 100-peso bills, Mr. [name omitted by the authors] gave [the money] to me eight days later here in Manizales" (Sumario 16, 237).

3. As far back as the 1930s, large ranchers had formed "private police forces" to fight cattle rustling, which the hunger and poverty of the Great Depression had raised to alarming levels. In 1946, when the Valle police—unlike that of

other departments—had been placed under Liberal control, Conservatives re-introduced the private police forces, with an eye on the 1950 elections.

4. *Pavear* (to turkey) or *puestear* (from *puesto*, or "post") means to lie in wait for someone on a road in order to kill him.

5. Around the same time, twenty-nine inmates escaped from a Buga jail. The prison breaks greatly alarmed the authorities, who blamed each other—for instance, Cali's prison warden and police chief blamed each other, the latter claiming he had sent the warden warnings that such an "assisted" escape was possible, along with timely reports that in northern Valle a collection was being taken to buy off the guards. So great was the fear of new escapes that 210 prisoners, before being transferred from Villanueva to Bogotá, were injected with morphine and tied firmly to their bus seats; they made the trip in a deep sleep (*Semana*, January 28 and February 11, 1960). Police statistics showed Valle and Caldas had the highest rate of escapes—30 percent and 14 percent, respectively, of all inmates (Policía Nacional de Colombia 1962, no. 5, 128).

6. We disagree with Jaime Arocha's claim that, in the end, administrators or sharecroppers were always victimized by the *bandoleros'* tax-collection system. Arocha says that the wealthy patrons, the region's *hacendados*, gradually transferred to the sharecroppers the burden of the economic support for the *bandas* and that sharecroppers and administrators became indebted to coffee merchants, who, in turn, ended up taking possession of the land. Nevertheless, Arocha recognizes elsewhere in his book that people were willing to take great risks to receive a *coloca* as a sharecropper or administrator. The large amount of information gathered for this book confirms that, although merchants commonly took over land in the first phase of the Violencia, in the *bandolero* period it was the sharecroppers and administrators who, because of their autonomy, benefited from their relationships with the *bandoleros* by receiving a larger share of the harvests and even by gaining possession of farms, although most of them did so only briefly (Arocha 1979, 178–182).

7. Tribunals everywhere were ineffective, since they lacked the power to impose sanctions if the parties failed to show a "willingness to reconcile."

8. The increase in "common" violence during the coffee harvest forced the army and the terrified landowners to take extraordinary preemptive measures.

9. In September 1962, the departmental secretary for political affairs issued a list of sixty-two *bandoleros* killed and another of twenty-one *cuadrilla* leaders who continued to operate in the department of Caldas.

10. Over time, these differences in political affiliation avoided a situation like that of the Brazilian Sertão, where *cangaceiros* might become *capangas* (killers at the service of *fazendeiros*) if the regional political situation and the physical need to survive so demanded (Singleman 1975–1976, 81).

5. The National Dimension: Political Debates

1. On May 16, 1957, *Tribuna* published a photograph that it claimed had circulated clandestinely, although widely, during Rojas's regime, and that carried the following caption: "The former director, accompanied, on his right, by León María Lozano, alias 'El Cóndor' and head of the *pájaros* in Valle, by

Lola Ceballos de Vélez and Gustavo Salazar García, the three persons who organized the dreaded institution in that section of the country."

2. This second amnesty (the first was decreed by Rojas Pinilla on June 13, 1954) was issued through Decree 0328, of November 28, 1958, the relevant articles of which read: "1. Persons who may have committed in the aforementioned departments (Caldas, Cauca, Huila, Tolima, and Valle del Cauca) the crimes referred to in Article 2 of this decree, prior to October 15, 1958, may request that the government suspend the application of criminal procedures against them, if they undertake to reincorporate into ordinary civilian life, to submit to the Constitution and the laws of the Republic, [thereby] observing good behavior under the surveillance of the authorities, and abstaining from any act that may disturb law and order or social tranquillity. . . . 2. The suspension of criminal procedures referred to in the first paragraph of the preceding article shall only be applicable to crimes committed within the territory of the aforementioned departments by private individuals, by any public official or employee, by members of the military or groups organized under the authority of bosses, if the crime or crimes attributed to them have been caused by: (a) the attack [against] or defense of the government or the authorities; (b) political animosity; (c) partisan violence exercised by reason of the conflict between the parties" (Molano 1978, 161–162).

3. An overview of the amnesty decrees can be consulted in Molano (1978).

4. In 1925, a similar bill had been submitted by the moribund Conservative regime, leading to a memorable debate, visibly led by a *caucano* poet, Guillermo Valencia, and Congressman Antonio José Restrepo. The oratory duel between them was published in a text titled *El cadalso en Colombia* (The scaffold in Colombia), which ended the controversy.

5. A September 30, 1957, editorial in *El Independiente* argued, in addition, that adding a statement regarding the death penalty to the plebiscite "would stir up a problem already settled by the public, which had witnessed the practical application of that sanction for many years and not only for heinous crimes but also for political reasons, which in fact should not fit in such a legal classification." Some members of the clergy, however, felt that the death penalty could be beneficial. Bishop Gallego Pérez, for instance, said, "as much as it may disgust traditional sentimentalism, the death penalty appears to be the supreme remedy to the barbarism and crime that have become customary in a broad area of Colombian territory." Father García Herreros stated: "I believe that merely putting the measure into effect would pull us out of this atrocious situation without 'the need to execute anyone'" (*Anales del Congreso*, June 23, 1961, 2236).

6. Of the most painful murders of MRL members during this period, the following merit mention: that of Valle del Cauca Representative Melquisedec Quintero (publicly attributed to the F-2, or secret police); that of Julio Gómez, a deputy in Tolima's assembly; and those of the president of the Farm Workers Union in Lebrija (Santander) and MRL leader José Gil Zafra (*Anales del Congreso*, April 16, 1962, 458, and July 25, 1962, 566).

7. The key document in this dispute was a speech given by Alfonso López Michelsen before the Ibagué Convention in November 1962, printed in a special brochure under the title *Conceptos fundamentales del M.R.L.*, No. 3. López emphatically recalled a warning he had made in a previous speech, delivered

in the Hotel San Francisco on March 20 of that year, when celebrating the electoral results: "We are not going to allow the discontent and frustration being incubated by the National Front to be forced to take refuge under the sign of the hammer and the sickle" (1962, 4).

8. Jaramillo availed himself of the mediation of a priest from the neighboring town of Armero, who delivered the proposal.

6. *The Fall of the* Bandolero *Empire*

1. Created in 1957, the commission was made up of two army generals (Hernando Mora Angueira and Ernesto Caicedo López), two representatives of the traditional political parties (Otto Morales Benítez, Liberal, and Augusto Ramírez Moreno, Conservative), and two priests (Fabio Martínez and Germán Guzmán).

2. The same flyer also asked for cooperation with the authorities and included other ways to distinguish the two sides:

"The army and police use standard-issue weapons; they do not use shotguns or .22-caliber carbines.

"The army and police do not ask for contributions in the form of money, products, or cattle. Anyone asking for these things can be deemed a *bandolero*.

"The armed forces do not ask any citizen's political affiliation.

"The members of a single patrol wear the same uniform, and there will be no differences of this sort among them. The army and police do not wear rubber (tennis) shoes but leather boots."

The Eighth Brigade's flyer ended with this appeal: "CAMPESINO, when you notice the presence of *bandoleros* [near] your house, reject them. Defend yourself with the means available to you. Bandoleros are cowards. Show them your courage" (*La Patria*, December 23, 1962).

3. One particularly illustrative case comes from a 1966 Infantry School introductory course on "irregular warfare." Using data from the B-2 (army intelligence), the school prepared a questionnaire to discover the origin and evolution of, and the tactics used by, the persons presented in the *Revista del Ejército* as *guerrilleros* and to the public as simple criminals. Desquite's *cuadrilla* was chosen for this exercise. The questions included the following:

"Do you feel that *Desquite* is carrying out a *war of insurrection?*"

"Do you feel that *Desquite is applying the tactic of guerrilla combat?*"

"What phase of *guerrilla evolution* do you feel *Desquite's cuadrilla* is in?"

"Indicate two methods *Desquite* uses to exert *control* over the populace."

"Do you feel the *cuadrilla* has *political and military* leadership?"

("Haga usted el análisis de una cuadrilla de bandoleros," *Revista del Ejército* 6, no. 26 (September 1966): 159–165; original emphasis).

4. The operation was preceded by psychological action to gain the peasants' sympathy and introduce informers; next, the area was sealed off economically and militarily; then the final assault was carried out with 16,000 "lancers," the elite counterinsurgency force. In a message to the MRL's members in Congress, Tirofijo denounced American participation and guidance of the psychological warfare as well as of the napalm bombardments (Ramsey 1981, 306–307, 313–314; *Anales del Congreso,* August 5, 1964).

On May 21 and 22, 1964, the press said a U.S. spokesperson had acknowledged U.S. involvement in the extermination campaigns against the Violencia in Colombia. The commander of the Sixth Brigade, Hernando Currea Cubides, who had also led the Marquetalia Operation, hastily denied the report, with what amounted to a confession of the known facts: "We have not received military support on the scale supplied to South Vietnam. The aid has been very limited, and only starting in the middle of last year did we begin to receive small-scale aid. That aid is more limited than what is given to other countries on the continent. There are no units of American special forces in our territory. *United States officers serve as technicians to help the Colombian army;* we have received new materials, such as radios, transport equipment, weapons, etc. But [the American officers] have not been deployed at any time in battle locations. *They stay in the schools and in the battalions giving instructions, but they have taken no part in the struggle against the Violencia"* (*El Cronista,* May 22, 1964; our emphasis).

5. Incidentally, this process reveals that the constitutional amendments that led up to the 1968 Reform translated not into full-fledged political centralization but merely into a new pact entailing the *gamonales'* recognition of the central power of the government and the latter's recognition of the relative autonomy of the *gamonales.* Other processes, such as agrarian reform, would be further additions in this same line of reconciliation.

Epilogue

1. Here we return extensively, with the pertinent adaptations, to the notions put forth by Gonzalo Sánchez in the prologue to the 1992 Spanish edition of Maria Isaura Pereira de Queiroz's *Os cangaceiros: La epopeya bandolera del Nordeste del Brasil.*

2. The following paragraphs have been taken in part and adapted from Donny Meertens 1995 (36–49) and 1998 (236–265).

Glossary of Terms and Abbreviations

Note: All terms listed are in Spanish unless otherwise indicated: Eng. = English; It. = Italian; Port. = Portuguese; Sp. = Spanish.

Agregado: Sharecropper; tenant farmer
ANAPO: Alianza Nacional Popular (National Popular Alliance)
Antisocial: Criminal, rebel
Aparcería: Sharecropping
Aparcero: Sharecropper
Aplanchador: Literally, "flattener," that is, an assailant who, rather than cutting his victim, demonstrates his superiority by clubbing the victim into submission with the flat side of his machete; the term referred to members of paramilitary organizations in Antioquia
Arroba: Unit of weight equivalent to about 25 pounds
Banda: Gang of between three and nine individuals (see Chapter 3)
Bandolerismo: Banditry
Bandolero: Bandit
Boleta: Extortion note containing threats and/or a demand for money
Boleteo: Extortion through the delivery of a *boleta*
Brigantaggio (It.):   Brigandage, banditry
Cangaceiros (Port.):   Brazilian bandits; armed men of the "Cangaço," or Brazil's "badlands," who were in the service of rural landlords in the first decades of the twentieth century
Carga: Unit of weight equivalent to about 300 pounds (or 12 *arrobas*)

Chulavitas: Originally, the Conservative police from the region of Chulavo, in the municipality of Uvita, Boyacá; the term was later applied to all sectarian police

Coloca: Employment on a *finca*

Corregimiento: Village lying outside a *cabecera*, or "municipal seat"

Corte de franela: Literally, "cut in the undershirt"; refers to cutting the ligaments and tendons of a victim's head

Cortijo: Farmhouse; in southern Spain, a farm or country estate

Cuadrilla: Two or more *bandas* (see Chapter 3)

Cuadrillero: Member of a *cuadrilla*

DAS: Departamento Administrativo de Seguridad (Administrative Security Department)

ERC: Ejército Revolucionario de Colombia (Colombian Revolutionary Army)

Finca: Farm

Foco: Cluster of guerrilla fighters

Galantuomini (It.):   Gentlemen, men of honor; "gallant men" who used French-imposed legislation in the first decades of the nineteenth century to take over large areas of land

Gamonal: Local or regional political boss

Hacendado (Eng./Sp.):   Owner of an hacienda or large rural property

Latifundista: Owner of a large and unexploited landholding; an absentee landowner

Ley de fuga: Literally, "flight law"; refers to the practice in Spain and Latin America of executing a prisoner and then claiming that the person was trying to escape

Minifundio: Small landholding

Minifundista: Small landholder

MOEC: Movimiento Obrero Estudiantil Campesino (Worker-Student-Peasant Movement)

MRL: Movimiento Revolucionario Liberal (Liberal Revolutionary Movement)

Muchachos del monte: Boys from the mountains; rebels

Pájaros: Thugs hired by the Conservative Party

Penca ancha: Heavy whip

Picada de tamal: Literally, "chopping into a *tamal*"; a technique for chopping up a victim's body into little pieces

SAC: Sociedad de Agricultores de Colombia (Society of Growers of Colombia)

SIC: Servicio de Inteligencia Colombiana (Colombian Intelligence Service)

Sumario: Investigative stage of a criminal proceeding

Usufructuario: Literally, "beneficiary"; a merchant, landowner, or boss who hired *bandoleros* to help him take over land or to carry out other coercive acts

Vereda: A rural neighborhood

Violento: Person who committed violent acts in the context of the twenty-year civil war

References

Newspapers and Magazines

Diario del Quindío, Armenia
El Campesino, Bogotá
El Cronista, Ibagué
El Espectador, Bogotá
El Relator, Cali
El Tiempo, Bogotá
Estrella Roja, Líbano
La Calle, Bogotá
La Mañana, Manizales
La Nueva Prensa, Bogotá
La Patria, Manizales
Revista Cafetera, Bogotá
Revista de la Fuerzas Armadas, Bogotá
Revista de la Policía Nacional, Bogotá
Revista del Ejército, Bogotá
Semana, Bogotá
Sistema. Bogotá
Tribuna, Ibagué
Voz Proletaria, Bogotá

Court Records: Investigations of the Leading Cuadrilla *Members*

Investigation of Chispas's *Cuadrilla*

1. Sumario por homicidio y robo. Sindicados: a. "Chaleco" y otros. Juzgado 280 de Instrucción Criminal. Initiated at Inspección Departamental de Policía "La Bella," Calarcá, July 14, 1961. Archivo Juzgado Primero Supe-

rior de Armenia. [Investigation of "Chaleco" and others on charges of homicide and robbery.]

2. Sumario por múltiple homicidio y otros. Initiated on July 28, 1959. Juzgado Primero Municipal de Calarcá, Radicación No. 32, Archivo del Juzgado Cuarto Superior de Armenia. [Investigation for multiple homicide and other crimes.]

3. Sumario por múltiple homicidio y otros. Sindicados: a. "Nobleza" y otros. Initiated at la Alcaldía de Pijao, September 3, 1958. Archivo del Juzgado Cuarto Superior de Armenia. [Investigation of "Nobleza" and others for multiple counts of homicide and other crimes.]

Investigations of "Desquite's," "Sangrenegra's," "Pedro Brincos's" and "Tarzán's" *Cuadrillas*

4. Sumario contra "Avenegra," "Desquite" y otros. Juzgado Primero Superior de Honda, Causa 245. Initiated on April 14, 1963. [Investigation of "Avenegra," "Desquite," and others.]

5. Sumario contra "Desquite," "Sangrenegra" y "Pedro Brincos." Juzgado Primero Superior de Honda. [Investigation of "Desquite," "Sangrenegra," and "Pedro Brincos."]

6. Sumario contra "Sangrenegra" y otros. Radicación No. 12,681, Archivo del Juzgado Penal Municipal del Líbano. [Investigation of "Sangrenegra" and others.]

7. Sumario contra "Tarzán" y otros. Causa 2175, Juzgado Penal Municipal del Líbano. [Investigation of "Tarzán" and others.]

8. Sumario contra Roberto González y Moisés Patiño Hernández por secuestro y extorsión. Radicación No. 43, Juzgado 111 de Instrucción Criminal del Líbano. Initiated November 1962. Archivo del Juzgado Primero Superior de Ibagué. [Investigation of Roberto González and Moisés Patiño Hernández on charges of kidnapping and extortion.]

Investigation of Efraín González, "Melco," and "Polancho"

9. Sumario por homicidio. Sindicado: a. "Melco." Radicación No. 1467, Juzgado Primero Superior de Armenia. [Investigation of Efraín González, "Melco" and "Polancho" on charges of homicide.]

Investigation of "El Mosco's" *Cuadrilla*

10. Sumario por cuádruple homicidio y robo. Initiated 1959. Juzgado Segundo Superior de Buga. [Investigation for quadruple homicide and robbery.]

Investigation of "Pájaro Azul" and "Cabo Yate"

11. Sumario por homicidio. Sindicados: "Pájaro Azul" y "Cabo Yate." Causa No. 1654, Juzgado Primero Superior de Honda. [Investigation of "Pájaro Azul" and "Cabo Yate" on charges of homicide.]

Investigation of "Pájaro Verde"

12. Sumario contra a. "Pájaro Verde" (lugarteniente de "El Cóndor"). Juzgados Superiores de Cali y Bucaramanga. [Investigation of "Pájaro Verde," "El Cóndor's" lieutenant.]

Investigations of "Zarpazo's," "La Gata's," and "Joselito's" *Cuadrillas*

13. Sumario por asociación para delinquir. Radicación No. 26. Initiated in Obando, La Victoria and Cartago. Juzgado Primero Superior de Armenia. [Investigation on charges of conspiracy.]
14. Sumario por asociación para delinquir. Radicación No. 5429. Initiated 1964. Juzgado Primero Superior de Armenia. [Investigation on charges of conspiracy.]

Other Investigations

15. Sumario por homicidio y robo. Radicación No. 8245. Initiated June 21, 1958, by Inspección Departamental de Policía Irra (Quinchía). Juzgado Primero Superior de Manizales. [Investigation on charges of homicide and robbery.]
16. Sumarios por homicidio y robo. Radicación No. 7408 y 8565. Initiated in Chinchiná, June 10, 1957, and January 26, 1965. Juzgado Primero Superior de Manizales. [Investigation on charges of homicide and robbery.]
17. Sumario por múltiple homicidio. Radicación No. 32, June 30, 1959. Archivo del Juzgado Cuarto Superior de Armenia. [Investigation on charges of multiple homicide.]
18. Sumario por homicidio. Radicación No. 006, Initiated 1962. Juzgado Cuarto Superior de Armenia. [Investigation on charges of homicide.]
19. Sumario por homicidio. Causa 1230. Initiated in Quimbaya, June 19, 1962. Juzgado Primero Superior de Armenia. [Investigation on charges of homicide.]
20. Sumarios del Tribunal de Conciliación y Equidad (1960-1961), Juzgado Superior de Armenia y Juzgado Superior de Calarcá. [Investigations conducted by the Tribunal of Reconciliation and Equity.]

Congressional Annals

Anales del Congreso (1958–1965). Bogotá: Imprenta Nacional.

Books, Articles, and Theses

Aguilera, Mario, and Bernardo Ramos. 1980. "La Violencia en Puente Nacional." Bogotá: Departamento de Historia, Universidad Nacional de Colombia. Mimeographed.
Alba, Tito. 1971. *Vida, confesión y muerte de Efraín González*. 2d ed. Bogotá: Tipografía Bermúdez.

Alvarez Gardeazábal, Gustavo. 1974. *Cóndores no entierran todos los días.* Guayaquil: Editorial Ariel Universal.

Aprile-Gniset, Jacques. 1991. *La crónica de Villarrica.* Bogotá: Opción and the Instituto Latinoamericano de Servicios Legales, ILSA.

Arango, Gonzalo. 1964. "Desquite." *La Nueva Prensa* 106, March 27, 1964, 63.

Arocha, Jaime. 1979. *La Violencia en el Quindío.* Bogotá: Editorial Tercer Mundo.

Arrubla, Mario, et al. 1978. *Colombia Hoy.* Bogotá: Siglo XXI Editores de Colombia.

Aya, Roderich. 1975. *The Missed Revolution: The Fate of Rural Rebels in Sicily and Southern Spain 1840–1950.* Papers on European and Mediterranean Societies no. 3. Amsterdam: University of Amsterdam.

———. 1978. "Theories of Revolution Reconsidered." *Theory and Society* 8: 39–99.

Bejarano, Jesús Antonio. 1981. "Campesinado, luchas agrarias e historia social: Notas para un balance historiográfico." Paper presented at symposium "El mundo rural colombiano: Su evolución y actualidad." FAES (Fundación Antioqueña de Estudios Sociales), Medellín, December.

Bernaldo de Quirós, Constancio. [1919] 1973. *El espartaquismo agrario andaluz.* 2d ed. Madrid: Editorial de la Revista de Trabajo.

———. 1959. *El bandolerismo en España y México.* Mexico City: Editorial Jurídica Mexicana.

Bernaldo de Quirós, Constancio, and Luis Ardila. [1933] 1973. *El bandolerismo andaluz.* 2d ed. Madrid: Ediciones Turner.

Betancourt, Darío, and Martha Luz García. 1991. *Matones y Cuadrilleros.* Bogotá: IEPRI (Instituto de Estudios Políticos y Relaciones Internales), Universidad Nacional de Colombia, and TM Editores.

Blok, Anton. 1972. "The Peasant and the Brigand: Social Banditry Reconsidered." *Comparative Studies in Society and History* 14, no. 4 (September): 495–504.

———. 1975. *The Mafia of a Sicilian Village 1860–1960: A Study of Violent Peasant Entrepreneurs.* New York: Harper and Row.

———. 1976. *The Bokkerijders Bands (1726–1776), Preliminary Notes on Brigandage in Southern Netherlands.* 2d ed. Papers on European and Mediterranean Societies no. 7. Amsterdam: University of Amsterdam.

———. 1978. "Over de Beroepen van de Bokkerijders in de Landen van Overmaze." *Tijdschrift voor Criminologie* 20, no. 3/4: N.p.

———. 1979. "Wie waren de Bokkerijders? Een dupliek." *Tijdschrift voor Sociale Geschiedenis* (Amsterdam) 14: N.p.

Bottia G., Luis F., and Rodolfo Escovedo D. 1979. La Violencia en el sur del departamento de Córdoba. Undergraduate thesis, Facultad de Ciencia Política, Universidad de los Andes, Bogotá. Mimeographed.

Braudel, Fernand. 1976. *El Mediterráneo y el mundo mediterráneo en la época de Felipe II.* 2 vols. Mexico City: Fondo de Cultura Económica.

Brenan, Gerald. 1967. *The Spanish Labyrinth: An Account of the Social and Political Background of the Spanish Civil War.* Cambridge: Cambridge University Press.

Buitrago Salazar, Evelio. 1956. *Caldas: Estudio de su situación geográfica, económica y social.* Bogotá: Ministerio de Trabajo y Seguridad Social.
————. N.d. *"Zarpazo," otra cara de la Violencia.* Bogotá: Imprenta de las Fuerzas Armadas.
Carrillo Ramírez, Alberto. 1976. *Luis Pardo: "El gran bandido."* 2d ed. Lima: N.p.
Chandler, Billy Jaynes. 1978. *The Bandit King: Lampião of Brazil.* College Station: Texas A&M University Press.
Chesneaux, Jean. 1973. *Peasant Revolts in China 1840–1949.* London: Thames and Hudson.
Comando del Ejército. N.d. *Casos tácticos de guerra de guerrillas en Colombia,* no. 18. 3 vols. Bogotá: Imprenta de las Fuerzas Armadas.
Devalle, Susana B. C. 1977. *La palabra de la tierra: Protesta campesina en India, Siglo XIX.* Mexico City: El Colegio de México.
Díaz del Moral, Juan. [1929] 1969. *Historia de las agitaciones campesinas andaluzas.* 2d ed. Madrid: Alianza Editorial.
Engelen, Theo. 1979. "De Bokkerijders: Banditisme tijdens het Ancién Regime 11. Een repliek." *Tijdschrift voor Sociale Geschiedenis* 14: N.p.
Escuela Superior de Guerra. N.d. *El Comunismo en Colombia: El fenómeno social de la Violencia.* Bogotá: Imprenta de las Fuerzas Armadas. (Contains document titled "Una franca apreciación de la situación de orden público en el país y la intervención del comunismo en las zonas de Violencia.")
Facó, Rui. 1965. *Cangaceiros e Fanáticos.* Rio de Janeiro: Editorial Civilização Brasileira.
Fajardo, Darío. 1979. *Violencia y desarrollo.* Bogotá: Fondo Editorial Suramérica.
————. 1981. "La Violencia 1946–1964: Su desarrollo y su impacto." *Estudios Marxistas* 21 (May–August): 39–59.
Franco Isaza, Eduardo. 1959. *Las guerrillas del Llano.* Bogotá: Editorial Librería Mundial.
Gabler, Carlos. N.d. "La lucha de clases y la Violencia." Bogotá: Departamento de Ciencia Política, Universidad de los Andes. Mimeographed.
Gilhodés, Pierre. 1974a. *Las luchas agrarias en Colombia.* 2d ed. Bogotá: La Carreta.
————. 1974b. *La question agraire en Colombie: Politique et violence 1958–1971.* Paris: Editorial Armand Colin.
————. 1976. "La Violence en Colombie: Banditisme et guerre sociale." *Cahiers du Monde Hispanique et Lusobrasilien* (Paris) 26: 69–82.
Gómez, Luis Eduardo. N.d. La violencia en el Líbano: Panorama general. Unpublished notes in author's family collection. Líbano, Tolima.
Guzmán Campos, Germán. 1968. *La Violencia en Colombia.* Bogotá: Editorial Progreso.
Guzmán Campos, Germán, Orlando Fals Borda, and Eduardo Umaña Luna. [1962] 1977. *La Violencia en Colombia.* 8th ed. 2 vols. Bogotá: Editorial Punta de Lanza.
Henderson, James. 1972. Origins of the Violence in Colombia. Ph.D. diss., Texas Christian University. Microfilm, Ann Arbor, Michigan.
Hernández Girbal, Fernando. "Bandolerismo de antaño." *Revista de Estudios Históricos de la Guardia Civil* (Madrid) 5: 137–149.

Hobsbawm, Eric J. 1959. *Primitive Rebels: Archaic Forms of Social Movement in the Nineteenth and Twentieth Centuries.* Manchester: Manchester University Press.

———. 1963a. "The Anatomy of Violence." *New Society* (London) 28 (April): N.p.

———. 1963b. "The Revolutionary Situation in Colombia." *The World Today* (London) 6 (June): 248–258.

———. [1969] 1981. *Bandits.* New York: Pantheon Books.

———. 1974. "Social Banditry." In *Rural Protest: Peasant Movement and Social Change,* ed. Henry Landsberger, pp. 142–157. London: Macmillan Press.

INCORA (Instituto Colombiano de la Reforma Agraria). 1958. *Informe del Secretario de Gobierno de Caldas a la Asamblea de Diputados.* Manizales: Imprenta Departamental.

———. 1963. *Informe de Gobierno de Caldas* (Sept. 1962–Sept. 1963). Manizales: Imprenta Departamental.

———. 1964. Microfilmed archive available at INCORA, Bogotá.

Kuzmanich, Dunav, Javier Orozco, and Jairo Obando. 1980. "Efraín." Mimeographed movie script. Later published as "Sietecolores" in *Cine de la Violencia,* ed. Isabel Sánchez, pp. 225–306, Bogotá: Centro Editorial Universidad Nacional de Colombia, 1987.

Lewin, Linda. 1979a. "The Oligarchical Limitations of Social Banditry in Brazil: The Case of the 'Good' Thief Antonio Silvino." *Past and Present* 82 (February–April): 116–146.

———. 1979b. "Oral Tradition and Elite Myth: The Legend of Antonio Silvino in Brazilian Popular Culture." *Journal of Latin American Lore* 5, no. 2: 157–203.

———. 1980. *Libro negro de la represión 1958–1980.* Compiled by Jorge Villegas and Gerardo Rivas. 2d ed., expanded. Bogotá: N.p.

Lima, Estacio de. 1965. *0 Mundo estranho dos cangaceiros.* Salvador, Brasil: Editorial Itapoa Limitada.

Longworth, Philip. 1978. "La revuelta de Pugachev: El último gran levantamiento cosaco campesino." In *Rebelión campesina y cambio social,* ed. Henry Landsberger. Barcelona: Editorial Crítica.

López Albújar, Enrique. [1936] 1973. *Los caballeros del delito.* 2d ed. Lima: Juan Mejía Baca.

López Michelsen, Alfonso. 1962. *Conceptos fundamentales del M.R.L.* No. 3. Brochure.

Marulanda V., Manuel. 1973. *Cuadernos de campaña.* Bogotá: Editorial Abejón Mono.

Matta Machado, María Cristina. [1969] 1978. *As tácticas de guerra dos cangaceiros.* 2d ed. São Paulo: Editora Basiliense.

Maullin, Richard. 1968. *The Fall of Dumar Aljure, a Colombian Guerrilla and Bandit.* Santa Monica: The Rand Corporation.

Meertens, Donny. 1979. *Jonkers en Boeren, de strijd om het land in Colombia.* Incidentele Publikatiereeks (Amsterdam), no. 13. Amsterdam: CEDLA.

————. 1995. "Mujer y violencia en los conflictos rurales." *Análisis Político* (Bogotá) 24 (April): 36-49.

————. 1997. *Tierra, violencia y género*. Nijmegen, Netherlands: University of Nijmegen.

————. 1998. "Víctimas y sobrevivientes de la guerra: Tres miradas de género." In *Las violencias: Inclusión creciente*, compiled by Jaime Arocha, Fernando Cubides, and Myriam Jimeno, pp. 236–265. Colección Centro de Estudios Sociales. Bogotá: Universidad Nacional de Colombia.

Ministerio de Trabajo. 1956. *Caldas: Estudio de su situación geográfica, económica y social*. Bogotá: Ministerio de Trabajo.

Molano, Alfredo. 1978. *Amnistía y Violencia*. Serie Controversia nos. 86–87 (Centro de Investigación y Educación Popular). Bogotá: Editorial Guadalupe.

Molfese, Franco. [1964] 1979. *Storia del Brigantaggio dopo l'Unitá*. 5th ed. Milan: Feltrinelli.

Moncada, Alonso. 1963. *Un aspecto de la Violencia*. Bogotá: Promotora Colombiana de Ediciones y Revistas.

Moreta, Salustiano. 1978. *Malhechores feudales*. Madrid: Editorial Cátedra.

Mossmann, Peter. 1979. "Campesinos und Ausbeutungsstrukturen im internationalen Konfliktfeld." *Sozioeconomische Schriften zur Agrarentwicklung*. Saarbrücken: Verlag Breitenbach, no. 34.

Octava Brigada. 1965. *De la Violencia a la paz*. Manizales: Imprenta Departamental de Caldas.

O'Malley, Pat. 1979. "Social Bandits, Modern Capitalism, and the Traditional Peasantry: A Critique of Hobsbawm." *Journal of Peasant Studies* (London) 6, no. 4 (July): 489–499.

Oquist, Paul. 1978. *Violencia, conflicto y política en Colombia*. Bogotá: Instituto de Estudios Colombianos.

Orlove, Benjamín S., and Glynn Custred, eds. 1980. *The Position of Rustlers in Regional Society: Social Banditry in the Andes, Land and Power in Latin America*. New York: Holmes and Meier Publishers.

Osorio, Guillermo. 1966. Diversos aspectos de la violencia. Undergraduate thesis, Facultad de Derecho, Universidad de Caldas, Manizales, Colombia.

Pang, Eul-Soo. 1981–1982. "Banditry and Messianism in Brazil, 1870–1940: An Agrarian Crisis Hypothesis." *PCCLAS Proceedings* 8: 1–23.

Pardo, Jorge Eliécer. 1979. *El jardín de las Hartmann*. Bogotá: Plaza y Janés.

Parra, José del Carmen. 1951, 1952, 1953. Unpublished personal diaries provided by Parra's relatives.

Partido Comunista de Colombia. N.d. *Treinta años de lucha del Partido Comunista de Colombia*. Bogotá: Editorial Los Comuneros.

Pecaut, Daniel. 1976. "Reflexiones sobre el fenómeno de la Violencia." *Ideología y Sociedad* (Bogotá) 19 (October–December): 71–79.

————. 1979. "Classe ouvrière et système politique en Colombie 1930–1953." 2 vols. Ph.D. diss., Académie de Paris-Université René Descartes, Sciences Humaines, Sorbonne.

Pitt-Rivers, Julian A. 1961. *The People of the Sierra.* Chicago: University of Chicago Press.
Policía Nacional de Colombia. 1962. *Estadística de criminalidad* 5. Bogotá: Fondo Rotatorio de la Policía Nacional de Colombia.
———. 1964. *Estadística de criminalidad* 7. Bogotá: Fondo Rotatorio de la Policía Nacional de Colombia.
———. 1965. *Estadística de criminalidad* 8. Bogotá: Fondo Rotatorio de la Policía Nacional de Colombia.
———. 1967. *Estadística de criminalidad* 10. Bogotá: Fondo Rotatorio de la Policía Nacional de Colombia.
Queiroz, María Isaura Pereira de. 1975. "Notas sociológicas sobre Cangaço." *Ciencia e Cultura* 27, no. 5 (May): 495–516.
———. 1977. *Os cangaceiros.* São Paulo: Editorial Duas Cidades.
———. 1992. *Os cangaceiros: La epopeya bandolera del Nordeste del Brasil.* Bogotá: Ancora Editores.
Ramsey, Russell W. 1981. *Guerrilleros y soldados.* Bogotá: Editorial Tercer Mundo.
Reglá, Juan. 1968. "El bandolerismo en la Cataluña del barroco." *Anuario de Historia Económica y Social* (Madrid) 1 (January–December): 281–294.
Revista Cafetera. 1964. "Proposición no. 21 del XXII Congreso Cafetero Nacional realizado en el año de 1960." *Revista Cafetera* (Bogotá) 16, no. 138A: 31–33.
Rivas Gómez, Fernando. 1970. "El bandolerismo en Cataluña y su persecución." *Revista de Estudios Históricos de la Guardia Civil* (Madrid) 10, no. 20: N.p.
Ruiz, Soledad. 1972. "La fuerza de trabajo en zona cafetera de Tolima." Bogotá: DANE (Departamento Administrativo Nacional de Estadística). Mimeographed.
———. 1980. "Desarrollo ideológico de los trabajadores rurales del Tolima 1959–1972." Departamento de Ciencia Política, Universidad de los Andes, Bogotá, Colombia. Mimeographed.
Sánchez, Gonzalo. 1976a. *Los "Bolcheviques del Líbano."* Bogotá: Editorial Mohán. 2d ed., Bogotá: ECOE-Pandora, 1980.
———. 1976b. "La Violencia y sus efectos en el sistema político colombiano." *Cuadernos Colombianos* 9 (first semester): 1–44.
———. 1977. *Las ligas campesinas en Colombia.* Bogotá: Editorial Tiempo Presente.
———. 1982. "El gaitanismo y la insurrección del 9 de abril en provincia." Paper presented at the Primer Seminario Nacional sobre Movimientos Sociales: Gaitán y el 9 de abril, Universidad Nacional de Colombia and Centro Cultural Jorge Eliécer Gaitán, Bogotá, April.
———. 1991. *Guerra y política en la sociedad colombiana.* Bogotá: Ancora Editores.
Sarasa Sánchez, Esteban. 1980. "El bandolerismo medieval en Aragón." *Historia* (Madrid) 16, no. 46 (February): 52–57.
Sarria Mondragón, Jesús Alberto. N.d. *La vida de Sangrenegra: El bandido más feroz de Colombia.* Pamphlet. N.p.

Shaker, Arthur. 1975. *Pelo espaço do cangaceiro jurubeba*. São Paulo: Editorial Símbolo.

Silva, Alberto. 1975. "O cangaceiro, herói do Terceiro Mundo." *Cultura* (Brasilia) 4, no. 16 (January–March): 13–19.

Singleman, Peter. 1975–1976. "Political Structure and Social Banditry in Northeast Brazil." *Journal of Latin American Studies* 7, no. 1 (May): 59–83.

Socarrás, José Francisco. 1958. "Psicoanálisis del 9 de abril: ¿Por qué fracasó el movimiento de masas?" *La Calle* (Bogotá), April 11.

Torres R., Camilo. 1963. "La Violencia y los cambios socioculturales en las áreas rurales colombianas." In *Memorias del Primer Congreso Nacional de Sociología*. Bogotá: Universidad Nacional de Colombia.

Urrea, Fernando. 1977. "Consideraciones sobre el tema de la Violencia." In *El agro en el desarrollo histórico colombiano*, ed. Francisco Leal et al. Bogotá: Punta de Lanza.

Vanderwood, Paul. 1981. *Disorder and Progress: Bandits, Police, and Mexican Development*. Lincoln: University of Nebraska Press.

Varallanos, José. 1937. *Los bandoleros en el Perú*. Lima: Editorial Altura.

Vásquez Santos, Jorge. 1954. *Guerrilleros, buenos días*. Bogotá: Editorial AGRA.

Vélez Machado, Alirio. 1962. *Sargento Matacho: La vida de Rosalba Velásquez, ex-guerrillera libanense*. Líbano, Department of Tolima, Colombia: Tipografía Vélez.

Villegas, Jorge, and Gerardo Rivas Moreno, comps. 1980. *Libro negro de la represión 1958-1980*. 2d ed. Bogotá: Fundación para la Investigación y la Cultura.

Womack, John. 1969. *Zapata and the Mexican Revolution*. New York: Knopf.

Zugasti, Julian. 1876–1880. *El bandolerismo: Estudio social y memoria histórica*. 10 vols. Madrid: Editorial T. Fortanet. Reprinted in one volume, Madrid: Alianza Editorial, 1982.

Index